ANA

CHINOOK

VALLEY

SCOBEY

DANIELS

PLENTYWOOD

SHERIDAN

AINE

PHILLIPS

• MALTA

• GLASGOW

ROOSEVELT

WOLF POINT

o

RICHLAND

SIDNEY •

MC CONE

o Zortman

o Landusky

o Carroll

Muscleshell City o

Kerchival City

GARFIELD

CIRCLE •

DAWSON

US

o Gilt Edge

STOWN

PETROLEUM

JORDAN

• WINNETT

GLENDIVE •

• WIBAUX

PRAIRIE

• TERRY

WIBAUX

MUSSELSHELL

DEN

LEY

GATE

• ROUNDUP

• MILES CITY

BAKER •

FALLON

HYSHAM

FORSYTH

CUSTER

YELLOWSTONE

o Junction City

TREASURE

ROSEBUD

EKALAKA

TER

o Coulson

BILLINGS

• HARDIN

CARTER

BON

D LODGE

BIG HORN

POWDER RIVER

• BROADUS

SHALLOW DIGGIN'S

SHALLOW
DIGGIN'S

Tales from Montana's Ghost Towns

Compiled by

JEAN DAVIS

ILLUSTRATED WITH PHOTOGRAPHS

THE CAXTON PRINTERS, LTD.
CALDWELL, IDAHO
1962

Library of Congress Catalog Card No. 62-8188

Printed, lithographed, and bound in the United States of America by
The CAXTON PRINTERS, Ltd.
Caldwell, Idaho
93754

To the memory of my father

INTRODUCTION

WHAT IS A GHOST TOWN? IT IS A HUDDLE OF ROTTING cabins on a mountainside; it is the towering ruins of vast mills or smelters around which life once swirled; sometimes traces of rotting foundations alone are left of a busy "city"; only the name may remain as a postmark on an old family letter or as a memory in the mind of a pioneer.

And the tales that have come down to us from these lost towns? Doubtless they are embroidered by the imagination of the teller; yet, even though minor details may be pure fiction, the chief incidents are fact; the thread that links folklore to history is unbroken.

When possible the tales are not rewritten here. The closer the story is to the source, the more authentic it is in detail, language, and spirit. Nor has there been any attempt to make this a definitive collection either of towns or tales. There are hundreds of the former and thousands of the latter not included. It is merely hoped that this compilation will serve to flesh the skeletons that lie on the plains and mountains of Montana, to recall the sometimes tragic, sometimes hilarious, always robust life of a century past.

CONTENTS

PART I
THE MINING CAMPS

PART II
TRADE & TRANSPORTATION CENTERS

CONTENTS

ILLUSTRATIONS

Picture Section following page 190

PART I

THE MINING CAMPS

Bell, book, and candle shall not drive me back,
When gold and silver becks me to come on.

SHAKESPEARE

1

GOLD CREEK

GRANVILLE STUART, ON HIS WAY BACK FROM THE California gold fields to visit his parents in Iowa, fell ill in July, 1857, at the head of Malad Creek. By July 17 he was so ill that it was feared he might die, and certainly it was known that he could not travel for many days, even weeks. Consequently, it was decided that his brother James and Reece (Rezin) Anderson would remain behind with him and the other eight members of the party would resume their journey.

He was severely ill for seven weeks and then recovered slowly. While in camp awaiting his recovery, the men became friendly with Jake Meek, a trader on the Oregon Trail and a former Hudson's Bay Company employee, who was camped nearby. As the immigrant trains lumbered past, some horses were stolen from one of the trains, and Jake was accused of being in league with the Indians to take the horses. The situation for Jake was an ugly one until the Stuarts came to his defense and upheld him stoutly. From then on a lasting friendship existed between them.

At the same time Brigham Young's "Destroying Angels," in open revolt against the government, were guarding all roads around Malad Creek so that, when Granville was sufficiently recovered to travel, the party found that it could neither proceed to Iowa nor return to California. They consulted with Meek who suggested that they go along with him and winter in the Beaverhead Valley some three hundred miles north. Then in the spring, when the Mormon war was over, they could proceed on their way. On the eleventh day of September, 1857, they packed their gear and started north. On the twenty-fourth of October they crossed the high ridge of Blacktail Deer Creek into the Beaverhead Valley—just in time, too, as that night a furious snowstorm swept down on them; wood and game being plentiful around them, they set up camp in elk skin Indian lodges and prepared to spend some time in the area. Here they remained comfortably established until Christmas.

Fifteen miles below them was another camp of mountain men including the Grants and ten or twelve others. Most of these men had families consisting of Indian wives and half-breed children who lived, as did the Stuarts, in elk skin lodges. Captain Grant, however, and his quarter-breed wife had a fine three-room log home.

The winter passed pleasantly. The white men visited back and forth, telling tales of the westward journeys, of hunting, and of the gold fields. Indians who drifted through the valley amused themselves and their white kibitzers with their gambling game of "Hands" or "Hide-the-bone," and now and then a teamster passing through would bring news of "the States." At Christmas time Captain Grant entertained with Christmas dinner consisting of buffalo meat, boiled smoked tongue, bread, dried fruit, chokecherry preserves, and coffee, a real feast to the men who had been living on unsalted meat and little else.

Just after Christmas, the Stuarts moved camp to the Big Hole and in March tried to cross the divide but were driven back by deep snows. Game was scarce, and they ate thistle roots boiled with what little meat they had.

In the tales that had circulated around the camps was one concerning Benetsee, a Red River half-breed, who had found float gold near Deer Lodge. Consequently, as soon as the weather permitted, the Stuart party started for Deer Lodge, arriving there April 7 to find not only plenty of game but milk available from a small herd of cattle owned by John Jacobs.

Just how much they were motivated by the lure of Benetsee's gold and how much by the prospect of drying game to last them to Fort Bridger will never be known. Stuart is probably sincere in saying that it was the latter venture that seemed more important as subsequent events proved them to be more traders than prospectors.

Nevertheless, a month after their arrival in the valley, they took what tools they had, an old square-pointed spade with the hand hold broken out of the top of the handle and a tin bread pan, and started up Benetsee Creek to prospect. Out of a shallow prospect hole they obtained ten cents to the pan in fine gold. This was "pay dirt," but they were ill-equipped for mining and had other business at hand. As they ate their supper around the campfire they decided to continue killing and drying meat to last to Fort Bridger, go there and secure supplies and tools, and return to the mines as soon as their eventful life would permit.

"This prospect hole dug by us," writes Stuart in his reminiscences, "was the first prospecting for gold done in what is now Montana and this is the account of the first real discovery of gold within the state."[1]

No sooner had Stuart made his claim of being the first to discover gold in Montana than from all sides defenders of other claims rushed to the fray.

Foremost among the contenders was Benetsee though he did not do his own contending. The creek was named after him; surely that in itself was proof. Stuart, a canny Scotsman, was not one to yield easily.

Francois Finlay, better known as "Benetsee," perhaps did find a few colors of gold in Benetsee creek, but his prospecting was of a very superficial nature and he was never certain whether he found gold or not. I first became acquainted with him in November, 1860. I had located at a point where the Mullan road crosses Gold creek; a village of Flathead Indians camped near me and with them was Benetsee, who made himself known to me. Naturally our conversation was about gold in Gold creek. I asked him if he had ever dug a hole and he said "No, I had nothing to dig with and I never cared to prospect." I am certain that this was true, because although we prospected on Gold creek and in all the gulches and streams leading into the creek, I never found the slightest trace of holes being dug or of any prospecting being done and the slightest disturbance of the sod would be noticed by us at that time.[2]

["Pshaw," retorted Duncan McDonald, son of old Angus of the Hudson Bay Company,] "As I have stated before about Benetsee Finlay which no one disputes in his finding gold on a creek named after him in the early days long before Mr. Stuart ever put his foot on the ground. . . . Sand Bar Brown yelled like hell if Finlay did find gold why did he not work the gravel? A child, a babe, knows better. That Finlay was a British subject and had an Indian, a Salish Flathead wife. That under no circumstances that he could

---

[1] Reprinted by permission of the publishers, The Arthur H. Clark Company, from *Forty Years on the Frontier*, by Granville Stuart (2 vols.; Cleveland, 1925), I, 136-37.

[2] *Ibid.*, p. 138 ff.

locate a claim and was further advised by the H. B. Co. to never mention gold for fear their fur business would be ruined, which is true. How did Stuart or why did he turn from his winter quarters north in the spring? . . . He found the gold, but Finlay had found it years before. . . ."[3]

Nor was Stuart the first to follow Benetsee's lead. In 1856 a party crossing the Bitterroot Valley to Salt Lake wintered with the Indians in Deer Lodge Valley and prospected a little where Finlay had found gold. They had better luck than he as they found several nuggets, one of which, worth about ten cents, they gave to old Captain Grant who used to show it off as the first gold found in Montana. Perhaps it was this piece, shown to Stuart while in the Beaverhead, that determined him to make a swing north on his way east.

Father de Smet, dedicated Jesuit missionary to the Flatheads in the 1840's, was aware of the presence of gold in the region; however, he was also aware that the knowledge, if generally known, would attract the greedy white man. Out of consideration for his beloved Indians and their simple way of life, he kept the secret to himself.

Poor unfortunate Indians! They trample on treasures unconscious of their worth, and content themselves with fishery and the chase. When these resources fail, they subsist upon roots and herbs; whilst they eye with tranquil surprise the white man examining the shining pebbles of their territory. Ah! They would tremble indeed could they learn the history of those numerous and ill-fated tribes that have been swept from their land, to make place for Christians, who have made the poor Indians the victims of their rapacity.[4]

---

[3] *Ibid.*, pp. 138-39 ff.

[4] Pierre Jean de Smet, *Life, Letters and Travels* (New York, Harper, 1904) II, 493.

In 1858 a party of prospectors entered the Big Hole Basin in the Beaverhead country. On Pioneer Creek they did considerable prospecting and found gold in paying quantities. They called the camp Pioneer and for a few years it was a major mining camp in what was then Idaho Territory. Although its fame was eclipsed by the strikes at Bannack and Alder, prospectors were active in the region up to the turn of the century.

These early prospectors, as well as those who first entered Grasshopper Gulch, found traces of much earlier mining. At the latter place there were traces of a "feed" and "tail" ditch. In one of these a fair-sized pine tree was growing, attesting to the very early digging of the ditch. It is assumed that Spaniards, penetrating north from Mexico in the sixteenth century, had done this mining long before Granville Stuart was born.

An entry in the Fort Owen journals for February 15, 1852, tersely states, "Gold Hunting found some."

In 1856 there showed up in Fort Benton, then the principal port of the Missouri navigation through Montana, a silent, grizzled trapper, John Silverthorne. He needed supplies to eke out his lonely existence, but he had no money. He did have a small quantity of yellow dust which he claimed was gold and asked the store-keeper to accept it in payment. The storekeeper, never having seen the stuff before, was reluctant but finally accepted it in payment for about twelve dollars and fifty cents' worth of supplies. When he shipped it to St. Louis, it was valued at fifteen hundred dollars. Silverthorne never said where he got the gold, but some believe that it came from the Kootenai country in Canada, not from Montana at all. Another expla-

nation of the dust is that Silverthorne, meeting Benetsee on the trail, exchanged some supplies for the half-
breed's gold.

One day while prospecting in the Butte area, William Allen and G. O. Humphreys made camp in Baboon
Gulch. Nearby they stumbled upon an old hole, obvi-
ously man-made, beside which lay elk horns that had
probably been used as gads and hand pikes to dig out
the gravel to a depth of four or five feet. Was this
the "Original Lode," as it was later named? Perhaps
there were other strikes to which some trapper or mountain man hoped to return but never did. It took the
Stuarts two years to get back to Gold Creek.

Although they had followed the gold rush, neither
James nor Granville Stuart apparently had the true
prospector's psychology. They never burned with the
fever for gold, and, when they finally returned to their
"strike," it seemed more to set themselves up as farmers
and businessmen than as miners. At Fort Bridger and
other stations they had acquired some furs, a considerable herd of horses and cattle, and a small assortment of Indian trading goods; these they loaded on a
wagon drawn by three yoke of oxen and in 1860 started
for the Beaverhead accompanied by their friend Reece
Anderson. The plan was to winter again in the Beaverhead and move on the next spring to the Deer Lodge
Valley.

After setting up their winter camp Reece and Granville decided to ride over to St. Ignatius to do a little
trading. Packing their bedrolls and trade items they
set off on the 460-mile round trip. On their way back
they were surprised to meet James and the others of

the party on their way to Deer Lodge. A band of hostile Bannacks had killed one of the Stuart cattle and, to avoid further trouble, for which they were ill prepared, they pushed on into the Deer Lodge Valley.

... I saddled up for a ride of sixty miles more, and putting a little food and bedding and our elk skin lodge on a pack horse, started, accompanied by Simmons and the young Indian.

At Cottonwood creek was camped Thomas Lavatta, Joseph Hill, and some others. ... I went down to Gold creek and begun cutting poles for a corral. Four days later Anderson and James arrived with the ox team, horses and cattle.[5]

Even in this remote area, two years had brought changes. A little settlement on Cottonwood Creek was growing. Many of the settlers here were Mexicans with names like Lavatta, Alejo Barasta, and Joe Pizanthia, and the settlement was often referred to as "Spanish Fork." It had other names before and other names later. The Indians called it "Soo-Ken-Car-ne" or "Lodge of the White Tailed Deer." Here herds of deer gathered to feed and rest comfortably in the tall grass and cattails that grew around the warm springs. The French trappers translated this into "La Loge du Chevreuil," the blunt Yankees into "Deer Lodge." To many it was "Cottonwood" because of the huge cottonwoods bordering the river. For a brief time in 1862 it was "La Barge City" after Captain Joe La Barge who had grandiose plans for a large trading center. On some early maps of Idaho and Montana it bears this name. Not until 1864, under the leadership of Granville Stuart, was the name Deer Lodge City finally established, wide

---

[5] Stuart, *op. cit.*, pp. 155-56.

streets laid out, a courthouse square platted and other far-sighted provisions made.

To the west of Gold Creek Higgins and Worden had established their trading post at Hell Gate. From here travelers passed more frequently through Gold Creek on their way to Fort Benton or Deer Lodge.

Johnny Grant's farm was assuming greater importance as a supply center for the increasing population and is often referred to at the time as Grantsville.

The tempo of social life increased somewhat, as is shown in Granville Stuart's diary:

January 1, 1862. . . . Everybody went to grand ball given by John Grant at Grantsville and a severe blizzard blew up and raged all night. We danced all night, no outside storm could dampen the festivities.[6]

July 12. With the emigrants today is a Mr. B. B. Burchett with his family. . . . Miss Sallie Burchett is sixteen years old and a very beautiful girl. Every man in camp has shaved and changed his shirt since this family arrived. We are all trying to appear like civilized men.[7]

July 23. Arrived at our town to-day a fine violin player accompanied by his handsome seventeen year old wife. . . . All the men are shaving nowadays and most of them indulge in an occasional hair cut. The blue flannel shirt with a black necktie has taken the place of the elaborately beaded buckskin one. The white men wear shoes instead of moccasins and most of us have selected some other day than Sunday for wash day.[8]

But it was still a lonely life. On March 1, 1862, James Stuart enters in the diary:

I brought with me the Indian woman ransomed from Narcisses, the

---

[6] *Ibid.*, p. 193.
[7] *Ibid.*, p. 213.
[8] *Ibid.*, p. 215.

Flathead. . . . I might do worse. She is neat and rather good-looking and seems to be of a good disposition. So I find myself a married man.[9]

Granville says, "Marrying is rapidly becoming an epidemic in our little village."[10]

On May 2, two months later, Granville married Aubony, a Snake Indian girl, "a fairly good cook, of an amiable disposition and with few relatives."[11]

Indians came and went through the valley which was traditionally neutral ground for all the tribes.

September 23. The Flathead camp passed on their way to hunt buffalo all winter. Am glad they are gone because of the d——d whiskey.[12]

April 5. Many Flatheads, Spokanes and Pend d'Oreilles are passing on their return from buffalo hunting.[13]

Between trading with Indians, planting and harvesting crops, begetting and raising families, the men of Gold Creek did a little mining.

June 12, 1861. Began to enlarge my prospecting out in the ravine, looks good.[14]

June 15. Dug some more, enlarging my cut in the ravine, got good prospects in beautiful gold.[15]

April (1862). Our little settlement at American Fork[16] has begun to take on the lively, bustling appearance of a new placer camp. Several parties were out prospecting with fair results. We have

---

[9] *Ibid.*, p. 198.

[10] *Ibid.*

[11] *Ibid.*, p. 206.

[12] *Ibid.*, p. 187.

[13] *Ibid.*, p. 203.

[14] *Ibid.*, p. 173.

[15] *Ibid.*

[16] This name had been adopted and was used for a short time instead of Gold Creek.

succeeded in getting one thousand feet of lumber, at ten cents per foot, whipsawed for sluice boxes. . . .[17]

May 13. Tony, Joe and Cossette dug on ditch. James, Jim and I washed with the sluices in the forenoon. In the afternoon they dug a hole to look for the pay streak.[18]

As mining activity increased, so did trouble with professional gamblers and gunmen. Granville Stuart had no time for gambling, but James couldn't resist a good game. In the diary he records:

August 23. I have lost three hundred dollars staking a man to deal monte for me in the past three days. Think I will take Granville's advice and quit gambling.

August 24. Our monte sharps are about to take the town. Getting decidedly obstreperous in their conduct.

August 25. Our stranger monte sharps opened a two hundred dollar monte bank and I broke it in about twenty minutes. About four o'clock in the afternoon two men arrived here from Elk City in the Clearwater mountains. They were in pursuit of our monte sharps for stealing the horses they rode from that place. One of the arrivals was armed with a double barreled shot gun heavily loaded with buckshot and a Colt's navy revolver. Their names were Fox and Bull. Bull had the gun. They slipped quietly into town in the dusk of the evening and meeting me inquired if the three men above described were there. Upon being informed that they were, they stated that they were in pursuit of them for stealing the horses. . . . They requested the cooperation of the citizens in arresting them. I assured them that they should have all the assistance necessary and went with them to look for their men. They found Spillman in Worden and Company's store and bringing their shot gun to bear on him, ordered him to surrender, which he did without a word. They left him under guard and went after the other two who had just opened a monte game in a saloon. Arnett was dealing and Jermagin was "lookout" for him. They stepped inside of the door and ordered them to "throw up their hands." Arnett, who kept his Colt's navy

[17] Stuart, op. cit., p. 205.

[18] Ibid., pp. 208-219.

revolver lying in his lap ready for business, instantly grabbed it,
but before he could raise it, Bull shot him through the breast
with a heavy charge of buckshot, killing him instantly. Jermagin
ran into a corner of the room, exclaiming, "Don't shoot, don't
shoot, I give up." He and Spillman were then tied and placed
under guard until morning.

August 26. Proceedings commenced by burying Arnett who had
died with the monte cards clenched so tightly in his left hand
and his revolver in the right that they could not be wrenched
from his grasp, so were buried with him. Jermagin plead that
the other two overtook him on the trail and gave him a horse to
ride and that he had no knowledge of the horses being stolen,
and what saved him, was Spillman saying that he and Arnett
had found him on the trail packing his blankets and a little food
on his back and that they gave him a horse to ride on which he
strapped his blankets. On this testimony Jermagin was acquitted
and given six hours to leave the country and it is needless to say
he left a little ahead of time. Spillman who was a large, fine
looking man was found guilty and sentenced to be hung in a
half hour. He made no defense and seemed to take little interest
in the proceedings. . . . He . . . walked to his death with a step
as firm and countenance as unchanged as if he had been the nearest spectator instead of the principal actor in the tragedy. . . .
It was the firmness of a brave man, who saw that death was in-
evitable and nerved himself to meet it. He was hung at twenty-
two minutes past two o'clock, August 26, 1862.[19]

Thus was enforced the first vigilante justice in Montana.

No one was getting rich from mining at Gold Creek.
Granville Stuart rather wryly says,

Doctor Atkinson is a most original character. He is always
traveling about the country with a pack horse and one or more
companions, prospecting. He carries a large pair of field glasses,
rides up the cañons keeping along on the ridges when possible, from
points of vantage he will take out his field glasses, take a look at
the surrounding country and declare, "There, the country looks

---

[19] *Ibid.*, pp. 218-20.

good. . . ." I never knew of his digging a hole or of panning a pan of dirt. He does buy into claims occasionally and then resells them. On the whole he was about as lucky as some of us who dig many holes and wash innumerable pans of gravel and succeed in "just missing the pay streak. "[20]

Coupled to the poor showings at Gold Creek were the persistent rumors of riches in other gulches.

September 30. Woody returned from Beaverhead mines. He reports that nearly everybody is making money over there. Everybody excited.

October 5, 1862. York and Irvine came from Beaverhead mines yesterday.

October 22. We went to the Beaverhead mines. . . . We found everybody making money and well satisfied. . . . We have decided to move over. . . . Hired William Babcock to haul about a ton of freight over for us.[21]

Like most Montana mining camps Gold Creek lived on, sometimes enjoying a revival of interest and activity with the advent of newer mining methods. The creek bed was washed and dredged until great piles of gravel filled the gulches. Today it still harbors a few inhabitants. The old log buildings hide behind false fronts; an abandoned gold dredge decays on the bank of the creek, and travelers rush past on Highway 10, oblivious to the fact that a little town, just south of the highway, still marks the cradle of Montana's great mining industry.

---

[20] *Ibid.*, pp. 206-7.
[21] *Ibid.*, pp. 225-26.

2

PIONEER

IF THE STUARTS OF GOLD CREEK WERE NOT SINGLE-minded in their search for gold, such cannot be said of the first miner to do extensive work where the ghost town of Pioneer now stands. In the summer of 1860 Henry Thomas, better known as "Gold Tom" and sometimes called the "Sutter of Montana," began working near the spot first prospected by the Stuarts. He worked prodigiously and alone.

He made a primitive windlass, and hewed out and pinned together with wooden pins and bound around with a picket rope, a bucket with which he hoisted the dirt while sinking the shaft. He would slide down the rope, fill the bucket with gravel, then climb up a notched pole aided by the windlass rope, and hoist the bucket of gravel. He encountered many boulders too large to go into the bucket. Around these he would put a rope and windlass them out. After we located at the crossing of Gold creek, I visited him several times and was amazed to see the amount of work he had done under exceedingly difficult conditions. He also hewed out boards eight inches wide and about seven feet long and made four little sluice boxes. He had no nails, but put them together with wooden pegs. He placed them near his shaft and then dug a ditch from the creek around to the sluice boxes, where he washed the gravel from his shaft and some of the surface dirt. He worked the summers of 1860 and 1861 but could not make more than one dollar and fifty cents a day and often less than that sum, owing to the great disadvantage under which he labored. . . .

He usually preferred to be alone, and would spend days and weeks in the mountains without other companions than his horses and trusty rifle. He was not at all misanthropic, and I never knew him to drink whiskey or to gamble.[1]

Although Pioneer did not boom immediately, its population eventually swelled to four thousand. The gulch was extremely rich and yielded as much as $20,000,000 in placer gold. While the gold lasted, the town had the usual establishments, pastimes, and problems, the latter caused, as in many mining camps, by an unbalanced ratio of men to women. One lovesick swain had the following published in the hope of furthering his suit:

> Take pity, Miss Fanny
> The Belle of Pioneer
> And grant some indulgence
> To a vendor of beer
> Whose heart rending anguish
> Will bring on decline
> Oh, God of creation,
> I wish you was mine.
>
> We'd live in a parlor
> Behind the saloon
> With sour-krout [sic] in plenty
> For our honeymoon;
> We'd have schnapps by the bottle
> To make it go down
> And live in more splendor
> Than any in town.
>
> There is Fowler and Fischer
> And Wallace of yore
> There's cows and there's chickens
> And many things more

---

[1] Reprinted by permission of the publishers, The Arthur H. Clark Company, from *Forty Years on the Frontier*, by Granville Stuart (2 vols.; Cleveland, 1925), I, 162, 165.

But none like your Perry
That sells lager beer
His tender heart is breaking
Each day in Pioneer.

· · · · ·

So now my dear Fanny
If you will incline
To join me in wedlock
Just drop me a line
And great expectations
With me you will share
Not to mention the sour-krout
And oceans of beer.
      PIONEER CITY, April 24th, 1871[2]

Gus Wisner, who spent more than sixty years at Pioneer, was one of the last veterans of '61. He was a "doodle bug expert" who had unshakable faith in the infallibility of his instrument.

The "doodle-bug" according to Wisner is similar to the "water witch." It is based on the theory that all metals give off electrical waves of magnetism. These waves, from certain metal in the ground, attract waves of a similar metal on the surface and cause a definite reaction.

When the "doodle-bug" operator wishes to find gold bearing ore, he makes a gold "doodle-bug." This is done by placing a small piece of gold in the top of a small wooden triangle measuring about an inch on each side. Two holes are bored at each end of the base of the triangle and into these are forced two willow sticks, or handles, about three feet long.

As rays from gold run north and south, the operator faces north and grasps the willow handles at their extremities. He holds the "doodle-bug" parallel to the surface and the palms of his hands are held upward, with the thumbs turned out. The fingers are lightly closed around the willow handles, but not tightly enough to impede its movement.

---

[2] *Missoula and Cedar Creek Pioneer*, April 27, 1871.

The operator walks north. When gold below the surface attracts, through its magnetic waves, the metal in the "doodle-bug," the instrument is slowly forced up without the aid of the operator's hands.

Mr. Wisner claims his is an infallible method of locating all kinds of metal. . . .

As for the operation of the "doodle-bug" only people of a certain type have the natural qualifications necessary for the "doodle-bug's" successful operation. One must have a certain amount of electricity in his body. . . .[3]

It was at Pioneer, Wisner relates, that W. A. Clark, Montana copper magnate, got much of his first start on the road to high finance. He came with a pack train of food supplies about the time of Wisner's arrival. The supplies sold at a high profit and later Clark became interested in the first bank in Montana at Deer Lodge with S. E. Larabie of that city as a partner.

Banking during the heyday of Pioneer was something startlingly different from the marble offices, adding machines, margins, stocks and bonds and debits and credits of the present day. Then the bankers books were probably under his hat and his vaults were his buckskin gold bags and his six shooter. . . .

Gold dust was then the only medium of exchange. It was used for currency and the miners had no way of knowing, from time to time, just what the real market value of their dust was. In this respect the bankers had the advantage.

The firms of Clark & Larabie would receive confidential quotations on raw gold from the mint at Denver. This price usually ranged from 20 to 25 dollars an ounce. The miners were made a standard offer of $18 an ounce for what they took from sluices. The difference between the payment to the miners and the current market price was the bankers' profit.[4]

After the white prospectors found themselves unable to make a living, Tim Lee, a Chinese known as the "mayor of Pioneer," brought in 188 of his compatriots

---

[3] Sid Stoddard for the *Lima Ledger*, April 25, 1932.
[4] *Ibid.*

who washed gold in the ground that had been once worked by the white men.

The Chinese carried away their tailings in baskets and built walls that still stand, a mute testimony to the industry of the Mongolian. Tim Lee was apparently a benign sort of nabob, but he is credited with having had a nervous trigger finger which got out of control twice under justifiable circumstances, it appears.

At any rate he had the respect of his white neighbors and is said to have been the only Chinese in the world to have been accepted into fellowship in a lodge of white Masons.

When Lee died a few months ago in Deer Lodge, he was given a funeral that the family of a white man of standing might have envied.

The mayor of Pioneer stood well with his own countrymen. He buried 172 of them at his own expense—whether in the United States or in the Flowery Kingdom the authorities are not agreed. . . ."[5]

When panning was no longer profitable, an English company, the Gold Creek Mining Company, Ltd., operated a dredge, locally known as the "drudge." The company was soon in legal difficulties that were not helped by the fact that the owners were foreigners. The Forest Service shut off the wood supply that furnished their fuel. Finally, they sold to Patrick Wall, of Butte and the Klondyke, who bought the whole town plus enough extra land to make up 7,000 acres, 6,500 of which were considered gold bearing. The area had already produced $20,000,000 in gold, and Wall was sure that he could recover another $20,000,000. The old town was to be removed and a new town built so that the rich gravel under the old town could be

---

[5] *Montana Standard* (Butte), October 27, 1929.

scooped up by the dredges. The new town was planned by Mrs. Wall.

Cabins for the workers were to be neatly constructed of carefully barked and mortised logs after the design of the Yukon cabin. The first business building was a hotel and dance hall, but the crowds that attended the dances were not prospectors and hurdy-gurdies but dredge operators and farmers with their wives and daughters.

Today the second Pioneer is a ghost town; three sturdy rock buildings, almost hidden by piles of tailings in the creek bed, look out windowless on the deserted streets, and a short distance up the creek one of the dredges stands rotting in the sun and rain.

3

BANNACK

EVEN IN THE VAST AND SEEMINGLY UNPEOPLED stretches of the Rocky Mountains of the early sixties, news of a strike spread like the Chinook that rushes down the eastern slopes of Montana's towering ranges. Far to the south in Colorado's waning mining camps a letter came from Granville Stuart to his brother Thomas: Better prospects here than anything you have seen there. One of the region's lonely wanderers approached the campfires of an immigrant train: They've struck it rich on Benetsee Creek. And in the rumors the wealth multiplied:

> Gold in the sands of the stream
> Gold in the gravel along its banks
> Nuggets the size of peas, of birds' eggs. . . .[1]

The news reached boats coming up the Missouri, wagon trains lumbering over the plains, mines in the Salmon River area of Idaho Territory. In the latter place it reached the ears of Jack White, a large, handsome man familiar in the Oro Fino and Elk City mines. He was a natural leader, energetic, courageous, enterprising. Gathering together six of the seasoned veterans of the mining fields, White ventured out into the

---

[1] *Dillon Tribune,* September 19, 1930.

wilderness of what later was Montana. If there was gold on Benetsee Creek, why not more gold on the creeks of the Missouri drainage? Time was not a determining factor to the prospector. He panned a stream. If the color wasn't there or wasn't good, he moved on. So the White party spent the summer of 1861. They roamed the hills and valleys of what is now southwestern Montana, what was then Idaho Territory. The nights were becoming chill and snow was on the mountains when, on the divide between the Big Hole and the Salmon rivers, the deposit in the turning pan matched the gold of the alder leaves along the stream.

By now their bacon and flour were almost gone; the snow that had been falling lower and lower on the mountains swirled into their camp. There was no chance to do much work before the ground froze and winter drove them to shelter. By mutual consent, they separated with the understanding that, come spring, they would meet again and develop the prospect.

Roy Herndon described that spring meeting in the *Dillon Tribune*, September 17, 1930:

Along in the early spring of 1862 a group of 6 men were seated around a camp fire up in the main range of the Rockies on the west side of the Big Hole. It was a wet, rainy evening just before dark. The camp fire, with its blaze of light, was the one bright spot in all that seeming endless wilderness. A small tent or two could be seen among the shadows of the trees and the steaming pots over the fire betokened the evening meal under preparation. They had left this spot late the fall before and were now just meeting at this, their rendezvous, and they had many tales to tell each other of what they had done and seen during the winter. There was old Jake Whelock who had spent the winter with "Rusty" Hill down in Salt Lake; Bill Sims and Tom Scovill had "holed up" over on the Salmon, where they had lived on fish and deer meat all winter and now were cravin' news and excitement; Sol Lambeth had gone down the Missouri and was full of yarns about the people comin' in on the river boats. Only one of the number was not present, their big leader Jack White. "Where do you suppose he is?" said Bill. "Do you suppose anything has happened to him?" said another. "Naw, you couldn't kill him with pizen. If he don't come it will be because he has found better diggin's, and if he does that, he will send us word." And while they talked thus they heard a loud "Hello" down the creek, and soon John White himself rode up and was greeted hilariously by the group.

"Well, Boys, how you all wintered?" was about the first words he said. "But first of all, lets eat. I'm starved." And while they ate, they talked.

"I'll tell you, men, I've struck it rich—a whole lot richer than we got here," and while they listened with open mouthed astonishment he told them the story.

"You see, as I was coming up here I passed over what some fellow told me was Grasshopper creek. I camped there that night, and next morning as it was raining I let my horses graze and I took my pick and gold pan and walked down the creek a ways to where I had seen some likely lookin' gravel, and I got three or four colors in the first pan, and before night I had a fairly good looking prospect hole, and the gravel all panned. Why, fellers, I got more gold in nearly ever pan than we ever got here and I think we ought to go back tomorrer. What d'say?" And so saying he displayed a small buckskin bag with some placer gold in it that he had panned from his new find the day before. The men all examined this "dust" with a lot of interest.

"Them's nuggets—them's not dust," said old Bill. "We can't get there too quick to suit me."

The early morning saw them on their way to the new diggin's which they reached the afternoon of the second day. As they staked their claims a family of Bannack Indians pitched their tepees close by and sold the boys a half venison so they could start work at once on their claims, and they named the camp "Bannack" from the name of the Indian tribe to which these Indians belonged.

Their work in the days immediately following proved that the ground was far richer than they had even dreamed of, and thus, the "Grasshopper Diggin's," "Bannack" or "East Bannack" with "White's Bar" as the first claim staked, came into existence. . . .

Work was well under way when wagon trains jolting over the Indian trail across Lemhi Pass from the Salmon River mines came upon the White diggings. They had started out for Gold Creek and, not being much impressed by what they saw at Grasshopper, continued on their way. However, Gold Creek looked no better, and they returned the long miles to Grasshopper.

Their provisions, low before they left Gold Creek, were now nearly exhausted. Most of them started the four hundred miles to Salt Lake, hoping to shoot enough game to keep them alive until they got there. Russell, who had decided to stay at the diggings, rode after them and persuaded them to return. Game was more abundant here than in the sage deserts to the south. If necessary, they could always eat their own stock, in better flesh if kept on the lush grass of the Beaverhead area than if exhausted from hauling heavy wagons over the rutted trails to Salt Lake.

They were saved from such an exigency by a large wagon train that arrived shortly afterward. It was led by a Mr. Woodmansee and had provisions enough to get the little colony through the winter which, fortunately, was mild.

In the spring Russell returned to Colorado with dust and nuggets from Bannack. Nothing else was needed; the rush to a new El Dorado was on. Those who had horses rode; those who didn't set out to trudge the endless miles, hoping, perhaps, to join some outfit along the way. Many of them became lost in the untrailed wilderness; some discovered other gold mines, and one helpful fellow erected a sign:

Tu grass Hop Per diggins
30 myle
Kepe the Trale nex the bluffe

And on the other side:

Tu jonni Grants
One Hundred & twenti myle

Through the fall and winter men, women, and even children poured into the area until the town of Bannack, several miles above discovery claim, teemed with five thousand people, including the Stuarts who had moved down from Gold Creek.

The noise of hammer and saw filled the air as houses, sluice boxes or cradles were hastily constructed. Ox teams and pack trains crowded every available space with their loading or unloading; auctioneers cried their wares, drunken Mexicans pranced their bucking mustangs for the edification of the crowd. Saloons ran full blast; the voice of the fiddle and the banjo floated out of the hurdy-gurdy dance halls, and the click of the gamblers' chips was loud and constant. Here and there some gentleman would be trying out his new pistol on a neighbor or relieving some luckless miner of his bag of dust. Drinking, fighting, gambling and dancing was the order of the day, indulgence blossomed into crime and the hangman's tree soon bore its fruit.[2]

The prospectors who formed the majority of Bannack's inhabitants were simple, honest men, moved in all their dealings by a basic code of justice. To set forth their creed they drew up and circulated in Bannack the "Miners Ten Commandments."

First commandment: Thou shalt have no other claim than one.
Second commandment: Thou shalt not make thyself any false

---

[2] *Mineral Independent* (Superior), September 1, 1921.

claims or any likeness to a mean man, by jumping one; for I, a miner, am a just man and I will visit the miners round about and they will judge thee; and when they shall decide thou wilt take thy pick thy pan thy shovel and thy blankets and with all thou hast thou shalt depart to seek other diggings but thou shalt find none.

Third commandment: Thou shalt not go prospecting before thy claim gives out. Neither shalt thou take thy money or gold dust or thy good name to the gaming table for monte twenty-one roulette faro lunsquent and poker will prove thee that the more thou puttest down the less thou shalt take up and when thou thinkest of thy wife and children thou shalt hold theyself guiltless though insane.

Fourth commandment: Thou shalt keep the Sabbath day holy and shall do no work other than cooking the pork and beans for the week's supply getting in firewood and doing the week's wash and baking the week's supply of bread.

[The fifth commandment is skipped, presumably because the Biblical command is accepted without revision.]

Sixth commandment: Thou shalt not drink mint juleps nor sherry cobblers through a straw nor gurgle from a bottle the raw materials nor take it from a decanter; for while thou art swallowing down thy purse and the coat from thy back thou art burning the coat off thy stomach.

Seventh commandment: Thou shalt not grow discouraged and think of going home before thou hast made thy pile because thou hast not struck a lead, nor found a rich crevice nor sunk a shaft upon a rich pocket, lest in going home thou shalt leave a job paying four dollars a day to take, ashamed, a job back east at 50 cents a day; and serve thee right. Thou knowest that by staying here thou mightest strike a lead and make 50 dollars a day and keep thy self-respect and when thou goest home thou shalt have enough to make thyself and others happy.

Eighth commandment: Thou shalt not steal the dust or the tools of another miner, for he will surely find out what thou hast done and will call together his fellow miners and they, unless the law hinders them, will hang thee or give thee fifty lashes, or shave thy head or brand thy cheek with an "R" like a horse, to be read by all men.

Ninth commandment: Thou shalt tell no false tales about good diggins in the mountains, to benefit a friend who may have mules, blankets or provisions and tools that he wishes to sell lest thy neighbor, deceived by thee into making the trip shall one day return through the snow with naught left but his rifle, contents of which he shall present to you in a manner that shall cause thee to fall down and die like a dog.

Tenth commandment: Remember thy wife and children that are in the east and be true to them in thought, word and deed. Avoid the temptation to become a squaw-man and to people this country with half-breeds, for while there is naught to be said against these boys and girls as individuals, the fact remains that they will give the Indians the benefit of their white training and thus make the redskins more dangerous to the white man.[3]

This took care of the situation in so far as the miners were concerned in their simple relationships; it did not take care of the professional outlaws who followed the stampede.

The settlement was filled with gambling houses and saloons where bad men and worse women held constant vigil, and initiated a reign of infamy which nothing but a strong hand could extirpate.[4]

The thirst for gold was shared by all classes and there was no vice unrepresented. Many types of character were developed; but as a general thing, the most aggressive and crafty, usually predominated. The Civil War also caused many to migrate to the mines of the Northwest. There were drifters who kept drifting, war or no war. Many deserters from the Union and Confederate armies made their way to the mining camps.[5]

It was not long before the worst of these elements developed an organization under the leadership of Henry

[3] *Dillon Examiner*, September 20, 1939.

[4] N. P. Langford, *Vigilante Days and Ways* (2 vols.; Boston: J. G. Cupples, 1890), I, 240.

[5] Oren Sassman, "Metal Mining in Historic Beaverhead" (unpublished Master's thesis, Montana State University, Missoula, 1941), p. 66.

Plummer. Of all Western bad men, Henry Plummer is one of the most interesting. He came from a good Connecticut background and impressed everyone he met with his attractive appearance and affable manners. Granville Stuart, surely no incompetent judge of men, happened to meet him in Gold Creek and noted in his diary:

On our way to Hell Gate at Beaver Dam hill we met two fine looking young men. One of them said his name was Henry Plummer, the other was Charles Reeves. . . . They were from Elk City on Clearwater, and enquired about the mines at Gold creek and at Beaverhead. They rode two good horses and had another packed with their blankets and provisions. We liked their looks and told them that we were only going down to Hell Gate and would return to Gold creek in a few days and asked them to return to Hell Gate with us and then we could all go up the canon together. They accepted our invitation and in a few days we all went up to Gold creek together.[6]

Others were also deceived by Plummer who managed to get himself elected sheriff of Bannack. From then on he led a double life, as sheriff and as outlaw leader. He was a common, even a romantic sight on the streets of Bannack. Usually arrayed in the finest buckskins and riding his magnificent horse, he was often accompanied by Buck Stinson dressed in the border style of buckskin and sombrero. In 1863 he married Eliza Bryan and seemed the ideal bridegroom. It wasn't long, though, before a few doubting citizens began seeing a relationship between Plummer's absences and the more daring of the many murders and holdups that were occurring frequently. His fortunes also seemed

---

[1] Reprinted by permission of the publishers, The Arthur H. Clark Company, from *Forty Years on the Frontier*, by Granville Stuart (2 vols.; Cleveland, 1925), I, 223 ff.

to rise and fall with stage robberies. To add to the
suspicions, it was obvious that he associated with some
of the city's most unsavory characters: George Shears,
a known horsethief; George Ives, a gunman; Whiskey
Bill and Mexican Frank, both "roadsters"; and last, but
certainly not least, the brutish Boone Helm, over whom
hung the frontier's ugliest suspicion, that of cannibal-
ism. Too often he had gone out with a partner only
to return alone and well fed after undergoing what to
another would have been starvation conditions. More
than one mining camp from Colorado to California
had given him the choice of getting out of town or
dangling from a rope. The result was that he found
himself, with a lot of other desperate characters, joining the mass murder schemes of Henry Plummer. More
than a hundred men were coldly shot down before the
aroused citizens took the law into their own hands.
Then, one bitter December day in 1863, about twenty
of Bannack's defenders, meeting in secret, swore the
following oath:

> We the undersigned uniting oursel in a party for the laudible
> purpos of arresting thievs & murders & recove stollen property do
> pledge ourselves upon our sacred honor each to all others & solemnly
> swear that we will reveal no secrets violate no laws of right &
> not desert each other or our standard of justice so help us God as
> with our hand & seal this 23 of December A.D. 1863.[7]

No one outside of the committee knew who the members were; in all their law enforcement they used the
mysterious symbol 3-7-77 as a signature of the committee. Not even today, although the Montana State

---

[7] *Hysham Echo*, September 28, 1933. Other versions with improved spelling,
claim to be the original.

Highway Patrol has adopted the symbol as its official insignia, does anyone apparently know for sure what it means. The most common explanation is that it stands for the dimensions of a grave: three feet wide, seven feet long and seventy-seven inches deep. Another explanation is that it meant to the man who found it on his doorstep that he had three hours, seven minutes and seventy-seven seconds to get out of town. Considering that many of those marked by the committee were given no such opportunity, it seems likely that this explanation is wrong.

Plummer, when he was arrested, begged for such an opportunity.

"Give me a few hours' start and my black horse, and I'll get out of town, leaving to you, Gentlemen, my weight in gold." The plea was useless, and from the gallows that he himself had erected for another, Henry Plummer went to his death, coolly and audaciously, as he had lived. "Now, men, as a last favor, let me beg that you will give me a good drop."

Following him to the gallows were thirteen of his followers, and only once did mob rule prevail. This was when Joe Pizanthia, "The Greaser," was executed. The Greaser had holed up in his cabin and, when two of the vigilantes approached to seize him, he shot them both, killing one and wounding Smith Ball, the other. The crowd, infuriated by the death of their man, borrowed a howitzer that had been stored under the bed in Governor Edgerton's cabin and proceeded to blast three holes through the outlaw's cabin. When the smoke cleared, they called to him to come out; getting no response a member of the party was given the privi-

lege of emptying his gun into Pizanthia. The body
was then dragged through the streets and finally thrown
into a huge bonfire where it was so completely con-
sumed that not even a bone was recovered. The next
day girls from the dance halls panned the ashes in the
hope that the Greaser had gone to his death loaded with
dust, but nothing was recovered.

No one knows what disposition was made of many
of the other road agents' bodies. Some were turned over
to their womenfolk and quietly buried in unmarked
graves. Plummer's was thrown into a pit with that
of Ives and a pile of rough stones was left to mark the
spot in Hangman's Gulch.[8]

Plummer's bones did not rest in peace. Five weeks
after the execution, Dr. John Glick, a prominent Bannack physician, decided to settle a mystery that had
long bothered him. At one time, under the threat of
death, he had treated Plummer for what appeared to
be a gunshot wound in the right forearm. However,
he had not been able to recover the bullet that he felt
sure was lodged in the arm. Now was his chance to
satisfy his curiosity. In the dead of night he dug into
the grave, severed the arm and cached it in a snow-
drift while he attended a dance that was in progress.
In the middle of the dance a little dog entered dragging the arm and laid it proudly at his mistress' feet.
In the ensuing furor, the doctor managed to retrieve
his grisly object and much to his scientific satisfaction

---

[8] It must not be assumed from this that the unprotected bodies were tossed
into the pit. Mr. French was paid forty-three dollars for making a coffin for
Plummer. His son, who still lives in Dillon, presented the receipt to the State
Historical Society.

found the bullet that he knew all along must be there.[9]

Later two drunks in Bannack decided to dig into the grave. They recovered the skull and, after pelting each other with it until they wearied of the game, they turned it over to the Bank Exchange saloon where it graced the bar for several years. Some say it was lost when the saloon burned, others that it was sent to someone in the East who may still have this precious memento of Montana's early history.[10]

The activities of the road agents and the Vigilantes has tended to overshadow other events in Bannack.[11] Actually those other events form a rich tapestry of the life of an early mining town.

The residents had some trouble with the Indians after whom the town was named, but this never reached the proportions that it did farther east. In 1863 a Bannack chief and his wife camped near the gulch. With them was a white girl whom they had captured after killing her parents. The stalwart citizens of Bannack determined to rescue the child. When the chief got word of this plan he assembled his whole army of warriors, numbering some three hundred, and lined them up in full battle array within sight of the courthouse and the blockhouses of the little town. The inhabitants, not primarily of fighting stock, were terrified. However, either through the clever strategy of some white man or just through good fortune, the Indians came into possession of enough liquor to mellow their belligerence. The girl was ransomed and, although the

---

[9] Homer Faust in the *Hardin Tribune Herald,* September 19, 1930.

[10] *Dillon Daily Tribune,* March 12, 1948.

[11] For a full account of Vigilante justice read Dimsdale's *Vigilantes of Montana.*

chief in a more sober moment made an abortive attempt to recapture her, the affair blew over with no
blood being shed on either side.

Sometimes the Indians were more sinned against than
sinning, as can be seen in the following letter from
James Fergus, a coffinmaker of Bannack:

> BANNACK CITY GOLD MINES
> IDAHO TERRITORY, Jan. 21, 1863
> Morning bright and pleasant; another coffin to make—three in
> a few days. . . . At four the coffin was finished. Went across the
> river to hang a door, was detained until dark, when suddenly
> six or eight shots were heard in rapid succession across the river
> instantly followed by the most unearthly screaming and wailing
> from some Indian lodges situated on Yankee Flat, occupied by a
> few helpless squaws and papooses of the lower class, inoffensive,
> doing no one any harm, and living among us by virtue of an under-
> standing or treaty made with the Indians last fall. I hastened
> over and found that some fiends had crawled up unperceived and
> fired into the lodges, and killed one or two old Indian squaws and
> wounded several of the papooses. Of course consternation ensued,
> and interpreters were sent for to ascertain from the Indians who
> had committed the horrible deed, and to assure them that the whites
> generally were not going to massacre them. Still more horrible to
> relate, while this investigation was going on in the Indian lodges,
> the murderers returned reinforced, and, regardless of the presence
> of the whites and the wailings and anguish of the bereaved savages,
> fired the contents of their guns and revolvers into the lodges wound-
> ing four white men—one mortally—and more Indian women and
> children. What an atrocious deed! What a savage murder! Here
> is work for the morrow. The miners are aroused at last, murderers
> are to be caught and punished and the Indians to be appeased or
> a thousand armed savages may pounce upon us at an unlooked for
> moment.[12]

Cultural, social, and political forces struggled to ele-

---

[12] *Rocky Mountain Magazine,* December, 1900, p. 266.

vate the town to some semblance of civilization. A private school was conducted for a short time in 1863. In 1864 a short term was again held during the winter. Later school met in the first church built in Bannack, and by 1909 Bannack had a busy, up-to-date school, but the need for it was fast waning.

Religion got its start when a colored minister, Mr. Woods, arriving with Hugh O'Neil's wagon train, preached Bannack's first sermon on April 20, 1863. Religion, though respected was never very popular in Bannack.

As usual, the first of these [Protestant clergy] to arrive was a Methodist, who might be classed among the old-time circuit riders. He was a good man, and sincere in his belief, but of scant education.

After being in Bannack for a while, he managed to interest a few of its residents in the desirability of holding church services on Sunday. . . .

There was never a large attendance at these services, and those who came strayed in at any hour, stayed as long as suited them, and then left. All hymns were given out line by line which, taken together with the uncertainty of keeping the pitch and remembering the words, complicated their rendering. . . .

. . . The dogs and cats, of which there were many, wandered back and forth from one room to the other, and were disposed to be quite friendly with the churchgoers, especially the choir members. One cat and our tenor became fast friends. Pussy helped the latter to while away the time between hymns. . . .

Miners working hard day in and day out, were not inclined to be spiritually minded and on Sunday nights sought to be diverted rather than instructed.[13]

The most wholesome of these diversions were community dances.

---

[13] Martha Plassman in the *Silver State Post* (Deer Lodge), November 13, 1941. Mrs. Plassman was the daughter of Edgerton.

There were two good fiddlers in camp, "Buz" Caven and Lou P. Smith, and something over thirty white women. Seven were unmarried, but did not remain so very long. We had a number of fine balls attended by all the respectable people and enjoyed by young and old alike. Best suits packed in the bottom of our "war bags" and long forgotten, were dragged out, aired and pressed, as best we could, and made ready for these festive occasions. A very few of the men who had their wives with them, sported white shirts with stiffly starched bosoms, but the majority wore flannel shirts with soft collars and neckties. These dances were very orderly; no man that was drinking was allowed in the hall. The young people danced the waltz, schottish, varsoviane, and polka, but the older ones stuck to the Virginia-reel and quadrille. There were usually about ten men to every woman at these balls so the women danced every dance. These gatherings were very informal and very enjoyable. Tickets were 5 dollars gold and there was no supper served.[14]

For the few respectable women these balls were about the only social activity and, perhaps to be distinguished from their gayer sisters, such women were inclined to favor sober styles and manners. Their print dresses were good enough for the occasion. If they had brought anything more elaborate with them, they usually kept it stored in their trunks or sold it at fancy prices to fancy ladies of the town.

Jewelry made from native gold was common and appeared in rings or broaches. The most favored design was a bunch of grapes and leaves in different colors of gold. Roses were also popular.

Commerce and communications were carried on with great difficulties. Beef was supplied from Johnny Grant's and Kohrs' ranches near Deer Lodge but everything else—food, clothing, mining machinery, and mail

---

[14] Stuart, *op. cit.*, p. 233.

—had to be brought in from "the States." If merchandise was hauled by way of South Pass and Fort Hall, the wagon trains had to cross the Continental Divide twice. If it came by water up the Missouri, then by land from Fort Benton, five hundred extra miles were added to the long trip. Freight rates were high and the supply of any item uncertain.

The independent merchant or freighter had to anticipate his market, and that market seems rather surprising today. Since mice, rats, vermin, and all other conceivable pests plagued the miners both in their cabins and in the mines, cats were much in demand. Ira Meyers, on his way to Bannack with a load of freight, spotted a cat and seven kittens when he stopped at a farm two days out of Denver. He offered the housewife two dollars and fifty cents for each one of the kittens. She was reluctant to part with one to which she had become especially attached, but offered to sell him the mother cat and all the other kittens for $2.50 for the batch.

Taking the clothes out of his trunk and putting them in gunny sacks, he converted the trunk into a cat house so that his new family would be comfortable on the long haul to Bannack.

All along the trail his outfit was the most popular because of the pets, and, when he reached Bannack, he sold one kitten for ten dollars in gold dust and all the others for fifteen dollars each. He could easily have demanded more, but one hundred dollars profit on seven cats seemed sufficient.

At first private expresses carried what mail was brought into camp, but in July, 1863, a weekly pony express coming from Fort Bridger, Wyoming, began carrying mail at the rate of fifty cents each item. Both mail and passengers were carried by Oliver's Express operating out of Salt Lake.

The first meeting of Masons in Montana was held in the winter of 1862-63. Eight men attended, and Leeson tells of the fate of some of these founders of Montana's Masonic lodges:

Copley, while acting as deputy sheriff, was killed in Bannack in the spring of 1863 by a Spaniard, whom he was attempting to arrest for murder. The miners of Grasshopper creek put a rope around the Spaniard's neck and dragged him up and down the streets of Bannack until he was dead. . . . Geary was shot by the Indians while on a prospecting trip near the head waters of Wind river, in company with Jim Stuart, Brother Bostick, and others. Knowing that he could not live long, shot and killed himself, in order that his companions might escape from the Indians with their lives. He was buried on a small stream, tributary [of the] Snake river, near where he was shot. . . . Bostick was shot and killed by Indians in the summer of 1864, while on a "revenge trip," as they termed it, through the Wind river mountains, in company with James Stuart and others—his companions fleeing for their lives.[15]

Besides their fraternal organizations, the citizens of Bannack were also interested in politics.

The miners . . . made a practice of observing the Sabbath, not as the sky pilot would have them, but by a cessation of labor in the gold diggings, devoting the day to pleasure and recreation. It was their custom to gather in some central place and be entertained by speeches on subjects of local interest.

One of the popular speakers at these Sunday afternoon meetings

---

[15] M. A. Leeson, *History of Montana, 1739-1885* (Chicago, Warner, Beers, 1885), p. 481.

was Con Orem, then the heavyweight champion pugilist of the
gold country, and the idol of the miners.

Orem loved what was the equivalent of that day to the spot-
light of more modern times. He talked almost as he fought which
was saying much for his oratorical powers.[16]

One Sunday afternoon someone demanded, "Why not start a
movement right here looking to the organization of another territory, and make Bannack the capital? . . ."

Con Orem was very much interested. He mounted a wagon just
outside the saloon and made a speech favoring the organization of
a territory. Several hundred miners listened and applauded.[17]

In the audience were Wilbur F. Sanders, a lawyer,
and his uncle, Sidney Edgerton, who had just finished
serving in the Thirty-sixth and Thirty-seventh Con-
gresses in Washington. To them was delegated the re-
sponsibility for arranging the political aspects of the
project, and the miners took upon themselves the task
of winning support and providing the financial aid
needed to send their representatives to Congress. Miners
from Bannack were sent around to the neighboring
"Cities"—Virginia, Summit, Nevada—to explain the
plan and raise money to finance it. Everywhere the
idea was received with enthusiasm, and $2,500 worth
of dust and nuggets poured in as contributions. With
this wealth in their pockets, the delegation set out for
Washington. Mrs. Plassman, daughter of the governor
to-be says:

My father and others took [gold] with them to Washington in
all its forms: in quartz, as gold dust and nuggets, nor did they
fail to carry ingots of the precious metal in proof that enough
gold was produced to call for the erection of quartz mills.

---

[16] *Dillon Examiner*, June 8, 1921.
[17] *Philipsburg Mail*, January 7, 1927.

These gold bars, according to my recollection, were about three or four inches long and two wide, and cast in molds after the gold was melted in a crucible. It chanced on a time that a crucible broke and its contents, running out, formed in cooling a golden mass about the charcoal used for heating. It was a beautiful object, and looked as though it might have been dug from the earth. Mr. Thompson, a merchant of Bannack, an active member of the first territorial legislature, and the designer of our seal, purchased the nugget (?) and gave it into my father's custody.

I have already told how gold bars were quilted into the front of the latter's overcoat by my mother, making that garment suspiciously heavy, and how he never permitted anyone else to carry it, or the suitcase which held the nugget, gold dust and other specimens, while he was on his way east. . . .

When the nugget arrived it played an important part in proving the wealth of the proposed new territory, where it was believed such masses of gold existed and could be dug from the ground with pick and shovel.[18]

The Territorial Act was signed by Lincoln in 1864, and Mr. Edgerton was designated governor.

Back home in Bannack the status of governor did not set Mr. Edgerton aside greatly from his fellow citizens. There was no "governor's mansion" for the citizens to battle over as there was almost a century later. Mrs. Plassman describes the home thus:

It was certainly not designed for a residence, as it consisted of but one long and wide room, with a kitchen annex. This had to be remodeled before we could move into it. In front there was a passable door . . . and that stood in the center, flanked by two windows. On the east side of the room midway its length, was a fireplace of rough stones, constructed in such a manner as to carry most of the heat up the chimney.

Just beyond this fireplace, a transverse partition of unplaned boards divided the front portion from the rear, which was then laterally partitioned into a large and a small room, the latter having

---

[18] Martha Plassman in the *Roundup Tribune,* September 20, 1928.

no windows, being lighted only by a door. In the large rear room, and in the kitchen there were but two windows. Glass was expensive, and therefore a luxury, not to be recklessly indulged in.

There was a fireplace in the small kitchen, but this we never used preferring to install our trusty sheetiron camp stove, which had given us such faithful service during our journey over plains and mountains. No furniture could be bought with two exceptions. A bedstead, which was installed in the large rear room where I slept, and three chairs were purchased for the front room. One of these had an ox-bow back.

Instead of bedsteads, bunks, made of boards, were nailed against the walls, and were more comfortable than the one bedstead we were able to find in town. We brought with us some matresses, and these failing to supply the beds, ticks filled with hay or straw took their place. After sleeping on the ground, or in wagons for three months, none of us were disposed to covet luxuries. . . .

. . . The window west of the door lighted a little curtained space my father used as his office. Of course nothing secret could be discussed there, but it offered the appearance of privacy, at least. Here lobbyists during the session of the first legislature came to further the interests of bills they wished to have passed, and today, in fancy, I can hear N. P. Langford recounting in a droning voice something about "leads, lodes, and ledges" which I did not understand, although the alliteration amused me.

The walls of the front room were covered with sheets my mother had providentially brought with her, but there were not enough of them to cover the ceiling. Blue cambric curtained off the space occupied by a bed, and the office section. It was under this bed that the mountain howitzer was stored together with its shells, which the Fiske party brought with them to Bannack. This was later used to shell the house of Joe Pizanthia, the Mexican who killed Copley. The men did not stop to mount it on its carriage but carried it in their arms to the top of the hill above the house. . . .

Our tableware continued to be the tin dishes and cups which had been in daily use on the plains, and spoons of the same once precious metal took the place of silver. . . . Style of living is relative at best. Our house was the best in town when we lived in it —what more could we ask? On the mountainside above Yankee Flat, men lived in dug-outs, and doubtless envied the magnificence of our residence, although they were probably more comfortable when it rained than we, under our dirt roof. . . .[19]

The next-largest celebration ever held in Montana's old capital city was staged in 1876. The late Thomas J. Farrel was marshal of the day. One of the most unique floats ever included in a procession was handled this day by Captain Todd, first cousin to President Lincoln's wife, Colonel Diemling, and Mr. Wilson, editor of the *Montanan*. Captain Todd owned a very large mule weighing about 1,800 pounds. This animal was hitched up with a burro and drew a float through the streets with Mr. Wilson perched on a high pedestal orating to the throng. Captain Todd was the driver.

James Williams, son of Captain Williams of the Vigilantes, had saved up enough money to buy a suit of clothes and came to town to attend the celebration. He purchased some firecrackers. A town boy saw the bunch sticking from his pocket, slipped up behind him and set them on fire, and Jimmy's clothes were in rags when he returned home.

One old-timer tells of a man by the name of "Cider" Nick making cider from dried apples on that day and selling the beverage at twenty-five cents a glass. Dried apple pies could also be bought at a stand on the occasion for seventy-five cents each.

But above and beyond all these diversions loomed the work of the miners. Arriving in Bannack in 1863, James Kirkpatrick, a tenderfoot from Wisconsin, leaves us this description of the work done by the miners as he saw it on his arrival at Grasshopper Creek:

---

[19] *Kalispell Times*, June 2, 1927.

Down by the creek, on either side, were miners rocking cradles, "rockers" they called them, guiltless, however, of infants, but shaking the precious dust from gravel washed by intermittent dippersful of water from the stream, a primitive though simple and economical method quite prevalent in the placer diggings of the West.

Some were "cleaning up" the results of the day's labor, "panning it out" in a shallow sheet iron, water-filled gold pan by a skillful rotary motion of the hands. We looked with wonder at the shining handfuls of wealth so simply recovered from the sand. . . .

Sluice boxes, with three twelve inch sides, open at the top, and twelve to fourteen feet long carried swift streams of water over removable slatted or auger-perforated bottoms for retrieving the gold shoveled into them all the day among sand and gravel.

. . . From four to six or more boxes formed a set. The coarser gravel and rocks were being forked out at the upper box by a boy or man standing astride.

The larger flakes of gold and the nuggets were usually detained in the upper boxes of the set while the finer particles with the ubiquitous black or magnetic sand lodged along the lower riffles.

Another kind of mining was being done wherein the water, gold, gravel and earth all went through the same kind of boxes but the material instead of being handled with pick and shovel was being undermined and sluiced down from the sloping hillsides along the creek by means of hydraulic hose and nozzles under tremendous pressure.

Water for rocking and for common sluicing was mostly obtained from the stream while that for hydraulic operations and bar diggings was invariably supplied by ditches meandering along the mountain slopes on either side of the gulch.[20]

Only after the "poor man's diggings" were all taken up was attention diverted to extracting the gold from quartz. This operation required more than a pan, a shovel and a sluice box. The ore had to be crushed and machinery for this operation, coming in as it had to by freight, was extremely costly. In the winter of

[20] *Dillon Tribune,* March 14, 1930.

1862-63, an enterprising blacksmith of Bannack, using old wagon tires as stamps, constructed the first stamp mill to work in the gulch. It had four shoes or stamps for crushing the ore, and was powered by a crude water wheel.

In all these operations the physical effort involved was tremendous. Miners would stand all day in the cold water of the stream; all the shoveling was done by hand; lumber for the sluice boxes was whipsawed from native timber. The only help that man had besides his two hands was that furnished by horses and mules that were used in hauling and road-making, but with these primitive methods, possibly one hundred million dollars in gold was taken from the Grasshopper area, and it was this gold from Montana that did much in financing the Civil War and bringing it to a successful conclusion.

An hour's meditation among the headboards of the old cemetery at Bannack summons up the ghosts of its stirring past. There is one that reads:

Nellie Paget
Age 22
Shot April 22
1864[21]

Nellie Paget wasn't her real name. Back in a little town in Illinois she was Helen Patterson, a good, respectable girl courted by steady Howard Humphrey. In 1862, promising to return to Howard within a year, she set off with her sister and brother-in-law to visit the gold fields of Montana. Arriving at Bannack, she

---

[21] *Ibid.*, September 19, 1930.

saw a new and glamorous life that might be hers. Whereas at home eligible men were scarce and often dull, here she found many who would pour gold dust into her little hands in exchange for her favors. Awakened to the power she held, she adopted the name Nellie Paget and entered the saloons and hurdy-gurdies as a dancing girl. Many men, including members of the Plummer gang, drank to her charms and fought over her smiles. One day in the saloon a miner, inflamed by her attentions to another, whipped out his gun and shot her through the head. Without great to-do her friends buried her in the cemetery on top of the hill.

Back in Illinois Howard had been waiting. Now and then men would pass through the little town on their way home from the gold fields. Of these he would seek news of his love. Four years went by before one returning prospector, knowing Nellie's story, bluntly informed Howard of the life she was leading. Furious at such slander, the faithful swain knocked his informant down and continued his wait. After fifty-seven years, as a broken old man, he decided to go West to find—and face—the truth. In 1917 he arrived in Butte; from there he journeyed to Bannack only to stand, hopeless and disillusioned, beside the untended grave of Nellie Paget.

South of Bannack lies the Horse Prairie Mining District, famous not for the wealth it produced as much as for the fact that here was the first appearance on Montana's stage of a man who was to play a dominant role in the state's political and economic development.

The first appearance of W. A. Clark was not impressive.

Gus Greater said: "I remember well seeing W. A. Clark, a little red-headed fellow, with his pack on his back, the day he left Bannack for Jeff Davis Gulch. He was wearing a soldier's overcoat, with one of the tails gone, that was said to have been caused by getting too close to a campfire, sometimes when he was cold."[22]

Clark himself describes his first activity in Montana:

We reached Horse Prairie Creek on the 7th day of July, where we went into camp just below the crossing on the way to Bannack. I saw a wagon and a tent a short distance away on the other side of the creek, so I went over and accosted the gentleman in charge of the establishment. He was evidently preparing to build a house, as a load of logs had been delivered nearby. . . . Afterwards, having located twenty miles above the point on Horse Prairie Creek, to engage in mining, I became well acquainted with this individual, whose name was Martin Barrett. . . .

The next morning we drove to Bannack, reaching there about noon, when we turned our cattle out to graze while we prepared something to eat. Our camp was on Yankee Flat, where there were a few cabins, one of which was afterwards noted as the home of Ned Ray, one of the desperate "road agents," or highway men.

While we were eating our meal a rather old man by the name of Baugh came over from the town and told us a story about an important discovery of gold which had been made about a days' drive from Bannack. He said the story of the discovery had leaked out and a stampede would take place that night, and said: "If you boys will take your wagon and haul a barrel of whiskey, a tent, some grub, and a few boxes of cigars, I will send a man along to show you the way. . . ."

Selby and I then accepted the offer of Baugh, and at ten o'clock that evening I drove over to Baugh's saloon and loaded up the "wet" goods, cigars, etc., and started with Baugh's guide, whose name was R. T. Kennon. They called him Dick; I knew him afterwards when living in Deer Lodge. . . . We found, however after starting, that Dick did not know anything more about the direction we ought to go than we did ourselves, but it turned out all

---

[22] T. J. Dimsdale, *Vigilantes of Montana* (Virginia City, M.T.: Montana Post Press, 1866), p. 209.

right, as we found some stampeders already on the way; some of them afoot, others on horseback, and all we had to do was to follow the crowd. Our route lay back to Horse Prairie Creek and westward to Red Butte, about ten miles from the crossing, where we stopped to prepare breakfast. In the meantime hundreds of people had passed us and we did not get into the camp we started for until late in the afternoon, when we discovered a man by the name of Roe Dorsett and party had discovered gold on a bar, which they were working by the means of ground sluices, but aside from this, I afterward found that there were no other bars and that neither the main gulch or any of the side gulches, with one exception, contained gold in paying quantities.

Baugh, our benefactor, rode into camp just after we arrived and set up his tent and dispensed to the hungry and thirsty crowd, in short order and no doubt at satisfactory prices, the goods we had hauled for him.

Having found all the ground staked, Selby and I the following day, started prospecting in the adjacent gulches, where we spent several days, but could only get colors in different places where we sank to bedrock. Upon leaving camp we told Baugh that we were going prospecting for several days and would then return. He said, "All right. I am going to do a little prospecting myself. If you boys find anything good stake me in and I will do the same thing with you." To which we agreed as it is a universal rule among prospectors.

Upon our return, after several days of fruitless search, we found nearly all the stampeders gone, but Baugh was still there. Sure enough, only a mile from the camp he had found a little dry gulch that gave encouraging prospects, and as he was an ex-rebel, he named it "Jeff Davis" Gulch, and true to his promise, he had located us both in, that is with claims 100 feet in length from rim to rim, according to the established rules prevailing in those days, and really we got the best ground in the gulch, which we proceeded to develop. Not being much inclined to do much himself, he offered to sell his interest, agreeing to give some time for payment. . . . We were obliged to strip off about four feet of waste before reaching pay dirt near the bedrock. As there was no water in the gulch, we were obliged to haul the dirt to the main creek, where we put it in our sluice boxes. There being no lumber with which to make the sluice boxes, I had to go to Bannack to purchase some and get some "grub" also, as we were running short about that time.

We were not in a very flush financial condition at that time. Upon my arrival at Bannack I found five letters from home that anticipated me and had been carried from Salt Lake by private express which had been established between that place and Bannack. The price of transportation of a letter at that time was one dollar each, and I had just five dollars value in Bob Tail dust (a term applied in Colorado to gold amalgam, the product of the mills of that country, and at that time it was the sole currency in circulation in Colorado). I had, besides, a fractional greenback currency of the denomination of fifty cents. I gladly parted with the five dollars for the letters; therefore, I was obliged to get credit for the lumber and some few other articles which we needed, and this I readily obtained. During our prospecting trip I found a very fine pair of elk antlers, which I brought to Bannack, and for which Cy Skinner, who kept a saloon and who was afterward hung by the Vigilantes near Hell Gate, offered to give me ten dollars and this I readily accepted.

Returning to the gulch, I found that my companion had commenced operations, and it was not long until we installed our equipment and began our experience at placer mining. We first got some logs and built a cabin about fifteen by twenty feet in dimensions, which was covered in the conventional style with a roof of split poles covered over with dirt, and which we found very satisfactory in absolutely dry weather. We took the hind wheels of the wagon, which we converted into a cart for the purpose of hauling dirt, one yoke of oxen being used. We had about a half-mile to haul the dirt to Colorado Creek, where we constructed three sluice boxes of lumber which I had brought from Bannack. The summer and fall months were very fine, and we worked almost uninterruptedly until the beginning of November. We usually observed Sundays and refrained from working. My partner, who was very fond of cards, usually passed the day and sometimes the night, at Dorsett camp a mile below.[23]

Clark soon sold his holdings to hydraulic operators who, in turn, after skimming the cream from the milk,

---

[23] *Dillon Examiner*, November 17, 1895.

sold out to Chinese operators in 1872. The thrifty, painstaking Chinese washed the gulches for the next two years, taking out as much as $36,000 in six weeks of operation. Today the name "Chinatown" or "China Diggins" still clings to the scene of their activities, but the little red-headed discoverer is remembered mostly for his vast financial empire, his political machinations, and the unsavory reputation of his bizarre family.[24]

[24] For a discussion of the Clark family read W. D. Mangam's *The Clarks, an American Phenomenon.* (New York: Silver Bow Press, 1941).

4

VIRGINIA CITY

VIRGINIA CITY WAS PERHAPS THE GREATEST OF MON-tana's mining camps and is today the only "restored" camp in the state. The mines that gave it birth were discovered in 1863 only a year after the discovery of Grasshopper Gulch. It was while they were at the Grass-hopper diggings that Barney Hughes, Henry Edgar, Harry Rodgers, Bill Sweeney, and Bill Fairweather de-cided to leave Bannack and seek their fortunes on the Yellowstone. On January 14, 1863, they left Bannack for Deer Lodge where they planned to outfit the expe-dition and proceed to the Yellowstone as soon as the weather would permit. About six weeks later they set out from Deer Lodge intending to strike the Yellow-stone country in the vicinity of the Gallatin River.

On the morning of May 1, the little party found itself suddenly surrounded by a sizable party of Crow Indians in full war paint and regalia. Being greatly outnumbered, the prospectors had no choice but to sur-render and hope for the best. Versions of their escape vary widely. One story claims that Fairweather the Fearless seized a snake in his bare hands and thereby so impressed the Indians that they released the party.

Another story is that the Indians were marching their prisoners around a sacred "medicine bush" when Bill, becoming impatient as he often did, seized the bush, yanked it up by the roots and hit the medicine man over the head with it. The outraged redskins demanded blood, but Chief Red Bear, a friend of the whites, harangued his fellow Crows for more than ten hours and so wore down their resistance that they let the captives go, probably rather than listen longer.

Still another explanation credits an old squaw who had befriended the captives with creeping up to them during the night, warning them that the braves planned to kill them the next day, and leading them to safety past their unsuspecting guards.

Whatever version is correct, the party escaped unhurt, and, although the Indians had kept their best horses and the bulk of their supplies, they were not destitute and continued to carry out their original plan, moving from one spot to another to "try their luck."

Henry Edgar's diary tells the outcome of their efforts.

May 26, 1863: Off again; horse pretty lame and Bill leading him out of the timber; fine grassy hills and lots of quartz; some antelope in sight; down a long ridge to a creek and camp; had dinner, and Rodgers, Sweeney, Barney and Cover go up to the creek to prospect. It was Bill's and my turn to guard camp and look after the horses. We washed and doctored the horse's leg. Bill went across to a bar to see or look for a place to stake the horses. When he came back to camp he said "There is a piece of rimrock sticking out of the bar over there. Get the tools and we will go and prospect it." Bill got the pick and shovel and I the pan and went over. Bill dug the dirt and filled the pan. "Now go," he says, "and wash that pan and see if you can get enough to buy some tobacco when we get to town." I had the pan more than half panned down and had seen some gold as I ran the sand around, when Bill sang out "I have found a scad." I returned for answer, "If you have one I have a hundred." He then came down to where I was with his scad. It was a nice piece of gold. Well, I panned the pan of dirt and it was a good prospect; weighed it and had two dollars and forty cents; weighed Bill's scad and it weighed the same. Four dollars and eighty cents! Pretty good for tobacco money. We went and got another pan and Bill panned that and got more than I had; I got the third one and panned that—best of the three; that is good enough to sleep on. We came to camp, dried and weighed our gold, altogether there was twelve dollars and thirty cents. We saw the boys coming to camp and no tools with them. "Have you found anything?" "We have started a hole but didn't get to bedrock." They began to growl about the horses not being taken care of and to give Bill and me fits. When I pulled the pan around Sweeney got hold of it and the next minute sang out "Salted!" I told Sweeney that if he "would pipe Bill and me down and run us through a sluice box he couldn't get a color," and "the horses could go to the devil or the Indians." Well, we talked over the find and roasted venison till late; and sought the brush, and spread our robes; and a more joyous lot of men never went more contentedly to bed than we.

May 27th: Up before the sun; horses all right; soon the frying pan was on the fire. Sweeney was off with the pan and Barney telling him "to take it aisy." He panned his pan and beat both Bill and me. He had five dollars and thirty cents. "Well, you have got it good, by Jove!" were his greeting words. When we got filled up with elk, Hughes and Cover went up the gulch, Sweeney and Rodgers down, Bill and I to the old place. We panned turn about ten pans at a time, all day long, and it was good dirt, too. "A grub stake is what we are after," was our watchword all day, and it is one hundred and fifty dollars in good dust. "God is good," as Rodgers said when we left the Indian camp. Sweeney and Rodgers found a good prospect and have eighteen dollars of the gold to show for it. . . .

May 28th: Staked the ground this morning; claims one hundred feet. Sweeney wanted a water—a notice written for a water right and asked me to write it for him. I wrote it for him; then "what name shall we give the creek?" The boys said "You name it." So I wrote "Alder." There was a large fringe of alder, growing along the creek, looking nice and green and the name was given. We staked twelve claims for our friends and named the bars Cover, Fairweather and Rodgers where the discoveries were made. We agree to say nothing of the discovery when we get to Bannack and come back and prospect the gulch thoroughly and get the best. It was midday when we left; we came down the creek past the forks and to its mouth, made marks so we could find the same again and on down the valley (Ram's Horn Gulch) to a small creek; the same we camped on as we went out and made camp for the night; a more happy lot of boys would be hard to find, though covered with seedy clothes.

May 30th: All well. Ate up the last of our meat for breakfast; will have supper at Bannack, ham and eggs. Away we go and have no cares. Crossed at the mouth of the Rattlesnake and up the Bannack trail, the last stage over the hill and down to the town the raggedest lot that was ever seen, but happy. Friends on every side. Bob Dempsey grabbed our horses and cared for them. Frank Ruff got us to his cabin. Salt Lake eggs, ham, potatoes, everything. Such a supper! One has to be on short commons and then he will know. Too tired and too glad.

May 31st: Such excitement! Everyone with a long story about the "new find." After I got my store clothes on, I was sitting in a saloon talking with some friends; there were lots of men that were strangers to me; they were telling that we brought in a horse load of gold and not one of the party had told that we had found color. Such is life in the "Far West." We have been feasted and cared for like princes.

June 2nd: Left Bannack this forenoon and came over to Rattlesnake. A crowd awaits us; crowds follow after us; they camp right around us, so we can't get away.

June 3rd: Move on down to Beaverhead River and the crowd gets more and more strong, on foot as well as on horseback.

June 4th: Down the river we go over two hundred strong. . . . We see it is no good to try to get away from the crowd, so we will camp where we leave the river. Made a camp near the Beaverhead Rock. "Miners" meeting called for this afternoon. I was chosen to state to the crowd what we had found. I did so and told them that we had panned out one hundred and eight-nine dollars altogether, showing them a sample of the gold stating what the prospect was and the extent of the gulch so far as we had prospected, what we knew it to be; told what we had done; the claims we had staked, and said "If we were allowed to have the claims as we have staked them, we will go on, if not, we will go no further." Some talk and it was put to a vote; the vote was in our favor, only one vote against it. At the meeting there was a set of laws adopted to govern our claims. A provision of the law passed was that the claims of our party should never be jumped nor taken from us and they are exempt from one day's work in seven required by law to hold claims. Well and good. They wanted to know where the gulch was, but as some were on foot and others on horseback with that advantage, they were told "when we get to the creek you will know and not till then." Everybody satisfied.

June 5th: Off and away across the long flat between the two rivers and camped at the same small creek the third time. We are fearful that when the crowd gets in, they may pull up our stakes. So some of the boys on the outside of the ring were told of the plan and Barney with ten or twelve will get out ahead to make them secure.

June 6th: This morning the crowd was told that we would be in the gulch today and to prepare for it. When we came to the creek and were going up I said to them "This is the creek." Such a stampede! I never saw anything like it before. I was left alone with our packs and took my time, for I know my claim is safe. After I crossed the small creek that comes in from the left, as we go up, Colonel Wood caught up with me. He asked me if I knew where he could get a claim. I told him "Yes, I'll show you where two bits was got, but only one pan was panned!" I showed him the place and he stopped and located a claim. Got back to camp at Discovery about 4 o'clock. The creek is all staked.[1]

As the stampeders followed their Pied Piper up the gulch out of Bannack their cry was "Five dollars to the pan and shallow diggin's." Every horse that could carry a pack was cinched, and miners afoot with blankets on their backs and coffeepots, frying pans, picks

---

[1] Helen F. Sanders, *A History of Montana* (3 vols.; Chicago, Lewis Publishing Co., 1913) I, 175-77.

and shovels hanging on them, brought up the rear.[2] Little did they realize that there was no need to hurry, that here was gold for all who came; two men, locating rather haphazardly, panned fifteen hundred to twenty-five hundred dollars' worth of dust per day, and the yield of the gulch during that first year of operations was $30,000,000.

Nevada City was the first town founded in the gulch, but its importance was soon eclipsed by Virginia City whose original name was Varina, in honor of the wife of Jefferson Davis. This bit of partisanship went unchallenged until the name was to be recorded on a legal paper. The judge was noted for his Northern sympathies as well as for his profane language. Coming across the name in the document, he slammed the papers on the table, "By ———, that name will never deface my records," he stormed, and, erasing it, he substituted the name Virginia City, a name that has persisted since.

Virginia City's difficulties with the road agents were essentially those of Bannack since these desperados preyed upon both camps, and the Vigilantes operated simultaneously throughout the mining area. The most colorful character executed by the Vigilantes at Virginia City was Slade. Slade had another name, but throughout the breadth of Montana he was simply known as Slade, a man to be reckoned with at all times, a man to be feared when drunk.

Long before Slade himself arrived on the Montana scene his name and the dried ears that he carried in his pocket were legendary throughout the West. When

---

[2] Oren Sassman, "Metal Mining in Historic Beaverhead" (unpublished Master's thesis, Montana State University, Missoula, 1941), p. 87.

the Overland Stage company was experiencing difficulty with road agents and horse thieves around Julesburg, Slade, because of his growing reputation of fearlessness, was the man chosen to solve the problems. In this position he replaced Jules Remi, "Old Jules," whose mismanagement and, possibly, villainy, had brought the company close to bankruptcy. In a matter of months, the new superintendent had so intimidated the thieves and ne'er-do-wells who hung around Julesburg that they moved on to the Rocky Ridge district; now freight and passengers moved safely through Julesburg.

Any man of Slade's nature made enemies, and chief among those set to "get" him as a result of his cleanup of the area was Old Jules, not only because Slade had taken his job but also because he had linked Jules rather conclusively with the thievery that the company had suffered along that section of the road. One day, catching Slade unarmed, Jules emptied his six-shooter into him, then seizing a shotgun emptied that, too, into Slade's body. Slade's friend, Boner, said, "The doctor picked out half a handful of lead from Slade and yet, when he was hanged, he carried several of Jules' bullets in him. I never saw a man so badly riddled as he was; he was like a sieve, and I don't see how he ever lived."

But he did live, and the whole frontier knew that between Jules and Slade it was a feud to the death.

As in many of the frontier legends there are variations in the details connected with the last act of the drama. One version tells how Slade "got the drop" on Jules and compelled him to surrender. He was then tied to a post, and Slade, an accomplished marksman, began torturing his human target. He shot him through the arm, then went in and had a drink; he came out, shot Jules in the shoulder, went in and had another drink. This routine was continued until Jules, riddled with lead even as he had riddled Slade, was dead and Slade was drunk. Slade then cut the ears from the corpse and slipped them in his pocket as souvenirs.

Another version, subscribed to by Mark Twain,[3] claimed that Jules was captured by friends of Slade and brought in; he was then tied to the post where Slade left him all night to contemplate the grim tomorrow. In the morning Slade went out and began nicking his victim here and there with his merciless, accurate bullets. Repeatedly Jules begged for an end to his misery, but not until his tormentor tired of the game was the fatal shot fired. Slade cut off his ears and left the body snubbed to the post for half a day.

E. M. Pollinger, a driver along the Overland, claims that Slade didn't kill Jules at all. He offered a five-hundred-dollar reward for Jules alive, nothing dead. Nelson Vaughan and John Frey captured Jules but wounded him before tying him to a horse to take him to Slade. On the way back, Jules died of his wounds and his captors, fearing to lose the five-hundred-dollar reward, tied the corpse in a sitting position against a post and announced the capture to Slade.

When Slade saw Jules he said, "But the man is dead."

"No, he's only playing possum," said Nelson.

"This will prove if he's playing possum or not," said Slade, and, taking out his knife, he cut off one of Jules' ears. When Jules did not flinch, he added, "Well, that proves it, but I might as well have the other ear."

---

[3] For Slade's impression on Mark Twain read Twain's *Roughing It*.

Whatever tale is correct, the fact remains that Slade did have his victim's ears, and these, displayed frequently, seemed to become a symbol of his brutality.

The removal of Jules left Slade in absolute authority in the area, and he loved the feel of power. He ruled his domain with ruthless despotism. More and more frequently, feeling above censure, he indulged himself in the wild drinking sprees that turned him into a destructive devil. At such times he would wreck business establishments, regale any who would listen with wild and at times lewd stories, and display to everyone the ears that became soft and pliable as old leather as a result of much handling. True, he was unwaveringly faithful in the execution of his duties. He never drank or caroused while on the job; also, whenever he destroyed property he was willing to pay for it as soon as he was sober. Gradually, however, he became so notorious that the press of Denver, where he often went for his binges, openly criticized the company for keeping him on the job. Then the army, whose backing was essential in this lawless area, issued what amounted to an ultimatum to the company to get rid of Slade.

Relieved of his high command, he turned again to freighting, and it was as a freighter that he reached Montana in 1863. His reputation had preceded him, and he was warned on arrival that the Vigilantes would tolerate none of his excesses. After his first spree in Virginia he was again warned, and, contritely, he promised to pay for the damages and to harm no one.

With his beautiful, high-spirited wife Virginia he established a home along the trail from Virginia City to the Gallatin Valley. Here on Slade Creek he built a substantial stone house, improved the trail into a road, and set up a tollgate. Doubtless his intentions were to settle down to a peaceful existence, but the excitement of Virginia City was too strong. In spite of his wife's protests, he frequently sought the bars and gambling halls where he caroused with a host of friends including Bill Fairweather of the discovery party. If he ran out of money, he merely laid Jules' ears on the bar, and the bartender, paralyzed by Slade's reputation, would consider them legal tender. He would ride through the nearby towns of Nevada, Adobetown, Junction, and Central, spreading terror and destruction as he did in Virginia. More than once he rode his horse, Old Copperbottom, through a saloon, shooting and wrecking as he went.

The day came when the vigilance committee had had enough. Slade had terrorized the town; he and his companions had been ejected from the theater for shouting obscenities at the actresses; they had roamed the streets all night singing ribald songs that linked prominent Vigilantes to certain scarlet ladies. Finally, at dawn, they waylaid a milk wagon coming into the city to deliver the morning milk. Slade, surprisingly, wanted some milk to drink—lots of milk—a gallon. The driver handed it over, but Slade, astride the wheel and none too steady in his condition, spilled some as he drank. The driver, going along with the joke, laughed uproariously only to have the balance of the gallon emptied over his head. According to Beidler, Slade and his friends then upset the whole wagon sending rivulets of milk down the wagon ruts of the street.

Even in spite of such conduct, Slade was given every opportunity to avoid the extreme penalty because he was liked and respected for many of his good qualities. He was warned to get out of town by his friend Toponce, but he ignored the warning. When he was served a summons of arrest, he tore it up, threw it in the street and spat on it, jeering at the power of the Vigilantes. Quietly word was sent out to Nevada that the vigilance committee was to meet. There were friends of Slade on the committee and some say Slade himself was a member. Nevertheless, the decision was taken to rid the community of its most troublesome member.

Two hundred miners assembled, and the task of summoning Slade was given to Williams, one of the few men whom Slade really respected. He approached his friend and said, "Slade, I want you."

"What do you want with me?"

"Come along and ask no questions."

At last Slade knew that his game was up. He pled for his life, not cringingly but eloquently. Seeing the committee unmoved, he cried in despair, "Oh, my dear wife!"

Others had had the same thought. Many in the growing crowd believed that the committee was making a mistake. They hoped that, if Mrs. Slade could arrive in time, she might save her husband as she had once saved him from the vengeance of Jules' hired killers. A messenger was dispatched to inform her of what was happening. Distracted, she mounted her fleet pony and, unmindful of loose rocks and treacherous gopher holes, she galloped to her husband's aid.

She arrived too late. The well-known "Men, do your duty" came minutes before she topped the hill above the city, and Slade, the ears of Jules still in his pocket, dropped from the scaffold. Her grief was boundless; she berated his friends for not having saved him. "No dog's death should have come to such a man," she stormed. Refusing to have him buried in Virginia City, she secured a zinc coffin in which the body, preserved in alcohol, was shipped to Salt Lake City on its way to Clinton, Illinois, the Slade family home. But it never left Salt Lake and is still interred in the Mormon cemetery there.

Mrs. Slade later married Kiscadden, a family friend, who, on that dark day in Virginia City, had tried to warn Slade to get out of town, and, after the hanging, had asked that the body be cut down and taken to the hotel so that Mrs. Slade would not find her husband on the gallows.

The execution of Slade was the only one that aroused charges of injustice against the Vigilantes. For years stories appeared defending him as a fearless frontiersman whose killings stemmed from the demands of his position and the lawlessness of the border. Jimmy Austin, old-time pioneer and admirer of Slade, declared years later, "They strung him up on Widow Dugan's gatepost in Virginia City. Slade did lots of good. They should never have hanged him." Whatever justification Slade may have had for his killings, he had none for his brutality and wanton destructiveness. Dimsdale probably sums up the Vigilantes' position when he says, "The death of Slade was the protest of society on behalf of social order and the rights of man."

As elsewhere, disputes involving the miners were settled simply and justly. When Dutch Jake posted the following notice on his claim, "Notese i clames de clames on dese here gulch here," the validity of the claim was challenged by a smart young lawyer who, incidentally, had unsuccessfully defended George Ives. Such words, declared he, were meaningless, and he sought to have Dutch's rights overruled. The miners knew, though, how Dutch talked and knew what he meant. He kept his claim.

Civilization came quickly to Virginia City in the form of a newspaper, the *Montana Post,* whose first issues detailed the trip of the founders, John Buchanan and M. M. Manner, from St. Louis to Virginia City. They had brought their press and machinery up the Missouri on the steamer *Yellowstone,* intending to establish a paper at Gallatin City. On the way they met another boat going down-river to the States. One of its passengers assured them that Gallatin's chief occupants were antelope and white-tailed deer. Virginia City with its ten thousand humans seemed a more likely location for a newspaper.

The trip in had not been free from mishaps. While still eighty miles below Fort Benton, the *Yellowstone* stuck on a sand bar. Everything, including the heavy press, had to be unloaded in an attempt to refloat the boat. The following day, aided by a rise in the river that resulted from torrential rains, the *Yellowstone* floated free, was reloaded, and continued its journey to the mouth of the Marias. From there to Benton transportation was by mule and ox team; from Fort Benton to Virginia City the undaunted publishers joined the caravan of mules, horses, and oxen that ploughed through dust and mud to the land of opportunity.

When they arrived they set up their press in a cabin cellar and got out the first issue of 960 copies. Before the ink was dry these were sold for fifty cents a copy and subscriptions were pouring in at five dollars each, "invariably in advance."

The *Post* became a mirror of thriving, roaring Virginia City and its satellite camps, in each of which a reporter was stationed.

HOLDUP

While the express coach was passing through Port Neuf Canyon between this city and Salt Lake, it was stopped by four robbers, and the inmates, four in number, were robbed of $27,000 in dust. . . . They were on their way to the states, having been here for some time in accumulating by industry that which at home would have made them comfortable. . . . This business is commencing a little early and prompt measures will be resorted to to put a stop to these daring outrages. Road agents, as they are called, can easily be dispensed with.[4]

To the editor of the Montana Post:

Sir: Having been insulted by Joe Bean, on the night of the 20th, in the California exchange, in his low, degrading style, he said he would fight me for one or two thousand dollars. . . . I hereby denounce him as a coward and challenge him to fight me for one or two thousand dollars, in four or six weeks, the money to be put up immediately on the receipt of the challenge.

(Signed) JOE REILLY

P. S. I wish him to put up or shut up.[5]

---

[4] *Montana Post* (Virginia City), August 27, 1864.
[5] *Ibid.*, February 25, 1865.

It can be readily seen that the prompt reporting of foreign or "state-side" news would be somewhat of a problem with communication to the outside world taking several weeks. The only means the *Post* had of securing such news was from other newspapers coming into Virginia. Naturally, then, by the time the *Post* published it everyone had read it in another paper. To solve this difficulty the editors worked out a plan with the local postmaster. When the express brought newspapers, a copy was immediately sent to the *Post;* distribution of the others was held up until the *Post* had set up three or four columns of "telegraph news." As soon as the *Post* was on the street and selling to the eager citizens, the postmaster would distribute the state-side papers. The protection of home-town industry is essential to the development of a community.

This arrangement was not long in effect for, in 1866, the *Post* announced in bold headlines:

THE TELEGRAPH LINE BETWEEN SALT LAKE & VIRGINIA IS FINISHED!.
MONTANA FORMS PART OF THE CIVILIZED WORLD!
CITIZENS HANG YOUR BANNER ON THE OUTER WALLS![6]

With such progress in Virginia City, deserted Bannack did not long hold its political distinction; in 1865 the territorial capital was moved to Virginia City.

Supplying food for the booming city was a constant problem that taxed the best efforts of that sturdy group of frontiersmen, the freighters. Alexander Toponce, one of these, tells how he brought fresh pork to Virginia City in time for Christmas dinner.

---

[6] *Ibid.,* November 2, 1866.

At Salt Lake we loaded our wagons with flour, tea, shovels, picks, and at Brigham City we added a lot of butter. We returned to Montana over the same route we had come down. The season was open, very little snow, and we had a quick trip.

Going through Brigham City on my first trip back to Montana I saw a dressed hog hanging up behind a store run by a man named Cotton Thomas. It was one of the biggest hogs I ever saw. Dressed, it weighed a little over 600 pounds.

"Thomas," I said to him, "What will you take for the shoat?"

"That little pig," says he, "will cost you six cents a pound, or $36."

I bought it and paid him $36 in greenbacks. There was no place in my wagon for it, so I got three men to help me and I put it right up on the top of the wagon cover, all spread out on top of the wagon bows, with his snout pointing toward Montana, and with a rope tied to each leg and fastened down to the wagon bed. The carcass was already frozen and stayed frozen all the way to Montana.

When we pulled into Virginia City the day before Christmas, 1863, that hog attracted more attention than all the rest of the train.

I stopped in front of Alex Metzel's butcher shop and Alex offered me a dollar a pound for the pig which I accepted in gold dust and reserved six pounds of the best chops for our supper.[7]

The winter of 1864-65 was one long remembered in Virginia City as the "beef-straight" winter. As early as October, unusually heavy snow began clogging the passes over which supplies reached the gold camps. As winter advanced the supply trains arrived less and less often, finally ceasing altogether. Except for beef, which was secured locally, food supplies, particularly flour, began dwindling alarmingly. Quick to take advantage of the unhappy situation, certain manipulators began quietly buying up available stocks of flour. Soon the

[7] Alexander Toponce, *Reminiscences of Alexander Toponce, Pioneer, 1839-1923* (Ogden, Utah: Mrs. Katie Toponce, 1923), pp. 70-71.

citizens found themselves in the grip of a black market. At the end of March flour was selling for $14-$18 per hundred; by April 16 it was $45, and the next day the price asked by some racketeers was $110. Flour riots were threatened and some looting occurred. This was too much to be tolerated by citizens accustomed to taking justice into their own hands. On the evening of April 17, a citizens' meeting was called in Nevada, and Virginia City was invited to send a delegation. Briefly the situation was explained; fifteen minutes later the committee was authorized to requisition all flour regardless of where it was or who owned it. It was then to be sold at the rate of ten pounds per person at a price of $27 for Salt Lake flour and $30 for St. Louis flour. The committee visited all places or persons known to have more than their share and, with the spirit of the vigilance committees impressed as it was on the community, they ran into little opposition. Of course, many ingenious hiding places were found by those who already were in possession of the precious commodity: in mattresses, under loads of wood, in cellars, haystacks, and outhouses.

The justice of the committee was shown in the case of James Gormley of Nevada. At great expense and hardship he had succeeded in getting forty sacks of flour across the pass by pack horses. He could prove that the flour actually cost him $43 per sack. Over his dead body would anyone sell it for $27. The committee, realizing that justice was on his side, permitted him to charge $45.

No matter how grim the situation might be in a mining camp, there was always injected into it a certain rough humor. In the flour crisis of 1864-65, one shiftless fellow had bartered his wife for $100 and two sacks of flour. She was a patient soul who had endured her husband's laziness and abuse. When a former sweetheart appeared in camp, though, she apparently showed enough interest in him to arouse her husband's jealousy —or cupidity. At any rate, a deal was made whereby the husband would get the money and the flour, the sweetheart would get the woman. An accommodating judge issued a divorce on the spot and the next day the reunited lovers were married. The scheming husband, before he could dispose of the flour, saw it seized by the committee and sold for $27 a sack.

The first supply train to get through consisted of twenty-three wagons, hauled by oxen, that arrived the twenty-second of May. Cheering crowds lined the road into the towns as the long line of wagons approached. All work was stopped while eager hands helped unload the precious freight. Other trains quickly followed and the "beef-straight" winter was a thing of the past, a memory to be laughed at over white bread and dried apple pie.

The divorce cited above was not the first in Alder Gulch.

The initial decree . . . was granted to a Mrs. Betsy Wiggs from her husband, Joseph, by a miners' court in 1864.

The high contracting parties had signed away the rights of single blessedness somewhere in Pike county, Missouri. They made a robust young couple, and having a couple of yoke of oxen, some bedding and cooking utensils which each contributed to the common store, concluded to go to Montana and grow up with the country. The trip was to be their wedding tour and they hoped

to make a fortune in the new west. They joined one of the immigrant trains and made the start.

During the first two or three weeks they had a Romeo and Juliet
time. But troubles soon came to cloud love's young dream. Just
how much the presence of a younger and better looking man than
the husband had to do with the trouble, the trial did not disclose,
but the young wife got out of sorts, neglected her cooking, wouldn't
shake the blankets before making the bed at night and refused to
help yoke up the oxen in the morning, and by the time the train
reached Alder gulch the young couple was ripe for the divorce
court, which was non-existent.

They were told, however, that all they had to do was to post
notices in three places for a miners' meeting to hear the evidence
and decide the case. So they finally agreed to sign and post the
notices, which were as follows:

> "Betsy and me has agreed to split blankits and rustle on
> different trales. She will take one and me tother. A miners'
> meeting is hereby called for nex Sunday on the flat just
> abov Nevada to here our storeys and give us splittin'
> papers, everybody cum.
>
> Signed,
JOSEPH WIGGS
BETSY WIGGS."

And everybody in Alder gulch did come, judging from the crowd
present. A presiding officer was chosen and a couple of fledgling
lawyers volunteered to represent the parties to the suit.

Joseph told his story, and Betsy told hers. Both were willing to
separate, but the sticking point was the division of the property.
There was not much of it, but the husband wanted it all. At length
the chairman cut matters short by telling the lawyers to "argy"
the case. At this juncture a well known, young rollicking miner
known as "Jeff Davis" in the gulch, mounted a stump and yelled
out:

"Say, Pard, whot will yer take for the gal and the things she
claims?"

"Two hundred dollars for all the truck except the oxen and
wagon and I'll throw the woman in," replied Joseph.

"Done if the meetin' will give yer both dividin' documents,"
shouted Jeff.

In less than 10 minutes the meeting had granted the divorce; Jeff had weighed out and paid Joseph the $200, and Betsy was blushing and smilingly hanging onto Jeff's arm, while that hero of the day led the way to the nearest saloon to "set up for the boys," Joseph joining in the drink at the bar, and uniting with the crowd in wishing the well-pleased couple health, wealth and prosperity.[8]

In 1869 word of the Montana placers, and particularly of Virginia City, spread among the Chinese of California. A migration immediately began that brought to Montana's gold fields several thousand of these intrepid Orientals. They usually left California by stage for Salt Lake, and there they either joined a wagon train or, if affluent, continued on by the big Concord coaches that made the trip regularly from Salt Lake to Virginia City. Rather early in the winter of 1869, a group of nine of these arrived in Salt Lake on their way to Alder. They had left sunny California and arrived in Salt Lake where the weather was almost equally warm and pleasant. Without hesitation, each paid the one-hundred-dollar fare demanded for the trip in the Concord coach. The driver, Briggs, noting that their clothing was scanty and light in weight, appropriate only for Southern climes, urged them to secure warmer outfits and tried to impress upon them the change in weather that altitude and distance might well make en route. Either they could not comprehend such a change or they had spent their last money on the fare for, chattering and gesticulating, they piled into the coach and insisted on being off immediately.

As the six spirited horses sped the coach northward, news was picked up along the way of blizzard conditions ahead. Again the driver, now joined by the two white passengers, tried to persuade the Chinamen to wait or to get warmer clothing; again they insisted on continuing as they were. The second day out, the blizzard swept down upon them. The temperature dropped rapidly, drifting snow filled the road. Half frozen already, the Chinamen huddled together in the bottom of the coach, relying on the heat from their bodies to keep them alive.

Finally the stage bogged down in the drifts; the gallant horses could no longer be whipped into facing the storm. Briggs and the other white men, feeling more adequate in the emergency, urged the yellow passengers to mount the horses and follow them while they broke trail back to Point-of-Rocks, their last stop. The Chinamen were terrified at the suggestion and indicated that they would walk behind rather than approach the horses. So the struggling file started out, the snow swirling around them, the cold chilling them through. After proceeding about a mile, the leaders stopped to catch their breaths and check up on the Chinamen. To their horror the latter were nowhere in sight. Realizing that any attempt to find them would only result in their own deaths, they pushed on to Point-of-Rocks, arriving there with badly frost-bitten hands, faces, and feet.

The next day, the storm having abated, they lead a search party back to the spot where the coach had stuck. Nearby, under a drift of snow, they found the nine Chinamen frozen stiff in a tragic huddle. Carefully they extricated the bodies; when they came to the last one, an almost imperceptible movement indi-

cated a trace of remaining life. Burying the eight in
a common grave, they took the remaining one to Bannack where the best efforts of the primitive region
were made to save his life. He was too badly frozen,
however, and died in a few days. To this day the
knoll on which the eight were buried is called China
Point.

This and many other tragic incidents did not deter
others from following the lure of gold. The *Mineral
Independent* describes Alder's Chinese colony:

The old Chinese Masonic temple at Virginia City has long been
down. It made history. Forty years ago it was the fraternity
house, church, brothel and gambling hall of the Alder gulch colony
of Chinese—the meeting place of 700 or 800 Chinamen. It is reputed to have been, at one time, western headquarters of Chinese
Masonry in the United States, but certainly it was dedicated to
other uses.

Murder was said to have been done within its walls, but never
were the officials able to fix crime upon the killers. Those who
enjoyed its hospitality and protection may have been witnesses to
tragedy, but their lips were sealed. Within the temple was hatched
a tong war in which every member of the colony was arrayed either
on one side or the other, and which caused the death in battle of
two men, and the murderers, although caught red-handed, and once
sentenced to death, through oriental cunning walked out of the
Virginia City jail under the eyes of the jailer, and escaped.

The temple stood on a little promontory at the town's entrance
—at right angles to where Wallace street of Virginia City begins.
It loomed high in the skyline, an oriental outpost on the borders
of western barbarism. It filled the eye of the wayfarer as the stage
driver gave his whip the final crack and dashed around the corner
and up the main street on the last leg of his journey.

After the white placer miners had taken the cream of the millions in gold which were washed from the bars of Alder gulch,
came the Chinese miners. They were very clever in placer mining.
They could make good wages where white miners would starve.

The first working of the sands of Alder gulch was carelessly done, and rich pickings were left for the Chinese. So along in 1870, when the white miners were seeking other diggings, the gulch teemed with yellow men. For a quarter of a century they worked over the sands at a profit, until, the diggings exhausted, they, like the white men who had gone before them, took their departure. Its votaries gone, there are none left to kowtow before the great Joss. Budda, neglected, turned his face away and the old temple vanished.

This Chinese temple was the social center of all these yellow men, flush with money, and it was a little paradise to them. Outside its threshold they were alien. Inside they were back in old Cathay, where they counseled and fought, fraternized and gambled, or made love, after their fashion. In one spacious room they burned incense and said their prayers to the old gods of China; another large room was devoted to the service of the Chinese Bacchus. Here amid the fumes of the demon of the red poppy they dreamed dreams of the land of the cherry blossom and the lotus, and forgot their lonesomeness in a strange and almost hostile land.

How many murders were committed in the temple and covered up, no white man knows. There were a number of mysterious deaths, and if they were killings the secret was always kept from the white officials, and no murderer was ever brought to book. If a Chinaman died the body was buried with much pomp and ceremony, his friends and enemies following the remains to the grave, scattering bits of red paper on which were mystic characters designed to scare the devils away, and give the soul that had just been freed, either through natural death, or the knife of an adversary, a good start and a chance. If the deceased had been notoriously healthy his passing was explained away to the inquisitive white men by the statement that he had choked to death on a chicken bone. There were many feasts at the temple.

Six Chinese companies operated in Alder gulch, and every Chinese in the diggings was affiliated with one or the other of them. Whether the companies were connected with the six great Chinese tongs in control of the Chinese colony in San Francisco is not known, but the impression prevailed in Virginia City that the connection was direct. The head of each of these companies was a martinet and his followers obeyed his orders implicitly. Their quarrels the head men settled among themselves. There were many differences over leases, and gradually there grew up two factions in this Chinese fraternity house, four companies aligning themselves against two, and among the white people these factions became known as the Four company and the Two company groups.

Finally, came a time when this feeling developed into intense hatred and it burst into open armed warfare when the Two company group secured control of a choice lease of rich ground which the Four companies had long been negotiating for. The heads of the Four companies held a conference and decided that the Two companies should either surrender this lease or fight. The Two companies replied by entrenching themselves about the ground in dispute and defying the stronger element. Every man in the Two companies was supplied with a rifle and plenty of ammunition. The Four companies armed their men and gave battle.

For two days they fought desperately, and the gulch resounded with the din of battle. There were probably 200 men engaged on the side of the Two companies and 400 men in the forces of the Four companies. People going to and from Virginia City made a long detour over the hills to keep away from the zone of conflict. Thousands of shots were exchanged, but singular to say, not an individual was even powder-burned.

Finally, when all the ammunition in Virginia City and the surrounding towns was exhausted, the Four companies decided to go back to the ancient methods of Chinese warfare. They prepared stink pots and sharpened pitchforks and made pikes. They put ugly masks on their warriors to give them a ferocious appearance.

When all was in readiness to the din of gongs beating and much yelling, they took the redoubts of the Two companies, practically at the point of bayonet. The forces of the Two companies were not strong enough to resist them. Two of the defenders were killed and the rest fled. The battle ended with a small Two company man fleeing down the gulch, closely pursued by a tall Chinese, armed with a sharpened shovel. Finally the small man stumbled and fell, and his adversary calmly cut his head off with the shovel and bore it back in triumph to his victorious comrades.

In the meantime, the sheriff of Madison county organized a strong posse and going to the battlefield, put 40 of the belligerents under arrest. The Virginia City jail was filled with chattering Chinese. Following the investigation, two members of the Four company group, Ah Wah and Ah Yen, were charged with murder.

An interpreter represented each side at the preliminary hearing. The interpreters were agreed that the Chinese witnesses would disregard the sanctity of the oath, and suggested that if the witnesses were sworn on the blood of a freshly killed rooster they would testify truthfully. There were over 100 witnesses, and the sheriff sent his deputies out to commandeer poultry. Before the hearing started the jail yard was filled with crates of roosters. As each witness was sworn he would be led out into the yard, the head of a rooster chopped off, and in the blood of the freshly killed fowl the witness would be sworn to tell the truth. As the trial proceeded the jail yard took on the appearance of a shambles, and many constituents of the sheriff ate chicken pie during the days following.

At the end of the hearing the magistrate bound Ah Wah and Ah Yen over to the grand jury. The grand jury indicted them for murder, and shortly afterwards they were tried in the district court. The accused were defended by such able lawyers as Col. Wilbur F. Sanders, Judge Henry M. Blake and Col. J. E. Callaway. At the trial the rooster oath was dispensed with, greatly to the chagrin of the chicken pie fanciers who were known to be of the sheriff's political affiliation.

During the trial Michael Hatfield, a juror, became so ill that he could not attend court. Against the protests of two of the defendants' counsel, the presiding judge decided to proceed with the trial with but 11 jurors. Ah Wah and Ah Yen were found guilty of murder in the first degree and sentenced to death.

The case was appealed to the supreme court on the contention that the conviction of a capital offense by a jury of 11 persons was unconstitutional. The supreme court upheld the contention and ordered a new trial. Ah Wah and Ah Yen went back to the county jail to await the slow working of the law. The full decision may be found in the report of the Territory vs. Ah Wah and Ah Yen, 4 Montana, 149.

About a year later the case again came up for trial. In the meantime an election had been held made up of the sheriff's constituents who did not partake of chicken pie at the expense of Madison county voted against him and he was defeated. A new prosecuting attorney had assumed office and a new district judge was on the bench. The case was called and the sheriff brought in two Chinese prisoners.

The judge asked the prosecuting attorney if he was ready to

proceed with the trial of Ah Wah and Ah Yen. He replied that
he was ready. One of the attorneys for the defense arose and inter-
posed an objection.

"Your honor," he said. "This is a trial for murder. If the defendants are adjudged guilty they may suffer the extreme penalty
of the law. The rule of law is that when a man is on trial for his
life he must be present. Otherwise the proceedings will not stand."

"Are these prisoners not the defendants Ah Wah and Ah Yen,
who are charged with murder?" asked the astonished judge.

"They are not our clients," affirmed the several attorneys for the
defense.

The prosecuting attorney, who had had nothing to do with the
previous trial, admitted that he did not know.

The sheriff was called before the court. He admitted that he
did not know positively that the prisoners were the defendants,
Ah Wah and Ah Yen. "Your honor," he said, "all Chinamen look
alike to me. If these men are not the defendants I do not know
who they are."

Counsel for the defense sat back chuckling. Chinese interpreters
and head men of the six companies were brought in and all affirmed
that the prisoners were not the men charged.

The prisoners were given their liberty. Afterwards the story
leaked out. The quarreling companies had adjusted their differences,
and resolved to save the men whose lives were in jeopardy. So they
matched eastern guile against western carelessness and won.

The Chinese had been allowed much liberty in visiting the prisoners. Two Chinese were selected who were of about the same size
and general appearance of the prisoners. They were sent into the
jail to visit them. Inside the cells, when the jailer was not watching, they changed clothes with the murderers, who walked out of
the jail before the eyes of the unsuspecting jailer, and escaped.

They were never apprehended.[9]

The unbelievable wealth of Alder Gulch flowed
through white hands, yellow hands, black hands; some
were honest, some thieving, but, regardless of their
color or character, few of the hands that scooped nug-

---

[9] *Mineral Independent* (Superior), August 21, 1941.

gets from the rich gravel managed to convert the glittering hoard into either luxury or leisure. For these men the wealth was too sudden and too vast; their judgment was overwhelmed by their good fortune. As easily as the gold came, it slipped through their fingers, or finding it here in thousands, they sought it elsewhere in millions.

Bill Fairweather of the discovery party, he who should have profited most by the find, scattered nuggets in the streets for the children, or, if in one of his malicious moods, threw them into the muddy streets of Chinatown and roared as the greedy Orientals rooted for them like pigs in a sty. For all who came he bought drinks, joining them until his reeling figure was a familiar sight in Virginia City. Desperadoes like Slade and Plummer appealed to his adventuresome nature. Shunning the growing civilization and order, he drifted north to Canada and Alaska only to return, ill and broke, to die a pauper at Robbers' Roost at the age of thirty-nine.

5

NEVADA

CONTEMPORARY IN SETTLEMENT WITH VIRGINIA AND just below it in Alder Gulch, Nevada City had the distinction of being Montana's first incorporated city.

It was at the height of its fame during 1863-64. Thousands of tenderfeet were wildly filing claims and as these claims were very shallow— in many instances the bedrock was only a few feet below the surface and "lousy" with gold—it was not long before thousands were in possession of well-filled pokes of clean, yellow gold.

This sudden rise from poverty to riches put the miners in a state of wild recklessness that bordered on frenzy. The saloons were crowded all night and the games of chance, faro, roulette wheel, stud and draw poker, keno, 21 caused many a struggle and fight for a chance to play. These honest and unsophisticated fellows soon fell victims to the slick-fingered cardsharp. They took their losses with little regret, knowing there was plenty more gold left in their claims, since everyone in those days imagined the supply was inexhaustible.

Old Nevada City's turbulent and amazing life, when thousands of seething, struggling and money-mad human beings of every nationality and country on earth, swarmed its single street by day and night, was probably without parallel on the continent.[1]

Like all frontiers, the mining camps of Montana attracted a variety of eccentric characters. Here where law was lax, where the individual was freed from many of the pressures of social standards, there were found

---

[1] *Kalispell Times,* June 19, 1941.

those who were unable or unwilling to find a comfortable place for themselves in organized society.

Marion McCarty, who has a place in the diary of Bishop Tuttle, was the elder son of a large family. . . . He was about 27 years of age, very eccentric and extremely visionary, and sort of a religious zealot. He was moody and taciturn and at intervals given to outbursts of great anger and religious excitement.

Once in the summer of 1867, a boy was with him. His peculiar actions and conversation interested the boy. One day he suggested they take a trip over to Brown's creek, some three or four miles distant and south of Nevada.

This locality is quite rough, with deep ravines and rocky cliffs. They were standing upon the edge of a ravine when he began to quote scripture and shout in a wild, roaring voice, and then, muttering something about "sacrifice" grabbed the boy around the waist and attempted to throw him over the cliff. The boy was wearing a coat several sizes too large for him, like all boys in those rough days, and in the struggle he slipped out of the garment and ran for home. Soon McCarty disappeared.

The freaks of fortune and the whirligig of fate of the prospector are often startling and truly amazing, and no one ever met the like of that which happened to wandering Marion McCarty. He was next heard of in Colorado, with his grub and blankets, pick and shovel and pan, ever on the search for gold. While traveling one day along an old, abandoned and nearly obliterated trail on the side of a mountain he suddenly threw down his pack and commenced to dig in the middle of the path.

There seemed no reason, as surface indications bore no evidence of mineral of any nature. However, with a few strokes of the pick there popped into view a small piece of float thickly sprinkled with native gold. At the depth of a few feet he uncovered a two-foot ledge carrying immense values in gold. He carefully covered up his bonanza, then staked and recorded. When he resumed his work the vein grew wider and richer and soon attracted capital. He was influenced by sharp practice, no doubt, to sell for $25,000, the buyers realizing a vast fortune from the mine. . . .

Scroggins, who owned a grocery and clothing store in Nevada, was of bulldog physiognomy, dirty red hair and little red evil eyes, beetling brows and pock-marked face.

White women, even at that late period, were few and at a premium, and Scroggins, who was along in years, and single life becoming tiresome and monotonous and having for some time unsuccessfully endeavored to attach a helpmate, finally, in desperation, married a young and handsome Bannack squaw. The ceremony was performed by a rough old justice of the peace, who, when he pronounced them man and wife, said:

> Here stand a white man and a squaw
> Married under the white man's law
> Up the hill and down the level
> Kiss your wife, you ugly devil.

This was too rich a thing for the boys to pass up so they decided to give the bride and groom a charivari. This one was somewhat original and out of the ordinary. A requisition for tin cans and cowbells soon had all the kids that could be rounded up hilariously at work, while in the meantime, a huge fiddle was constructed in the shape of a trough some 20 feet in length and 4 feet in depth. Lariats, dipped in resin, were tightly drawn over this cavern. A sapling pole 15 feet long served as a bow, which was strung with strands of rope similarly dipped in hot resin.

Having now everything in readiness, the crowd gathered silently in front of the store at midnight, and at a signal from the leader of the band, a noise bellowed forth on the silent and sleeping city that fairly shook the earth. Pandemonium broke loose, with a sweep of the big resined bow, wielded by a half dozen men, the like of which was probably never heard before on earth. The unearthly racket of tin cans, cowbells, and the deep, rasping of the bullfiddle was continued incessantly until the store door opened, revealing a white and haggard face, hair apparently standing on end from panic, fright and collapse due partly to the thought that the Vigilantes were after him. The pitiable condition of Scroggins so affected the crowd that a hasty conclusion of the entertainment was voted and they quietly dispersed. . . .

[There was an odd character,] Sim Grim. He was of huge frame, weighing some 250 pounds, feet amputated at the insteps. He was of lamb-like disposition, yet rugged and rough in a western way.

He was an inveterate horse racer and originated the man-against-horse race. The race was conducted in the following manner: The race was usually 50 yards to a perpendicular pole, then turn and race back.

Grim was obligated to ride the smallest cayuse which could be found. The horse nearly always reached the pole first but in making the short turn he would lose so much ground that the foot racer, on the homestretch would, often, outdistance the rider and be declared the winner.

Many dollars changed hands in these contests and for thrills and excitement no other outdoor sport was compared with it. The fun and thrills were afforded by the rider who, in his quick effort to make the turn as quickly as possible and secure an even break with his opponent, would often find himself and his horse rolling over in the dust.

One of the greatest races that ever took place in Montana, for interest and excitement, was pulled off in the fall of 1867. The match was made in Nevada City and a good purse was hung up for the winner. More money is said to have changed hands in this race than on any other like affair in the state. A foot racer was pitted against the rider of a mule and the distance was ten miles.

The start was at Virginia City, through Nevada City to Junction, four miles below, nearly at the mouth of the gulch. The race course was the main road, full of dust, rocks and gravel. The foot racer was given a half-mile start. The road was lined throughout its entire length by thousands of men, women and children. A thunderous shout heralded the getaway—the shouting of the men and the screaming of the women echoed and reechoed up and down the gulch and over the distant hills. The nervy foot racer maintained the lead with heartbreaking speed, stimulated to greater efforts as they neared the goal, by the loud-pounding hoofs of the mule which seemed to the runner to be actually riding him down.

With a last effort and with a burst of speed that put him over the line and to victory, the man fell unconscious, blood gushing from his mouth, nose and ears. He was carried in triumph on the shoulders of the winners and his admirers the four miles to Nevada City where he was handed a purse of gold dust. . . .[2]

An incessant warfare had always waged between the white man

[2] *Ibid.*

and the Chinaman. "No Chinks allowed" was the slogan and many an individual battle occurred, but at this period the hatred for the pigtails had gradually subsided into a sullen acceptance and a fight was looked upon as a rare event.

A fight took place between a white man and a Chinese in the dry dusty street on a hot summer day in 1867. The principals, both diminutive size and weight, became involved in a quarrel that ended in a real scrap. This soon attracted a crowd of some 100 Chinks, armed with knives and an equal number of whites armed with six-shooters to see fair play.

The fight lasted over two hours with little advantage on either side until the white man managed to get the Chink's pigtail wound around the latter's neck and was slowly and surely choking him to death when the Chinks threw up their hands and rescued their fellow-countryman.[3]

Adobetown, that " 'wen' grown on the body of Nevada," was a mile from the larger town and was the slum area of the city; here hovels and semi-caves replaced the cabins of Nevada; if possible, the streets were narrower and dirtier, the inhabitants more villainous and grimy. Nevada is being restored to its former splendor; it is hoped that Adobetown, too, will be restored so that the world will know the living conditions among the "other half" of a mining town.

---

[3] *Froid Tribune,* May 18, 1923.

6

SUMMIT

IN THE VICINITY OF VIRGINIA CITY TWO OTHER TOWNS of importance in the sixties were Summit and Union City.

The spot called Summit seemed designed especially for a mining camp. Nature has seldom placed so much wealth, so easily to be gotten, in so small a space. . . . Summit City soon showed a goodly cluster of log houses. Most of these were one room affairs, seven or eight logs high with dirt roof, fireplace with ample chimney built along the outside, a door and no window. After a time, when glass could be provided, a window was made. The spaces between the logs were chinked with strips of wood or small lodge pole pine, and then mortar made of mud was applied. . . . These cabins were warm in winter and cool in summer. Soon log structures of several rooms were built providing comfortable homes for families. . . . It is probable that 200 people spent the winter of 1863 in Summit. This number had grown to 1000 or more by the advent of the winter of 1864-65.[1]

Now two-story houses appeared, and many men brought their families to live in the community. Social life was active, and it was decided to have a Christmas party to which everyone should come. At the mouth of the canyon named Hungry Hollow there lived a good-looking but somewhat notorious woman. No one would volunteer to bring her to the party. Some insisted that, as to her, exception should be made; she

---

[1] Lew Callaway in the Virginia City *Madisonian,* September 12, 1930.

should not be allowed to attend the party along with
the decent people of the community; others, perhaps
conscience-ridden, refused to cast a stone. Finally, it
was decided to draw lots to see who should bring her,
and the lot fell to Amos Hall, a handsome and prominent gentleman of the area. With some misgivings
Amos walked the four miles to Hungry Hollow to
extend his invitation and received an enthusiastic acceptance.

Great preparations were made. The fiddlers were the
best, and, while there was a scarcity of ladies to fill the
quadrille, gentlemen with decorated left arm bands
supplied the deficiency. Amos had gone for his lady
in a bobsled and was agreeably surprised to see her
modestly dressed. No one at the party appeared to
better advantage than she. She spoke in a low, well-
modulated voice, used flawless English, and charmed
everyone. At midnight each gentleman presented his
lady with an appropriate gift, a gold nugget. When
Amos escorted his lady home, she dismissed him with
the utmost propriety, assuring him that she would
always treasure her Christmas present.

The bedrock at and above Summit was shallow—that is, close
to the surface of the earth, but shortly below Summit it was quite
deep. In the vicinity of the town and above it, in Alder gulch
proper, the gold was coarse, nuggets being encountered with gratifying frequency. Nuggets weighing two ounces or more were not
unusual, and occasionally one was found worth several hundred
dollars.[2]

During 1865 prosperity ran high, but after this, as

---

[2] *Ibid.*, September 12, 1930.

the veins played out, the town lost population. Although two new mills were erected in 1872, the days of the placer camp were gone and the place was well on its way to being a ghost town. Today only a few ruins remain at Summit, but seeing them is well worth the short trip up the mountain from Virginia City.

7

UNION CITY

UNION CITY, CHILD OF THE ORO CACHE LODE DISCOVERED
in 1864, was, in many ways, the antithesis of its neighbor, Virginia City. The miners who worked the Oro
Cache and the arrastra in Spring Gulch were staunch
Union men, Union, that is, in a political not a labor
sense. The main street was Lincoln Boulevard, and the
American flag flew on every national holiday, an example to Virginia City where, in 1863-65, the Stars
and Stripes were not universally accepted.

Furthermore, Union City wanted none of the loose
living sanctioned in Virginia. It had no saloons, and
the Montana Gold and Silver Mill was not permitted
to operate on Sunday. Perched as it was in "the hop-
per," a little basin at the end of a steep and winding
path up the mountain, it was able to maintain an aloof
purity.

McClure, visiting the "city" in 1867, found there

nearly every leading nation in the world . . . represented. . . . The
sturdy Cornishman, the imperturbable Welshman, the impetuous
son of France, the quiet Swede, the wandering Swiss, and the
brawny Russian, all mingle their broken accents in their evening
gatherings, as they smoke their pipes in the wealth of contentment.[1]

---

[1] A. K. McClure, *Three Thousand Miles through the Rocky Mountains* (Philadelphia: J. B. Lippincott & Company, 1869), p. 209.

He noted also the picturesque speech of the Union miners, rich in the colloquialisms born of the prospector's life.

In all classes, from the most learned to the least favored in letters, the same expressive Westernisms are in common use. . . . If a man is embarrassed in any way, he is "corraled." The Indians "corral" men on the plains . . . the unfortunate politician is "corraled" by the mountaineers, the gulchmen or the settlers . . . and the gambler "corrals" the dust of the miner. . . . "Git" is another favorite and most expressive of Western terms. It is the invariable word by which the hero of the whip and lines starts his teams. . . . "You git" is the most emphatic notice that can be given any luckless chap to leave the room or ranch, or to escape a revolver; and "You bet" is the most positive manner of affirmation. Everything is an "outfit," from a train on the plains to a pocketknife. It is applied almost indiscriminately,—to a wife, a horse, a dog, a cat, or a row of pins. A "lay-out" is any proposed enterprise, from organizing a State to digging out a prairie dog. Anything that has been tried, from running for Congress to bumming a drink, has been "prospected" or "panned out"; and "he didn't get a color" expresses the saddest of failures.[2]

To describe an utterly worthless character in this jargon one would say, "I have panned him out, clear down to the bed rock, but I can't raise a color."[3]

The names of nearly all of Montana's early cities reflect this picturesque language applied either to their location, their history, or their peculiarities. So we find Hoggum and Cheatem, names reflecting the miner's scorn.

The city bearing the romantic title of Hoggum is a little mining camp near the Missouri River, some thirty miles below the junction

---

[2] *Ibid.*, pp. 210-11.

[3] A. D. Richardson, *Beyond the Mississippi* (Hartford: American Publishing Company, 1894), p. 486.

of the Madison, Jefferson and Gallatin. The mining gulch in which it is situated was discovered last spring; and it is charged that a few parties "hogged up" the whole of the pay claims before the usual stampede thereto was fairly inaugurated, and the disappointed adventurers named the new camp Hoggum and turned away from it in disgust. A little branch camp near the main one is known only as "Cheatem"; and the whole outfit is regarded by the itinerant miners as a sort of fraud upon the profession.[4]

Many of these expressions still persist in the language of the West today, giving it a colorful link to the area's past.

---

[4] McClure, *op. cit.*, pp. 246-47.

8

ARGENTA

MANY ARE THE TALES TOLD ABOUT MONTANA'S SILVER dollars. Canadian business firms do not like to accept them because of the cost of shipping them back to the United States. An Eastern service station attendant, being handed one, slipped away and quietly called the police to come out and arrest the counterfeiter. But they are loved by Montanans who think of them as a state tradition. So they are, for less than a century ago, out of the smelters of Argenta, came their gigantic counterparts, great disks of precious silver to startle and entrance the world.

The St. Louis smelting furnace ran out the argentiferous galena at Argenta into base bullion, which their cupel furnace reduced to disks of pure silver as large as new moons. As these broad disks of white metal were displayed in the bank windows of Eastern cities, the fame of Golconda and El Dorado paled before the rising glories of Argenta.[1]

Argenta was started with the discovery by A. M. Esler in 1865 of the Legal Tender, the first silver-lead mine in the state. At first the town was named Montana City and, as such, was chartered in 1865.

We, Henry Lovewell, James Duane Doty, Asheal K. Eaton . . .

---

[1] Joaquin Miller, *An Illustrated History of the State of Montana* (Chicago: Lewis Publishing Company, 1894), p. 691.

and our associates and assigns have this day claimed occupied and
have laid out and surveyed and by these presents do possess and
hold the following described tract of land consisting of three
hundred and twenty acres for a town site to be named and called
Montana. To wit commencing at a certain stake plated on the south
bank of Rattlesnake Creek near the mouth of a certain dry gulch
or Ravine a short distance below a lone pine tree running in a
southerly direction one-half mile. Thence Easterly one mile, thence
Northerly to Rattlesnake Creek thence up said creek to a point of
beginning.[2]

In 1866 the name was changed to Argenta to better
indicate its wealth in silver.

As usual, miners swarmed to the spot. At one time
three thousand persons crowded the streets of Argenta.
Yet, there was a difference between the populace of
Argenta and that of, say, Bannack. The same difference existed between Silver Bow and Butte, the copper capital. In both towns gambling was wide open;
whisky was preferred to water; hurdy-gurdies ran all
night. The difference lay in the characters spawned
by "the poor man's diggin's" and the salaried workers
of organized business. In the poor man's mines, a lone
individual could pan or sluice from the earth a glittering fortune or worthless sand. He was responsible only
to himself, and his fortune depended solely on his know-
how, his efforts, and his luck. He belonged to a breed
apart—nomadic, self-reliant, solitary.

Quartz mining could not be done on any kind of
profitable scale without the backing of wealth for
equipment. Even the primitive stamp mill at Bannack,
with its wooden stamps shod with the iron from worn-
out wagon tires, was not something that each indi-

---

[2] Beaverhead County Mining Records—Book A.

vidual could own and operate. Men worked for other men, were hired and fired, and, consequently, became regimented, settled, and far less interesting.

Once in a while a bit of bizarre action would take place in Argenta but the prosaic citizens called the participants "madmen," whereas in Bannack they would have been individualists.

The night was clear and cold and the peaceful people were wrapped in innocent slumber when a tremendous uproar broke loose. Two crazy men were found to be on the war-path. Joe Setler, a crazy sheepherder, with a repeating gun paraded Main street while a heathen called Wum Kum, entirely naked and flourishing a blood-stained Bowie-knife, and yelling like a demon, attempted to take the center of the town by storm. The alarm being given, all of the able-bodied men of the burg turned out to suppress the attack—some in their haste appeared on the scene clad only in their shirt tails.

Constable Bray, armed with a riot act in one hand and a revolving pistol in the other, advanced to the attack in front, while Justice French at the head of a posse of citizens executed a brilliant flank movement on Setler and the Chinaman, capturing them without shedding blood. Both the crazy men were disarmed and securely tied with rope, when quietness was restored to the town.[3]

Most of the time the citizens settled back into the busy routine of producing silver. There were four saloons, two hotels, a restaurant and two stores. School "terms" were held for the children. A term never lasted more than three months as it was difficult to maintain enrollment or to keep teachers for long in an unorganized society. Teachers were paid either by local subscription or by benefit dances held in a home or in a saloon. The usual salary was twenty dollars a

[3] *Dillon Tribune,* September 19, 1930.

month plus room and board that was furnished week about by different families in the town.

Still [the] successful mining did not pay. The high price of labor and all needed supplies, the cost of separating the worthless lead, and the enormous expense of shipping the silver by the overland coaches, beset, as they were, by "road agents" and hostile Indians, largely overbalanced the value of the silver produced. But numerous mines have been discovered at Argenta. Some have furnished large quantities of good ores; three smelters have followed the pioneer smelting and cupel furnace, and yet the heavy freight on fuel and base bullion consumes too much of the profits. But still the owners of the hundred mines in this old camp are hopefully working and waiting for the locomotive to bring them cheap coke and coal and to take away the trainload of bullion they could easily produce every week. Meanwhile the miners delve and rest. The furnaces and mills have a sort of spasmodic life; sometimes they glow with the melting ores, sometimes they take a long, hopeless sleep. Silver is down, and Argenta must wait the better market for the white metal. Her hundred mines must rest and their timbers decay. Her furnaces will scarcely glow with the flowing metal until silver becomes a "precious metal" once more.[4]

---

[4] Miller, *op. cit.*, pp. 691-92.

9

STERLING

A NAME; A FEW SCATTERED BUILDINGS LOOMING GHOSTLY IN THEIR emptiness, and a history recorded only in the memories of its few surviving founders; this is all that remains of Sterling, a once thriving gold camp tucked away in a wild and lonely ravine six miles south of Norris in Madison county....

Even women found their way into this lonely camp, as did the professional gambler. At night the narrow streets were aglare with lights from saloons and dance halls. . . .

The history of Sterling presents a brief, but stormy narrative. Like a mushroom it sprang up over night and then was abandoned by its 500 or 600 inhabitants in favor of more prosperous fields. The rush came in 1867, shortly before two New York financiers erected a stamp mill for the purpose of refining ore from the nearby prospects. . . . With a few exceptions the ore turned out to be low grade.

The latter discovery, however, was not made until several small fortunes had been sunk in machinery and other equipment. . . . At one time five stamp-mills were working full blast, each within a stone's throw of each other and owned and operated by different companies.

About two hundred yards south of Sterling were the holdings of the Midas company. Less than 100 men were employed there, but they refused to be considered part of the neighboring town and named their camp Midas. Sterling at one time boasted a population of 600 miners and their families, with three saloons, two hotels, a livery stable and numerous other business enterprises, legitimate and otherwise....

The farm of Bill Reel now includes the site of both the camps. . . .

Within plain view of the old ruins, Reel has erected his modern ranch home and although he is still interested in mining (his father was a prospector) most of his efforts are devoted to ranching. "For many years," Reel said, "gold dust was the only money known in this part of the country. It was easy to get and easy to spend."

It was no uncommon sight in those days for miners to walk up to a bar and drawing a well-filled sack from their clothing toss it carelessly on the bar and call to the house to "drink 'er up." In later years when the town was abandoned and buildings formerly occupied by saloons were being torn down, two prospectors leased the ground and accumulated a fair-sized grub-stake by panning the dirt beneath the floors.[1]

In 1881, when Sterling, still in its vigor, was a principal station on the stage route from the Gallatin country to Virginia City, it was the scene of a shocking but romantic murder followed by the prompt and relentless action of early Montana justice. William Douglass, a Gallatin Valley rancher, had fallen hopelessly in love with his pretty housekeeper, Alice Earp. She did not share the feeling, and being an independent frontier lass, was not intimidated by his desperate threats and pleas. Packing her bags, she caught the stage to Virginia City.

The *Midland Empire Farmer* continues the account:

Shortly after she left the ranch, Douglass decided to go after her and bring her back. He saddled up and by hard riding overtook the stage at the old mining camp of Sterling, which was also a stage station where passengers obtained meals. He arrived just as the passengers were re-entering the coach after having eaten their noon-day meal.

Jim Delaney was the stage driver, and had mounted the box. Miss Earp was sitting beside him and the other passengers were

---

[1] *Anaconda Standard*, October 23, 1921.

inside. As the stage started, Douglass rode up and yelled to Delaney to stop, which he did. Douglass then ordered the young woman to get down off the stage. She refused to do so, saying that she was going home to her mother.

Douglass said that if she didn't get off the stage and come with him he would "send her to a home in the grave" and, as he made the threat, drew a six shooter from his pocket.

The girl, however, still refused, huddling against Delaney. Douglass opened fire. She tumbled forward into the stage boot and Douglass, waving his gun, defied anyone to arrest him. Just then Dave O'Brien and another man drove down the hill from the Pony road on their way to Virginia City. O'Brien, unarmed, leaped from his buggy and approached Douglass who was still on his horse, commanding him to dismount and surrender.

"Are you an officer of the law?" asked Douglass.

"Officer be d———d," thundered O'Brien. "It doesn't take an officer to arrest a skunk like you. Get down off that horse or ———"

Douglass meekly alighted, gave up his gun. He was bound hand and foot by O'Brien and numerous men who came to his assistance after the prisoner had been disarmed, tossed into the stage coach and taken to Virginia City.

Miss Earp, in the meantime, unconscious and sorely wounded, had been taken from the stage and given first aid treatment. A light wagon was obtained in which to take her to Virginia City and a messenger sent ahead by horseback to bring a physician to meet her on the road. That messenger rode 30 miles in two hours, crossing two mountain ranges on the way. The girl, however, became so low that it was deemed inadvisable to take her farther than Meadow creek and there she died the following day despite the efforts of the doctor who came to her aid at the behest of the messenger.[2]

Conveniently, the district court of Virginia City was in session, and the day after the shooting Douglass was

---

[2] *Midland Empire Farmer,* February 3, 1938.

indicted, tried, found guilty, and sentenced to hang. He offered no defense, and when confronted by the gallows stepped forward without a word to have the noose dropped over his head. Asked if he had any final words, he merely shook his head.

A couple of weeks later a New York paper to which Douglass had subscribed received this notice from the postmaster at Bozeman: "Your paper addressed to William Douglass is dead in this office. Cause, he was hanged in Virginia City Friday. Present address unknown. Try Halifax."

10

TRAPPER CITY, LION CITY, GLENDALE

NEAR A TOWERING MOUNTAIN IN THE BEAVERHEAD Billy Spurr and his partner, James Bryant, located a claim, the Forest Queen, during the summer of 1872. No work was done on it, and the following season Bryant decided to relocate the claim in his own name before he left on a trapping expedition with a group of men including Jerry Grotevant.[1] The party, all on horseback, came up to the spring just above the old claim, pitched camp, and made their location. As they worked, their horses stood patiently, heads down, tails flicking the horseflies off their sides and flanks. As the day grew warmer, the swarms of flies increased. Under their torment the horses became more restless; they tossed their heads, snorted in protest, and switched their tails more furiously. Finally, unable to endure the assault longer, they bolted into the bushes, hoping thereby to brush off a few of their tormentors.

The men, ready by now to continue on their trapping expedition, set off to search for their mounts. The day was hot, the terrain rugged. Before long Jerry Grotevant sat down dejectedly to rest. At his feet the sun glinted on a rock. Picking it up he recognized native silver ore, and further search revealed the out-

---

[1] Both the time and characters vary in different versions of this tale.

cropping of a rich ledge. Excitedly he gathered together his companions who, after staking claims, sent
a sample of the ore to Denver for assaying. The report came back, that, although there was silver present, the real value was in lead.

Not even a wagon road led into this remote area,
and ore from the Trapper mines had to be packed out
by mule train. "Uncle Billy" Hamilton, that colorful old frontiersman who knew more of Indian sign
language than any other white man, had the contract
to pack the ore down to a point where it could be
picked up for freighting to Corinne, Utah, the nearest railroad station. From there it was shipped to Denver where it was smelted. In a short time ten thousand
dollars' worth of ore had been taken out; the fame of
Montana's lead mines had been established, and capital from as far away as Indianapolis became interested.
In Indianapolis was formed the famous Hecla Mining
Company that dominated the mining activities of the
area for the lifetime of the towns.

As the mining activities spread out beyond Trapper, richer ore was found nearby and the town of Lion
City came into existence and attracted the population
of the area. The naming of Lion Mountain and Lion
City also is connected with straying stock. It seems
that Jerry Grotevant had a white mule that he valued
greatly. One day it wandered from the camp and
Jerry's friend, Joe McCreary, of the original discovery
party, set off to look for it. As he reached a cliff he
saw the mule on a precipice above him, but, seeing it
from an unusual angle, he mistook it for a mountain
lion. He rushed back to camp to report the menace

to Jerry, who, grabbing his gun, set off to slay the predator and add a handsome trophy to his hunter's collection. When he discovered that the "lion" was his white mule, he and the other miners were determined never to let Joe forget his ridiculous mistake. They named the mountain Lion Mountain and the town that grew up at its base, Lion City.

The expense of getting the ore out was making heavy inroads on the profits. In 1875 Charles Dehler and Noah Armstrong built a twenty-ton furnace at the crossing of the stage road over Trapper Creek. Here another town sprang up.

In the letter from Glendale to the *Butte Miner*, May 7, 1878, we learn of the naming of this new town.

The next question was what should the place be called? The men building the road to Lion Mountain in derision of the pilgrims occupying the place, called it "Soonerville," and posted up mile stakes saying, "One mile to Soonerville," but the pilgrims payed them back in their own coin, by naming the cañon they occupied "Sucker Gulch," which name has "stuck" ever since. In naming this place one of the party selected Clifton, and another, Glendale, and as neither was willing to give way to the other, it was proposed that the words Clifton be written on one side of a chip and Glendale on the other, and it be then thrown over the walls of the assay office, and the name found uppermost should be the name of the camp. It was done and the child was called Glendale. . . .

Bull and mule trains hauled ore to the new town for smelting and hauled supplies back to the mines. At Glendale the bullion was made into ninety-pound bars; at times thousands of these bars were stacked in the smelter yards waiting to be transported to the railroad. The smaller smelter was replaced by a fifty-ton smelter and as many as fifty teams shuttled back and forth between the town and the mines. Later a tramway was built to replace some of the teams.

The old Hecla tramway . . . was the scene of many thrilling rides. The tramway was four miles long. A brakeman rode each car on its downward trip, and was supposed to retard the speed so the cars would remain on the track. But many times they jumped off. The ride was especially hazardous in the winter time, even though the track was covered with snow sheds most of the way.

Mules pulled the cars back up to the ore house at the base of Lion mountain. The ore was moved from the mine, high up on the mountainside, to the loading chutes below, in buckets carried along on a cable. The mountain was steep to the Cleopatra mine, and a rope was strung along the trail to enable the miners to pull themselves up hand over hand. At one time there was a flight of stairs at the steepest part, so nearly perpendicular that it resembled a ladder. It was burned, however, and was never replaced.

The workings of the Cleopatra mine were intensely cold. The miners who worked there wore heavy gloves, clothing and over-shoes. That made it uncomfortable for the miners but advantageous to the owners, in those hammer and drill days, for the boys had to keep hitting the steel in order to keep warm. The production from the double hand teams was particularly heavy, for the man who twisted a drill for 15 minutes was anxious to get his circulation started again when it came his time to swing the double jack, and thus operations were well nigh continuous during a shift.[2]

Glendale thrived. Its population reached two thousand; it had a Methodist church, a school with two hundred pupils, three hotels, two dry-goods stores, seven or eight grocery stores, thirteen saloons, two drugstores, a jewelry store, a confectionery, a brewery, a weekly newspaper, and a lumberyard.

---

[2] *Hardin Tribune Herald*, April 23, 1937.

It lived a long life for a mining town, but, after producing approximately eighteen million dollars' worth of ore, the mines were finally closed in 1905 as a result of long and costly litigation. With the closing of the mines the town died. Today there are picturesque ruins at old Glendale: the smelter smokestack, the beehive-like domes of the smelter ovens. Until fire destroyed it in 1959 the old Knippenberg mansion, built in 1881, stood, a ghost of its former glory when Mr. Knippenberg, superintendent of the Hecla properties, took immoderate pride in its six fireplaces, sterling silver doorknobs, and rich carpeting.

At Hecla, a companion of Glendale, can still be seen some old "stoneboats," those cumbersome but effective vehicles used for transporting rock and ore. However, the ghost towns in the gulch above Glendale are much less accessible than most others since the one-track road to them is rocky and deeply rutted.

11

PONY

VERY FEW PEOPLE LIVING IN PONY OR THAT VICINITY WOULD recognize the significance of the name, Tecumseh Smith. A little weathered desert rat and prophet of the placer pan, "Pony" Smith had prowled from gold camp to gold camp in quest of that elusive "lucky strike" which, mirage-like, haunts the horizon of the prospector's life.

From Virginia City he came over the Tobacco Root mountains to Sterling and prospected up what is now Pony creek to about the location of the Strawberry mine where he found rich colors in the placer sands. He began working there, and others followed to get some of the gold at "Pony's Diggings."

In 1875 the Strawberry mine was located to tap the mother lode of part of "Pony's" placer find, and the town of Strawberry sprang up, two miles above the present site of Pony. Two years later the present town was laid out and construction work started. The man for whom it was named, the little prospector, "Pony" Smith, drifted to other gold fields in his quest of a bonanza.

At about this time the Clipper and Boss-Tweed mines were staked, mines which, during 40 years of continuous running, have produced five million dollars of gold, the greatest production of the yellow metal, possibly, from any one group of holdings in the state. . . .

The purchase of the Strawberry-Keystone group by a Helena syndicate headed by A. M. Holter, in 1889, and the development work of this company, the Pony Mining Company, started the big gold boom in Pony. The railroad branch of the Northern Pacific trunk line at Sappington was started that fall and completed the following spring, giving rail facilities to the mining camp.[1]

---

[1] *Hardin Tribune Herald*, November 3, 1933.

The decline of Pony, unlike Diamond or Granite, was neither sudden nor complete. In 1907 quite an impressive little booklet, *Catalogue of the Pony Public Schools,* praised the town and its location:

Nowhere in this great Empire of the West has nature been more lavish in her display of beauty, grandeur and sublimity than in the quaint, picturesque, little city of Pony. Splendid residences, beautiful lawns, resplendent with a wealth of flowers, inviting shade trees in profusion, two hissing, turbulent mountain streams, pine-covered mountains on either side, and you have the striking features of the center of the picture. . . .

Entrancing as are the scenic attractions, Pony has a more substantial basis for its prosperity. Within a radius of seven miles are greater and richer mineral deposits than in any similar area in Montana. This is not alone the opinion of the writer. Practical mining men have with a remarkable unanimity expressed the same opinion.

The account continues to extoll the fine homes, the $10,000 school offering four full years of high school and possessing a library and a laboratory. At that time it was by far the handsomest and most commodious school building in Madison County.

Today there is still an elementary school at Pony, but the high school students go to Harrison. Many of the once-fine homes have fallen into a state of disrepair or have been dismantled. The few remaining citizens, probably challenging the "ghost town" label, hope for a revival of the mining industry or for a new industry that will bring back the vigorous days of the old town.

12

LAST CHANCE GULCH

KNOWN AS "THE GEORGIANS," UNCLE JOHN COWAN and John Crab, from Georgia, D. J. Miller, from California, and Reginald (Bob) Stanley, from London, were among the early arrivals in Montana Territory. They had mined at Alder and, while there, heard rumors of a fabulously rich strike on the Kootenai River of northwestern Montana. With many others they set out for the new land of "tearing torrents and gleaming gold."

Reaching the Hell Gate Valley they encountered a party of prospectors headed by Jim Coleman returning from the Kootenai fields. These men informed them that the Kootenai district was much exaggerated, in fact, was insignificant, and that disappointed and disgruntled miners were leaving the district. What little gold had been discovered already had been mined out. That ended the adventure for Miller and his companions.

They had flour and bacon sufficient for three months in their parfleches and hated to return to Alder. Here, near Hell Gate, three rivers joined—the Bitterroot, the Clark Fork or Hell Gate, and the Blackfoot. The Bitterroot Valley was known to contain little gold, but the summer before one of the party had been in the Blackfoot country with Captain Fisk's party of prospectors, and, at that time, free gold had been found in small quantities there. Why not follow the Blackfoot and

its tributaries to the peaks of the mountains, then descend the eastern slopes and prospect to the Missouri
River? They had a rough grasp of the lay of the land
and a more or less imperfect knowledge of routes and
localities.

Bidding Coleman and his companions good-by, they
followed the Hell Gate River upstream. They diligently
panned the Little Blackfoot region when they reached
it but found nothing but colors.

They traveled up this stream through some of the
country's most beautiful regions, but the way grew
steeper and more heavily wooded, the trail fainter and
finally nonexistent. Even the weather turned against
them. Usually sunny and mild at this time of year,
it was cold with either fog or rain. It was a despondent
group that slipped their packs to build a little fire from
what dry brush they could pick up. As they gathered
around the fire to rest, they discussed whether they
should pursue their original plan or take the shortest
route back to Alder.

As they were sitting dejectedly in the wilderness,
Crab glimpsed through the trees an outcropping of rock
on what might be the summit far above them. He
made his way to it and returned, scrambling breath-
lessly down the steep slope to the others. It was the
divide; beyond lay a valley and a great river, surely
the Missouri. His report was met with skepticism, particularly in so far as the identity of the river was concerned. But Crab was sure and offered to bet his pony
that he could reach the Missouri in a day's journey.
For that day camp was made below the summit, and

the next morning the four stood looking down on the magnificent spread of the Prickly Pear Valley.

. . . Their gladdened eyes swept the wide expanse of beautiful plains with its threading streams fringed with green-boughed cotton-woods. Bunch grass, fresh and luxuriant, waved everywhere, and herds of antelope, in scores and hundreds, fed unmolested—those nearest turning about and facing the party, wondering what the intrusion of man upon their long unmolested preserves meant.[1]

The descent was steep at first, but the country was more open and soon became flatter. The four travelers were the first white men known to cross the main range of the Rockies by the particular pass at the head of Little Blackfoot Gulch.

Miller and his friends reached a gulch which they called Seven-Mile Gulch and the creek Seven-Mile Creek. They panned the gravel here but still found only colors. They killed an antelope for meat and prepared their supper. After supper they discussed plans for future operations and decided to travel northward along the skirts of the mountains and prospect the streams as they went.

Before setting out, however, two of the party panned the sand at their feet and were surprised to find strong colors. Up and down the stream they worked, but the first promise didn't hold up.

"The whole country seemed filled with colors; every-where were colors, but no gold," said Stanley.

They were not far from where the great placer deposits later were discovered by them, but they had no hint of the fact, and

---

[1] Reginald (Bob) Stanley, returning to Helena nineteen years after the dis-covery, recounted his impressions of the event for the *Helena Herald*, November 6, 1883.

so they turned northward to resume their weary search for the auriferous metal and the fortune that was slow to materialize. As they traveled they prospected everywhere but made no strikes.

They traveled up the Dearborn River when they came to it, and later prospected on the Sun river and the Marias to the headwaters. They found colors, but no gold deposits of value, and in that region their experiences were complicated by a totally new factor. The country was overrun with grizzly bears. They were not interested in bears, particularly grizzlies, and the silvertips and their brown congeners were both bold and obtrusive.

Their presence rendered the situation of the prospectors even less attractive than it had been. It was unsafe to consort with such ferocious and powerful animals, and the prospectors began to feel that the country would be a good one to leave, particularly since it produced no gold.

They had been warned by men familiar with grizzlies not to attack the latter, and the winter before at Nevada camp, they had seen a man whose cheek had been torn off by a grizzly and heard his account of their ferocity. However, one of the men could not resist taking a shot at a bear one day. The grizzly, badly wounded, charged the camp, and for a time gave the prospectors a real scare.

After that they decided to end their northward march, and return to Alder gulch for the winter. Besides the bears there were other even more cogent reasons why they should adopt this course. Their bacon and flour were running short, and the volcanic mountains further south had been replaced by flat table-topped peaks which suggested a sedimentary origin excluding the presence of gold.

As they turned their steps to the south, their thoughts recurred to the creek where they had found such strong colors, and since that was on their way to Alder gulch they concluded to finish their prospecting for the season with another whirl at it. One of them said:

"Well, Boys, that little gulch in the Prickly Pear is our last chance. If we don't strike it there, we'll have to streak it for home."[2]

---

[2] *Rocky Mountain Husbandman,* August 8, 1929.

When they finally got back to the spot in the Prickly Pear Valley, July 14, 1864, they made camp near their old site and proceeded to sink two prospect holes. When they panned the dirt, the nuggets rattled against the sides of the pan! Here, at last, their quest was ended. Too excited for sleep, they sat around their campfire late that night dreaming of the golden torrent that would pour from their Last Chance Gulch.

Other gulches in the area proved equally rich: Grizzly Gulch, named after a huge grizzly who made nightly visits to the chokecherry bushes that grew along the path, Rattlesnake Gulch, named after a monstrous rattler whose ten rattles decorated a post after the snake was killed. During July and August this gulch and others, too, swarmed with the reptiles who sought the warm rocks and thickets on sunny days in such numbers that the banks seemed to wriggle with them.

Stanley tells the following incident:

Filing a whip saw one Sunday afternoon, preparatory to getting out sluice box lumber, the "harmonious strain" attracted the approach of a huge "rattler." It was soon circling about in a giddy circle, with head well up, eyes glistening with unwonted brightness, and its skin taking on a vivid brown lustre. There was about it an indescribable inquisitiveness which added to the novelty of its antics. The performance closed when the music ceased, and a convenient stone was used to dispatch his snakeship.[3]

Other animals abounded in the gulches. Stanley continues:

Wolves and coyotes made the nights hideous with their howling and barking, the more venturesome coming within a few rods dis-

---

[3] *Helena Herald*, November, 1883.

tance of the party's sleeping place. From its frequency this kind of serenading grew wearisome, and it was mitigated for the time only by the firing of rifle volleys at the pack. . . . A demoniacal saturnalia in Last Chance was that on the occasion of their killing a horse. The animal, sick and helpless from a snake bite, showed a leg puffed like a bolster. The wolves gathered about and fought for their prey. The chorus of howls and yelps that sounded through that lingering night was such a pandemonium of savagery as the ears of man were never saluted with before.[4]

The discoverers decided to keep quiet about the strike, and, when two of them went to Alder for supplies, they told only a few of their closest friends. The result was that, instead of a great stampede, there were only small ones for the balance of 1864. Even then, by midwinter, there were over 115 log cabins in the gulch.

When the camp was still small in October, 1864, the miners who were in the gulch decided that laws and other matters of general interest must be attended to. At their first meeting, mining regulations were settled. At the second meeting the matter of a more appropriate name for the town was brought up. Levity marked the discussion with such names as Punkinville, Squashtown, Tomahawk, Tomah, and others being suggested. The candidates for the honor had been narrowed to Tomah and Helena when John Somerville, a "tall, jovial frontiersman from Minnesota," is supposed to have declared, "I belong to the best country in the world, and lived in the best state in that country, and the best county, Scott, in that state and the best town, Helena, in that county, and by the eternal the town shall bear that name." To this day, no one is quite

4 *Ibid.*

sure that this is the true explanation. Some say Helena was chosen because it meant "a place far in the interior." Others believe it honors some lady.

News of the wealth of Last Chance couldn't be kept for long. By 1865 the town was booming.

The camp on Sundays was the scene of intense animation and activity. The streets were crowded with gaily shirted miners. Mexicans with bands of broncos careened through the main business thoroughfares. The shouting oratory of auctioneers was heard above the din of tramping horses and the noisy explosions of bibulous throngs of men. Broad doored saloons, gambling and dance houses, were open and in full blast day and night. In the afternoon a general stampede of horsemen took place toward Ten Mile, where racing was indulged, if there was not a prize-fight or other attraction at the Fighting Corral. Among all this, when violence threatened, or bloodshed occurred, the Committee of Safety had some occasional work to do, and Hangman's Tree became a well known rendezvous.[5]

Altogether thirteen of those early-day desperadoes gyrated slowly from the end of a rope tied to the sturdy limb of Hangman's Tree. One of these was a Chinaman according to Tommy Thompson who lived in Last Chance as a boy. The body hung there for three days "and it drew quite a crowd."

This Chinaman killed a white man in a brawl in Chinatown, confessed and was taken to Hangman's Tree and strung up.

I was just a kid going to school, but I remember the Chinaman's wife used to bring food every day and place it in his mouth. I guess she was feeding the spirit.

The body remained hanging for three days as a lesson to the other Chinese of the city. Hundreds of people drove out to Hang-

[5] *Ibid.*

man's Tree, every evening in their carriages to see the body. No one seemed to think it was particularly horrible.

On the fourth day they cut down the body and gave it burial. The wife placed a lot of food on the grave, which was quickly eaten by some of the youngsters around town.

Hangman's Tree? Why we kids used to crawl all over that thing when we were going to school. We'd crawl out on the branch they used to hang people on and look at the grooves the rope dug into the bark on the branch.

Too bad they cut down that old tree.[6]

Too bad, indeed. The people of Helena were up in arms over the desecration of their most historic landmark. Dr. Shippen, an earnest, popular minister bought the land on which the tree stood and cut it down soon thereafter, on September 8, 1875.

But he was not prepared for the chain of events that followed his act of vandalism, for no sooner had the news reached the ears of the people of Last Chance than a wild-eyed mob rushed to the minister's home with threats of lynching him.

Just how the doctor appeased that crowd it is hard to say, but finally the people moved sulkily away, and from that time on the minister was a marked man. The tree had gone, it is true, but it had left behind a grim dignity, while the minister was asked no more to officiate at weddings or to attend the last rites of the dead....

At last, unable to break down the disapproval under which he had fallen Doctor Shippen moved to Butte a year after he had destroyed the tree, and he did not visit Helena again until almost 32 years later, April 26, 1907—old and broken. The announcement in the paper next morning chilled him, which said: "Dr. Shippen visits city; 'Twas he who 32 years ago destroyed Hangman's Tree —did not appreciate its historic value."

[6] *Kalispell Times*, September 8, 1938.

It can be imagined that the doctor did not prolong his visit, but returned to Butte to his work. But the wound of Hangman's Tree had been opened again and the reporters in Butte rushed to get the story.

"When I moved to Helena," he said, "I bought the lot upon which Hangman's Tree was located . . . my home was there . . . a flood in Dry gulch swept down upon the place and washed the earth away from underneath the root of the tree . . . which towered above my barn in which I had a carriage and horse . . . left with but one root . . . the tree was insecure and a menace to my property. A man with a load of wood was going toward town . . . I asked him how much he would take to cut down the tree. Well when the news reached town a riot almost followed. Scores of people visited my home, and in a short time had taken most of the tree as souvenirs. . . .[7]

The fame of his crime spread throughout the territory until everywhere he went he was known as "the man who cut down Hangman's Tree!" Finally he moved to Oregon and died there, the forty years of service to Montana counting as nothing compared to the enormity of his desecration of the sacred tree.

One of Helena's Committee of Safety was X. Beidler, who floated here and there in the territory seeing to it that bad men came to their just end. Since he had an uncanny ability to be where trouble was, he was on the streets of Helena on that fateful election day when Negroes were first given the right to vote—given the right, that is, by the Federal government, not by the territory of Montana.

. . . Before the polls opened a mule skinner named Leech, an athletic specimen of physical power, who was working then for Kirk-

---

[7] Florence Lemert in the *Midland Empire Farmer* (Hysham), August 6, 1936.

endall & Co., met "Nigger Sammy," as he was called, a janitor about town, and asked if he

WAS GOING TO VOTE

Sam replied, "I haint doing nothin, Marsa" and throwing open his coat, added "and I haint got nothin." But Leech heeded not his pleadings and shot him dead. This occurred on the site of the Cosmopolitan Hotel. I was standing by my horse at the corner of Wood and Main Street. I leaped into the saddle and dashed down the street, when I heard the shot and saw the smoke. Throwing the reins to a boy I dismounted and seeing Leech there, his pistol in hand, saw that I must exercise some tact. So I said, "hello seems somebody has shot a nigger and there's one vote less." This distracted Leech's attention until I could grab his pistol hand, my gun was in my belt then. A struggle ensued, and we writhed and twisted, around among a crowd of two or three hundred people, but I was careful to keep the muzzle of his gun turned on the outsiders until I got it, then Jim Brewer and Burt ———two powerful men who happened to be near, got on either side of him and the procession started for the old jail on Wood street. The crowd shouted that "only a nigger had been killed," and demanded the release of the prisoner. But I was on the trail with a six shooter in each hand, and swore that I would shoot the first man who interfered. But when we got Leech to the jail, I hadn't enough clothes on me to dress a china doll.

THE SEQUEL

Later in the day a friend of mine named Goldberg had occasion to remark in Bill Mathew's saloon that it was a daring arrest. A big gambler said it wasn't, and that I was a coward and that Goldberg was a coward. Goldberg reached over the bar, seized a champagne bottle and cracked it over the fellow's head, and he was carried to his room by his friends. When his wounds had been dressed, the gambler started out with a six shooter, looking for Goldberg, whose friends came to me and said I must take the fight off his hands. So I went out on the war path, got the drop on him, got his gun and sent him back to bed, telling him I would have to kill him if he didn't go. He went.[8]

---

[8] *Helena Independent*, May 13, 1886.

The stamp of the ghost town of Last Chance and the ghost life of early Helena are everywhere apparent in Montana's capital city. Now and then, with decreasing frequency, a newspaper item will recall an incident of the old days. Such was the death notice of "Whiskey Cider," whose real name, Sam Jong Tai, was forgotten even by his countrymen. He entered the gulch on the heels of the first rush. For many years he prospected around the area acquiring on several occasions fortunes that would have made him wealthy in his homeland. But Whiskey Cider, like many other prospectors, had a weakness for gambling. Poker and fan-tan repeatedly stripped him of the dust and nuggets that would have paid his way home. At the age of eighty-two he died in poverty in a little room on West Main Street. Friends, both American and Chinese, contributed funds for a decent burial and, with the rites of his native land, but far from his celestial ancestors, he was laid to final rest in the Chinese plot of Forestvale Cemetery.

Helena's main street is still "Last Chance Gulch." The gulch is underlaid with gold and the "gully washers" that pour torrents of rain down the gulch at times carry gold dust in the silt that settles in the streets. Considerable financing for the Placer Hotel was derived from gold separated from the gravel excavated for the basement. They say that for the hoboes of Helena's jungles a few hours of gulch panning is more likely to replenish their pokes than a day's panhandling on Last Chance.

MARYSVILLE

THE GOLD FOUND AT LAST CHANCE, FOLLOWING THE earlier discovery at Montana City, was only a sample of the great deposits that, during the next few years, were discovered in the rich area surrounding Helena. Nearby strikes produced Marysville, Unionville, Gould, Basin, French Bar, Rimini, and blended into the deposits around Blackfoot City, Beartown, Garnet, and Coloma.

The history of Montana's ghost towns, chilling by the very fact of their being ghost towns, is further marred by the violent death and broken hopes of most of the original discoverers. So it is with relief that history records one who made his strike and lived to enjoy it. His is a Horatio Alger tale. Thomas Cruse, when he entered the gold fields, was as green as the Emerald Isles from whence he came. He had no education and no money. Yet his engaging personality and his unshakable faith that he would someday strike it rich made grubstakes easy to come by—at first. Grubstake after grubstake went off to the hills with "Irish Tommy," and Irish Tommy came back, his poke empty, his supplies gone. Finally even his best friends lost faith in his ability. He was a kid. It took the old-timers, sensing gold from the formation of the rock, to find the right spot. It looked as if he might have to go to work and forget his dream, but, like many engaging Irishmen before and since, he had inspired a woman with his faith; with her backing he followed his Irish luck to the fabulous Drum Lummon site.

Now when he went to town he was Mr. Cruse, not Irish Tommy at whose rough ways and Irish brogue people laughed. He took almost $150,000 out of his mine, then sold it for over a million and a half dollars. He founded a town, which he called Marysville after the first three Marys who lived there; he gave the town a bank. Finally, as one of the most respected citizens of the state, he moved to the capital city where he lived out his long life, a happy example of the boy who went from rags to riches.

After the Drum Lummon was discovered, Marysville was the scene of a wild stampede until its inhabitants numbered over five thousand. Log cabins soon gave way to frame houses; a large six-teacher school was built that continued in operation for many years. Churches were established, and Marysville had two newspapers, one of which, the *Gazette,* claimed "the largest circulation in Marysville of any paper in or out of Montana, and any man who says differently is a black-mailer and a libeller." This paper reported the Fourth-of-July celebration of 1894 as follows:

Marysville looked her prettiest and best, decked out in all the gorgeous decorations of flags, bunting and evergreen, she put on the air of a metropolis. The rushing crowds that passed along her streets made one think he was in a hustling, thriving city.

The parade took place at 9:30 a.m. It was headed by the Drum Lummon band of 16 pieces with Ed Young as leader. Next came

the car of state and the secret societies, which marched through
the principal streets of the town to the grand stand. . . .[1]

There followed dinner and the usual races and con-
test, the prize list reaching twenty and thirty dollars
in some cases. The climax event, the grand ball, was
glowingly described in the *Gazette:* "It was one of the
largest balls we ever attended and a more orderly select
crowd never assembled in Marysville. It shows among
other things the high estimation in which the Marysville band is held by Marysville society people." A final
note in the account was a gratifying one for the town
law: "There were very few cases of intoxication and
only one or two fights."

Other miners struck it rich, too; the Penobscot mine
was discovered by Nathan Vestal the year after Cruse
opened the Drum Lummon. Vestal realized more than
$400,000 from the ore and the sale of his property,
but, unlike Irish Tommy, he gambled away his fortune.
His easygoing disposition, his generous spending, and his
love of cards soon reduced to nothing the wealth from
the mine that produced the largest gold bar in the
world, a great mass of the precious metal that weighed
240 pounds and was worth $80,000. When he was
broke, he went back to the mine he had once owned
and worked at miner's wages.

In the wake of the prospecting came the Chinese,
washing the gravel at times, but more often washing
the dirty clothes of the miners who would rather pay
for such trivialities. Often the industrious yellow men
planted their little gardens to supplement, at exorbi-

---

[1] *Marysville Gazette,* July 5, 1894.

tant prices, the meat and flour diet of the camp. Their celebrations lent an exotic touch to the West. At these, with much chanting and howling, they drove away the bad spirits with their joss sticks. Sweetened pork and choice delicacies such as small white mice dipped in honey, were offered up to these spirits with the understanding that they would not disturb the Chinese family during the coming year.[2]

The railroad, that bringer of prosperity and permanency to many mining camps, came to Marysville, but, as the mines were worked out and the population dwindled, the rails were torn up to be used elsewhere. Business establishments were abandoned, school was closed. Today the old Drum Lummon mine stands, a grotesque skeleton along the highway, to remind the less than one hundred people who remain in the town of the former glory of Marysville.

---

[2] *Silver State Post* (Deer Lodge), August 27, 1936.

UNIONVILLE

DOWN THE GULCH FOUR MILES SOUTH OF LAST CHANCE, the Whitlach, Yellow Boy, Black Swan, Black Alder and other claims attracted their groups of miners. The trade and postal center for these was Unionville, a hustling village of several thousand inhabitants. It was a cultural and educational center with citizens who raised one thousand dollars for a Baptist church.

The Whitlach alone shipped four million in gold, but the lead vein soon ran out. In 1876 Unionville's first building, the Whitlach boardinghouse, was destroyed by fire. Other buildings were deserted one by one, and Unionville joined the ranks of ghost towns.

Years later, however, it enjoyed a brief day in the limelight—literally. In 1926 it was chosen by Famous-Players Lasky Corporation as the background for some of the mining scenes of "The Growler Girl," a stirring tale of Placer Pete and his two beautiful daughters.

Incidentally the making of the picture will offer opportunity for a number of Montana folks to enter the movies. Besides the seven principal characters, Mr. Hyland will use 25 or 30 men gotten up to represent the old time placer miners, a few extra women and two girls for "supers," to enact the roles of the daughters of Placer Pete.[1]

[1] *Roundup Tribune,* August 12, 1926.

CLANCEY

CLANCY, M. T.
December 18, 1874

WHEN WE CONSIDER THE IMPROVEMENTS WHICH HAVE GONE ON
and are constantly going on in this camp, we come to the conclusion
that this is one of the future cities of Montana. From the solitary
house of fifteen months ago, we now count two stores, one hotel,
one billiard saloon, one in course of erection, two butcher shops,
one feed and livery stable, one shoemaker shop, and one blacksmith
shop. Last but not least, on the list of improvements of the burg
is the "School House on the Hill" which is a credit to the builders
and an honor to the town. For the furnishing of the same everybody and his wife, the bachelor and his sweetheart, and his or her
friends, are going to have a grand ball on the 22d as you have
already had due notice. One of our fellow townsmen, S. S. Harvey,
proposes to contribute his share towards the ball by tendering the
use of his stable and sheds, to any of you Helenaites, or any other
man, who comes to the party with a team. . . .

So, if the Ladies' Fair has left you fellows any greenbacks, come
to Clancy on the 22d, and besides a good time, help a good cause.[1]

The mines on which the optimism of Clancey was
founded were so rich that a profit could be made even
after shipping the ore to England for refinement. In
spite of its richness, paying ore was soon exhausted and
by 1880 the population had dwindled to seventy-seven
persons.

There was an attempt to bolster the economy by the

---

[1] Letter to the *Helena Weekly Herald*, December 24, 1874. A bit late to do
the ball much good!

introduction of Montana's first woolen mill, the Jefferson Valley Woolen Mill. Competition with long-established mills in Europe and eastern United States was too keen, however, and the Jefferson Valley mills, like several later attempts to establish a milling industry in Montana, soon closed, ending Clancey's last hope of being a permanent town.

16

WICKES

NESTLING AMONG THE ROCKIES AT AN ALTITUDE OF 5,621 FEET is Wickes named for George T. Wickes, a contractor and mining engineer of New York City, who, with his partner, J. Corbin, operated in this vicinity long years ago. . . .

About the time the Great Northern was built, Wickes was a thriving busy camp of 1,500 people. Five dance halls, running day and night, and 22 saloons flourished, and fights were so common that a man would not rise from his seat to see who was fighting. Cards strewed the main street so thickly that for several years a man with a team cleared the street every morning.

For 26 years 360 miners with lunch pails daily wound their way up the north hill where the old Alta mine is located. Little does the traveler think as the train puffs up the mountainside that $32,000,000 of lead, gold and silver ores have been taken out of the hill above him, or that this mountain has over 30 miles of tunnels honeycombing its depths.

In the gulch, old smoke stacks stand as monuments to the dim past, where a smelter operated until 1889, when it was moved to its present site of operation at East Helena. . . .

Wickes had a fire in 1901, which destroyed the greater part of the town, followed by another fire in 1902 when the town had partially rebuilt. . . .[1]

As you visit Montana's old camps or talk to the old-timers, the tantalizing question will invariably come up, "How much gold remains undiscovered? Is there a 'Mother lode' still to be found?"

In 1946 Ed Leahy, a practical mining engineer of

[1] *Roundup Tribune*, November 24, 1927.

Butte, was fascinated by the old camps and their pos-
sibilities. In his private plane he would fly over their
locations taking 35 mm. kodachromes. Often he would
land and search the site to obtain samples for assay.

During one such flight he took pictures and samples
from the area around the old Alta mine at Wickes.
The samples assayed looked promising. During the next
few days he looked at the pictures so much that he
practically had them memorized. He could close his
eyes and see the narrow-gauge railroad winding down
the side of Alta Mountain, a steep seven-thousand-foot
peak honeycombed with tunnels and covered with ant-
hills of waste that marked its countless earlier diggings.

He decided to work the stubborn old Alta; even
though others had failed repeatedly, he moved in dozers
and other equipment. One day near the top of the
mountain the dozer blade uncovered what appeared
to be a wooden tub. It turned out to be a wheelbarrow
used some seventy years before when the Alta was giving
up its riches.

The old barrow, made entirely of wood even to its
wheel, fell apart as he picked it up. He examined the
upturned earth for other relics but instead found a
chunk of galena rock high in lead content. In the next
two months Leahy and his associates took out $30,000
of ore, and the property continued to produce ore running as high as $150 a ton.

17

MONTANA CITY

AT THE SAME TIME THAT THE STUARTS WERE LIVING
in Gold Creek, mining operations were begun at Montana City.

Histories of Montana have little to say about Montana City for
the reason that gold was not found in any great quantities and the
deposits were soon worked out, but from what little has been written
of this operation it appears that gold was found there in the middle
of July, 1862.

A man whom history has known only as Harlbert, one of a party
of prospectors who came up the Missouri river, discovered the Prickly
Pear diggings at the point where Montana City was afterwards
built. Harlbert was not very popular with his fellow miners for
the reason that he had for a partner a negro with whom he ate and
slept, a fact which greatly prejudiced him in the minds of his
fellow adventurers.

While it does not appear that there was any great rush to these
diggings, several hundred men were engaged for a considerable
time in working the gravel along Prickly Pear creek, [centering
their activity] at the point where the town of Montana City was
built.

Evidently the miners of that locality expected big things of
this district, as a townsite company was incorporated and a townsite was laid out within which many crude log and frame structures
were erected.[1]

Their expectations seemed moving toward realiza-
tion when their city was named as the first county

---

[1] *Mineral Independent* (Superior), September 25, 1941.

seat of newly created Jefferson County, but Montana City suffered much the same fate as Gold Creek. Lacking great wealth herself, she found her streets deserted when the strikes at Grasshopper, Alder, and Last Chance were made.

Today nothing remains of the town except the serrated ground from which the miners took the gold.

18

BEAR GULCH

ABOUT TEN MILES WEST OF DRUMMOND THE ALERT motorist may see, north of the highway, piles of tailings that obscure the view up Bear Gulch; on the south a sign explains briefly the great rush to the wealth of Old Bear. Here gold was discovered in 1865 by the Jack Reynolds party. Guayness, a Mexican, located the first lode and a year later the male population of the gulch was one thousand, augmented by many more in the surrounding gulches.

Beartown, the metropolis of the area, was located only a few miles up the gulch. Although men from all nationalities crowded into the area, the Irish formed a heavy majority, and Beartown rivaled Butte in its reckless living. Soon in the older, more conservative communities of Deer Lodge and Missoula, the population of Beartown had won the name of the "Beartown Roughs," a name well deserved since they raised hell from one end of the region to the other.

The newspaper in Missoula carried a column from Beartown, and the news revealed the town's activity.

Considerable excitement was created in the pastoral hamlet of Beartown a few evenings since by the surreptitious introduction into camp, by some outside barbarian, of a singular fluid known as "benzine botheration." One of the "Fathers of Israel" there resident incautiously partook of the dangerous compound, which pro-

duced an effect upon his usually placid brain of the most unexpected character. He proceeded to demolish the windows and doors
of a *maison d' joie* at the upper end of town, and emptied a double
barreled shot-gun among the inmates. The citizens threw themselves into a hollow square for the purpose of restraining these unlawful proceedings, when the "little discussion" with clubs and
six-shooters became general. Shortly after the smoke of battle had
cleared away, the Guardians of Public Morality held a special meeting to take steps for the enlargement of the village graveyard.[1]

Most of Beartown's dead were interred in the Deer
Lodge cemetery, and on such occasions, the good citizens of Deer Lodge kept close to their homes. According to "Sandbar,"[2] upon such occasions the utmost
hilarity and good feeling prevailed. The lamented was
considered merely incidental to an occasion. His hearse
was a dead-axe wagon, and the driver the most reckless and sombre-visaged prospector in the camp. But
the cavalcade which attended his obsequies was imposing, in both numbers and equipment. Horsemen before and behind. Stops were made for refreshments at
all settlements along the road. Money was spent in
extravagant sums. A Beartown funeral was an event.
Deer Lodge city surrendered to it. The gates of its
beautiful cemetery were thrown open, and the unfortunate party got everything that was coming to him in
the way of ceremony and regrets. Then followed a
memorable night. Indeed, to the astounded visitor at
least, the universal rejoicing seemed to signalize a great
event. It did.

One such funeral was that of Micky Finn.

---

[1] *Missoula and Cedar Creek Pioneer,* May 25, 1871.

[2] Frank Brown was known throughout the territory as "Sandbar" after he had
survived an Indian ambush on a sand bar.

"It was in Bear Gulch in the winter of '70. At that time there were no wagon roads, only trails, but Bear Town was a prosperous mining camp, cutting straight across as we did, in the neighborhood of 35 miles from Deer Lodge. We were drifting and hoisting pay dirt to wash in the spring; and the diggin's were deep.

"Mike Flynn—we called him Micky Finn—lived the third claim below us and in the winter he got sick. We visited him several times and finally Micky died.

"Micky was a good Christian and his partner had promised him that he would bury him in consecrated ground. We miners agreed upon the advice of Joaquin Abascal, to get our horses and bury Micky in Deer Lodge in the consecrated burying ground.

"We started out one morning from Micky's cabin. We had the corpse rolled up in a blanket and thrown over an Arapahoe pack saddle. One of the boys led the horse that was carrying it behind his own. There was quite a string of us.

"Near the mouth of Bear creek we found a man who had his rip-saw set up in the woods. Some of us stayed there to saw enough lumber to make a coffin for poor Micky, while some of us went into the Bitter Root to Baron O'Keefe to borrow an old democrat wagon and harness. We had quite a time breaking the cayuses into harness, which wasn't very strong. It was made of Shaganapy, which is a kind of Indian leather.

"Well, we put the corpse in the coffin and placed it in the wagon in the back. Next morning when we got ready to pull out for Deer Lodge we had another circus gettin' the horses started, but after breakfast the procession started, those on horseback going ahead. It was quite a procession. We traveled until we got to Gold creek. At Pioneer bar there was some ground sluice and we found there was a saloon.

"As it was late in the afternoon some of the boys went in and had a drink. And pretty soon they went in and had another drink. Then we concluded that as poor Micky had never had a wake we would bring him in an hold a real Irish wake. We got some candles and brought the coffin in and set it on two beer kegs. We took off the lid and lighted the candles and there was poor Micky a layin' in there. We had some real good singin' and drinkin' all night. The boys all got pretty tired and so we made our beds on the floor around the coffin.

"In the morning as we had to go on, we had a miner make us

some coffee and we started out on our journey toward Deer Lodge. The boys were pretty well worn out so that in the afternoon the storekeeper said to me and Jim to ride on ahead and see the priest and tell him we was comin' and to dig the grave for Micky. So the two of us spurred up our horses and got to Deer Lodge and saw the father and told him to show us the place to dig the grave. He was very kind to us and gave us some supper. Then we dug the grave and it was pretty dark. It took us a while to finish and when we were done the father came out with his cassock and his book and told us that the work was done in a good workmanlike manner.

"As we were waiting for the procession we finally saw it coming down the valley. All of us stood in respectful position ready for the burial of poor Micky. And finally as the wagon pulled up, Lord and behold the corpse was gone. I tell you we sure felt badly. The two drivers said that comin' down the hill the wagon had run up on the horses' hind quarters and of course they reared around acting as though they wanted to shake hands with the driver. We all felt pretty bad and were ashamed of ourselves. The father said for us to go to Deer Lodge for the night and in the morning some of us could look up the corpse and bury it.

"We all went to Deer Lodge and had a meeting in Pete Valiton's brewery. The next morning Jim and I and two more started out from Deer Lodge in the wagon. At the top of the hill we found the place where the horses had acted up and after a long search we finally found the coffin down in the creek bed where it rolled. And there was poor Micky standin' on his head. We had an awful time gettin' the water out of the coffin, but we brought the body up reverently to Deer Lodge and buried it with proper ceremonies."[3]

The Guardians of Public Morality, Beartown's provision for a vigilance committee, took care of many matters, legal and moral.

"SOILED DOVES" AT AUCTION

In accordance with instructions received from the Guardians of Public Morality of the city of Beartown, M. T., we will dispose of by public vendue, on the 1st day of May, 1871, at 2 o'clock,

---

[3] *Silver State Post* (Deer Lodge), March 19, 1942.

p.m., opposite the store of D. Manton, in said city, to the highest bidder for cash, three charming young ladies, whose morals have been slightly damaged by sea-water in transit from New York. The articles are almost as good as new, and will be sold at a sacrifice to close consignments.

HENRY LAMB & CO., *Auctioneers.*[4]

Two weeks after this notice appeared in the Missoula *Pioneer,* the column from Beartown carried the sequel to the story:

"ONTO IT" — POSTPONED

We had quite a lively time here on Sunday last. Tangle-foot had aroused the pugnacious disposition of several pillars of our community, which resulted in an impartial discussion with clubs and things by way of a joke.

The sale of the three *nymphs du pave,* advertised to come off here on the 1st inst., has been postponed on account of the scarcity of purchasers.

A GUARDIAN OF BEARTOWN MORALITY[5]

The committee also had to take a hand in the matter of one John Manning. Mr. Manning's conduct had caused the following to appear in the *Pioneer* of March 2, 1871:

The following is a "specimen brick" from the many such soothing *billet doux* recently received by Mr. John Manning of this town: It proves that the fools are not all defunct at present writing:

Mr. Jno. Manning—*Sir:* I see you paying particular attention to one who is *to good to ever recognize* you more than a *dog*—you know that you are too *base* to *rascally* a *fiend,* to *even* merit her *scorn much less* her *smiles.*

You know that you are a *gambling, horse-racing scoundrel.*

---

[4] *Missoula and Cedar Creek Pioneer,* April 27, 1871.

[5] *Ibid.,* May 11, 1871.

But describing your *damnable attrocities* which you know even *better* than myself is only useless, I have sworn that you never shall be more to her than you are now, leave the town within ten days or I will deprive you of that which *cannot be restored*. "I *mean* your life." I do not wish to have your blood on my hands, but one so *good*, so *pure* whose soul is *white* and *unpoluted*, must be protected from such fiends in human form as you. You have nothing to keep you—leave at once or I will send your soul to eternity.

Go, or beware.

PROTECTOR

Mr. Manning must have heeded the warning and fled to Beartown for, on March 23, the *Pioneer* published the following:

IN EXILIUM PRO BONO PUBLICO

The following correspondence is self-explanatory. When last heard from the "poor exile of Erin" was contemplating suicide with a boiled carrot:

BEARTOWN, March 15, 1871

MR. EDITOR: As we have for the last week been much troubled, and the peace and quietude of our burg much disturbed, by the obnoxious acts and presence of the notorious John Manning . . . we, the undersigned, having formed ourselves into a special committee, at the residence of Mr. Van Grundy, unanimously

Resolved. That, for the future well being of this community, the said John Manning be, and he is now hereby transported beyond the vicinity, precincts, suburbs and environs of the city of Beartown, Deer Lodge county, Montana Territory.

And be it further resolved, That the said John Manning be, and he is hereby furnished with a "wakiup," fish-hooks, grasshopper bag and other implements, to enable him to sustain life until he reaches his former abode among the benighted aborigines of Missoula, where he properly belongs.

And be it further resolved, That this committee do earnestly pray the exemplary city of Beartown will not again behold the external anatomy of the said John Manning until he has inaugurated a severe and searching course of personal reformation, thereby fitting himself for an unmolested residence in our peaceable, orderly and temperate community.

CUSTODIANS OF BEARTOWN MORALITY

Although it might seem that Beartown, M.T., would be far removed from events on the other side of the Atlantic, the loyal hearts of the Irish, wherever they might beat, rallied to the cause of Erin's independence when the following notice appeared in the *Missoula Pioneer,* April 20, 1871:

BEARTOWN, M. T.
April 17, 1871

The Irishmen and lovers of freedom in Beartown have lately organized themselves into the Order of United Irishmen of the Irish Confederation which had for its head the lately released Finian prisoners. The object of the new Brotherhood is to unite all Irishmen and friends of independence in the United States into one grand body, so as to aid their brethren at home to liberate their Fatherland from English tyranny. *All* Irishmen and lovers of freedom throughout Montana should form themselves into societies of the new Brotherhood. The men of Beartown have set a good example to every Irishman who loves freedom and hates tyranny. . . .

From Beartown prospecting activities moved farther up the gulch and into adjoining canyons. In nearby Elk Creek, gold was found that, although not quite so rich as the nuggets in Bear Gulch, nevertheless sometimes yielded thousands of dollars per running foot. Reynolds City, an exact replica of Beartown in so far as manners and morals were concerned, sprang up to serve the needs of Elk Creek miners. Here occured a story that could have served as the pattern for a Virginia City or Central City melodrama.

In the early fall of '65 there arrived at Reynolds City hotel a stranger by the name of J. B. Taylor and with him a pretty woman, to all appearances his lawful wife. Both were well dressed and showed good breeding. Two days were sufficient to establish Taylor's reputation as a gambler, whose hands were often quicker than the eyes of the dealer. After three weeks his "wife" turned out to be mistress, for he deserted her and left her destitute. She told how he had beguiled her by lies and promises into leaving a home where she was always happy. Stung by grief and shame she sank deep into the shadows of a miners' brothel, where men forgot they had sisters. The poor woman could not return to her own because it would kill them to know. Here was a way to hide herself and stifle the pangs of memory with riotous pleasures, it seemed her only chance and she took it.

Then one day came Glen Lindsay, a young fortune hunter from Wyoming. He had been raised in a different atmosphere and respected a woman if she desired it. Stopping for a drink in the hurdy-gurdy, he asked a bystander who the little lady with the sorrowful eyes might be.

"That's Letty," came the reply, "she and one J. B. Taylor thought they wuz in love, but it didn't last long."

Lindsay won his way into the hearts of his fellow miners, became enamored of Letty and persuaded her to give up the old life. She was merely to be a drinking partner with the boys until Glen could "shake down" enough dust to build a cabin. Friends told him of his folly in choosing such a woman, but he would not listen and said it was their fault for not helping her.

One evening when spirits were high in the noisy hall, J. B. Taylor quietly strode in with the air of a man who was never defeated. The music stopped, everyone in the room turned their eyes toward the tall stranger, who had been seen but once before and yet was remembered perfectly. Taylor walked straight to the corner where Letty was talking over half drained glasses with a grizzled miner. He pushed the whisky flask and glasses to one side, sat down on the table and pulled at the tawdry, ruffled dress which Letty was wearing. With a sneer of contempt, he said:

"So this is the wife I thought I'd married. I suppose," and he waved his hands to include all the men standing about, "that you have as much claim on her as I have."

There was a murmur in the room. "If we had, we wouldn't leave her to starve," said one miner.

The woman's steady gaze at Taylor betrayed an unholy fear of him and yet revealed a half tender remembrance of her first love.

It was Glen Lindsay who stepped from among the onlookers, grabbed Taylor by the collar and dragged him to the floor. In an instant there was seen the flash of a revolver, a puff of smoke, and Lindsay fell dead at the feet of the one for whom he gave his life. Before anyone could recover from the shock, Taylor had fought his way to the door and made a polite exit with two ugly looking barrels trained upon the crowd.

J. B. Taylor later was host to a little surprise hanging party given in his honor in Deep Gulch not long after his appearance at Reynolds City. The death of her lover brought about a complete change in Letty, and affecting the somber garb of a widow, she earned a scant living by the needle.

Just outside of Reynolds City and to the left of the road there stands a brown worm-eaten board which marks the grave of Glen Lindsay who, with unimpeachable chivalry, truly loved, bravely lost. . . .[6]

Farther up in the mountains, Garnet and Coloma were established about two miles apart. In 1897 Coloma was one of the busiest towns in the area, its saloons and hurdy-gurdies open all night, its stores doing a thriving business in supplying the miners. In 1892 Samuel Ritchie discovered rich ore at Garnet in the "Old Shaft" of the Nancy Hanks mine. Not until 1896 did production in the Nancy Hanks reach its height; then it produced $960,000. The old Dewey mine was located nearby and produced three hundred dollars and more per ton.

Of all these towns, Beartown died most completely. As early as 1871, the correspondent from Bear noted plaintively:

---

[6] Coleman H. Mulcahy in the *Billings Times,* October 25, 1928.

Our burg is very dull and lonesome at present—in fact, a regular deserted village. There is not even a decent knock-down, shooting scrape, or other characteristic item, to enliven the monotony of existence. The time was when manly sports of this nature, were incidents of every day occurence. Alas! Old Bear, how you have fallen.[7]

Today nothing is left where this town, whose population at one time probably numbered five thousand, was located. Many are still attracted to the site by the story that, before leaving Beartown, a Chinaman buried a large baking powder can filled with gold, intending to return for it. He never came back, and the hundreds of seekers who have honeycombed the cliff where it was supposed to be buried have never found it.

Coloma's life, too, was as short as it was merry, although there is still some mining activity around the old town.

Garnet alone lived on for many years. As late as 1948 an auction in Garnet attracted a large crowd, some who came as collectors, others to reawaken nostalgic memories and renew old friendships.

[Today] crowds again thronged the streets of Garnet, giving that ghost town another short day of life when T. A. Davey sold by auction his store supplies and hotel furnishings.

Nestled among the hills of the Garnet range about 15 miles northwest of here, the vacant buildings of Garnet, which once housed miners of the old Musigerod mine, echoed to the chant of the auctioneer as buggies, sleighs, carts, harness, light miner's tools and gold pans were put on the block, bringing memories to the purchasers and cash to the seller.

Here one could obtain black cambric cloth, marked to sell at 29 cents per yard, for a small sum. Most of the shoes in stock had pointed toes and many were of button style. Among the items to

---

[7] *Missoula and Cedar Creek Pioneer*, May 14, 1871.

be seen and had were ladies' shirt waists, which were once fashionable, and laces of every description. A large wheeled coffee grinder and also several different types of scales were inspected by most of the visitors. . . . Among the old timers present were Mr. and Mrs. Royal who had furnished music for three nights of dancing at the opening of the Wells hotel, from which the furniture was sold at this sale.[8]

Only recently was the Garnet school closed. Mr. Stoddard, who has prospected up and down the length of the Rockies and who lives on in Garnet, will assure you in his flawless English that the country is still rich in ore. Living in his little cabin surrounded by the abandoned, rotting cabins of the once bustling town, he is confident that the wealth is still there even though the false-front shops of Main Street have long ago disappeared.

The old hotel still stands, its formal-patterned red wallpaper faded and torn, its stairways and floors decayed and broken. The twenty or so log cabins that are still there offer one of the best remaining examples of a placer ghost camp. Although roofs are sagging or fallen, and the strong odor of rats hangs over the abandoned debris, it is not difficult in the imagination to see Garnet as it once was, busy by day with the hard work of the mines, and gay by night with gambling and revelry.

---

[8] The *Missoulian* (Missoula), July 15, 1948.

BLACKFOOT CITY

BLACKFOOT CITY WILL SOON BE UNSURPASSED AS A MINING TOWN. Everything is in its favor for here is indeed a miner's paradise. The finest grass grown is in this valley. Horses can travel on it as well as on grain. Even freezing weather cannot harm it and stock can come out of the winter fat and strong. This country is full of game. Mountain buffalo,[1] bison, elk, black and brown bears, black and white tailed deer, prairie chickens, grouse, and quail abide here in great numbers. The town lies at the base of an abruptly wooded mountain on a level table land, admirably calculated for a large and permanent city with every facility for fuel and water at hand. A solid and substantial fortune awaits any man of energy who plants his stake here and no more important service can be rendered to the community than the erection of a big town at a point where heavy goods can be brought in by water, avoiding the weary journey and casualties of a pilgrimage across plains. Let no man say there is not gold here, for the ground is full of it and indeed the grass roots are heavy with it, while the bars are lined with nuggets.[2]

This is the glowing account of one of the prospectors who struck it rich in Ophir Gulch, and, indeed, most of what he said was entirely true. Shortly after pay dirt was discovered Blackfoot City was a thriving mining town with a broad main street and cross streets leading to the ranges on each side of the gulch. Although it grew rapidly, the very richness of its sur-

---

[1] Unidentified.
[2] Jean Moore in the *Grass Range Review*, November 28, 1938.

roundings were a threat to its permanent population as miners were likely to stampede at any time, perhaps packing their frying pans and gold pans late at night prior to an early morning's move to some new discovery.

During its first year it boasted among its population seven good traders, two blacksmiths, two doctors, a combined carpenter and coffinmaker, a Chinese laundryman, and several liquor dealers, as whisky was considered a staple comparing in importance with flour, bacon, and beans. Prices were high but not as high as in many other camps.

Whisky, candles, flour, and heavy boots headed the list for selling value. Freighting charges were at first exorbitant, but decreased considerably with competition. A customer, who in answer to his question as to why he should pay forty cents for a small needle received as an answer that he was paying nothing for the needle, just forty cents for the freight and a bargain at that.

The wealth of nearby Carpenter's Bar was incredible. Here gold was deposited over a twenty-square-mile surface. A belt of leads on the north side of this auriferous range ran to Snowshoe Gulch and it was from these mainly that the gold was deposited. Men worked night and day on Carpenter's Bar, were always on guard against claim jumpers, and declined to give out information concerning their claims. A party sinking a prospect hole in Deadwood Gulch dug directly down to a three-thousand-dollar nugget. The gold found in all the diggings was coarse at the upper part of the gulches, gradually becoming finer when near the mouth. Nuggets were reported to have been as common as gold dust in Blackfoot territory. At Pence's Discovery a group of miners, playing handball, substituted a nugget worth $11,880 for a ball.[3]

Small towns sprang up at many of the bars and gulches for the accommodation of miners who found it too inconvenient to ride in to Blackfoot City as often as they needed supplies. There were many stores, some in small lean-tos and some simply set up in the brush. One of the smallest but most flourishing businesses was "Whiskey Keg Store," located at McClellan Gulch. As the name implies, the store itself was nothing more than a large whisky keg from which supplies were handed out as customers demanded them.

Blackfoot residents possessed a deep loyalty to their gulch or bar in which their claims were located. A miner of Poor Man's Gulch, describing his fellow workers, said,

> "Poor Man's gulch is full of real prospectors, not green puny men from the states, but stout, hard working men, mostly of middle age who have served long apprenticeships; men who work more and swear less than our eastern frontier men and a great majority are very strong for the union."[4]

A clannish spirit existed between the so-called Pikes Peakers and the Californians. Reported a miner from Jefferson Gulch, "A Californian is broad shouldered, bronzed and exceedingly intelligent looking and godlike in appearance."[5] Needless to say, the describer was a Californian.

---

[3] Unverified.

[4] Moore, *loc. cit.*

[5] *Ibid.*

As in many mining towns, Blackfoot occasionally experienced troubles with the Indians, the first and probably the most serious occurring on June 28, 1865, when Captain Burns, Frank Angevine, John Alley, the King brothers, and several others whose names are unknown, were attacked by Indians who resented the white man's using too much timber and wild game. A meeting of citizens was called with Judge Brond presiding. In a war speech, he declared it necessary that the governor declare martial law throughout the territory for thirty days and that all able-bodied men fight the disturbers of peace. The following Monday and Wednesday rumors were afloat of prospectors being found dead and of freight lines being corralled by Indians who were camped in heavy concentrations on the Sun River. Orders were immediately dispatched by the governor to organize a force of five hundred men to dispel the Indians. This word must have reached the red men by smoke signals for, when the army assembled and searched the area, the enemy had disappeared.

Crimes of passion and vengeance, of greed and fury fill the pages of Montana's violent early days; yet few, if any, seem as blood-chilling as the calculated murder of Captain Dodson of American Gulch. Dodson's son, Clinton, living in the Black Hills of South Dakota, had for some time not been favored by fortune. In the summer of 1899, accompanied by a Navy deserter, Oliver Benson, he set out in a rickety old wagon to visit his father. There were many rickety wagons on the rough roads of the West, but the canvas of this one had been patched with black oilcloth, a fact that was later to serve in tracing its owner.

When the boys reached American Gulch one of the first tales they heard was that a mild-mannered old prospector, Cullinane, had $15,000 hidden in his cabin. After one unsuccessful attempt to interest a third party in a scheme to kill and rob the old man, Clinton and Oliver met Persinger, a jovial, irresponsible Missourian, in Helena. He was down on his luck and was persuaded to accompany them back to American Gulch.

Arriving there August 8, they hid their outfit in the brush, decided that Benson should stay to guard it and that Clinton and Persinger would see what could be done about getting $15,000. They were gone all day; nervously Benson waited. At last, the pair arrived, but instead of $15,000 they had $15 and a gold watch. They had hidden themselves in the brush near the cabin and, when Cullinane returned from his claim, had shot him down. On the body they found the watch and money; in the cabin, which they ransacked thoroughly, they found nothing.[6]

Hitching their horses to the wagon with the black patch, the trio fled eastward, passing through Helena on their way.

A week after the killing Cullinane's partner returned from a prospecting trip. In the barn he found Cullinane's horse half dead from hunger and thirst. Hastening to the cabin, he found it in disarray; searching the surrounding area, he soon found his partner's body half covered with leaves and brush.

The alarm being given, the miners, with whom old

---

[6] The story persists that Cullinane's fortune still lies hidden in the gulch.

Cullinane had been popular because of his honesty and gentleness, were in a frenzy. One and then another began recalling the movements of the trio in the black-patched wagon. By prompt and clever action, the outfit was spotted near Gallatin and the three criminals seized and bound. Benson, having the least to fear, told all; Clint Dodson was named as the trigger man and got 99 years in Deer Lodge prison. Each of the others got ten years.

The trail of blood did not end in that prison cell. Dodson had, as a cell mate, James Fleming, alias McArthur, who was just about ready for release after having served time for burglary. Dodson conceived the following plan: When McArthur got out, he would go to American Gulch, murder Captain Dodson, Clinton's father, in such a way that it would look like suicide, and leave a suicide note confessing that the elder Dodson had murdered Cullinane. By this scheme, Clinton would be pardoned, and he and McArthur would make their way to Texas, robbing trains as they went.

Each step in the plan worked smoothly. McArthur won Captain Dodson's confidence by offering to buy some of his land. They spent several days together both in American Gulch and in Helena. In Helena, McArthur, after robbing his host one night, returned to the claim to wait until the old man came back. It was a week before the captain returned; during that time McArthur had gone out rarely, but one day he had borrowed some ink from a neighbor. The ink had been frozen, but in that remote place, it was still considered usable.

On February 15, several inhabitants of the gulch

noted Captain Dodson's return, but, being winter, it was five days before anyone began wondering at his not being seen around. When someone went to investigate, his frozen body, a rifle pointed where his head would be if he were standing, and a string attached from his finger to the trigger, was found in his cabin. A suicide note confessing to the Cullinane murder was on the table. It took no Sherlock Holmes to detect the fallacies in the setup. Beneath the head of the corpse was a pillow and a neatly folded pair of long johns; the note was not in his handwriting; furthermore, it had been written in ink that had been frozen.

Again neighbors began remembering. McArthur had occupied the cabin before Dodson's return; he had borrowed the ink; someone had heard shots in or near the cabin on February 15; someone else saw McArthur leaving the gulch shortly after the shots were heard.

Montana justice found the murderer a week later hiding at the home of a friend in the Bitterroot. Before he stepped to his death on the Deer Lodge gallows, he told the entire scheme; Clinton Dodson was hung as an accessory before the fact the following spring.

To balance such grim business as this and the hard work of placer mining, the Blackfoot citizens required some form of amusement, and it was often originated on the spot. The miners' natural gambling instincts often created much of their fun. Even a dog fight was not passed up but, instead, would draw a sizable crowd with bets running from one to three hundred dollars. The California Minstrels found Blackfoot City a promising place and played to good audiences, not because of any particular ability on their part but because its residents welcomed any outside entertainment. On July 4, 1865, a congenial fellow with the appropriate name of Hugh Happy, his patriotism fired by the Fourth-of-July celebration and several drinks of firewater, was dismayed when he was unable to find a single flag floating anywhere. Asking everyone he met for an explanation of such a disgrace, he was informed that the town did not boast a flag. Never, while Hugh Happy was a citizen, could Blackfoot City accept this ignominy. He purchased yards of red, white, and blue material, and within an hour's time the Stars and Stripes were floating proudly in the breeze.

Another bit of Blackfootiana concerns a camel. In 1854, under a grant of $30,000, Secretary of War Davis was directed to import camels from Africa to see if, transplanted, they would be satisfactory as military beasts of burden. After two years of planning, the camels embarked, complete with six Arab attendants and a Turkish camel M.D. to keep them healthy. There were nine dromedaries, twenty-three camels, and one calf. These were to form the nucleus of a camel ranch if the animals proved valuable under the changed conditions. They were highly satisfactory, and forty-one more were imported with plans to bring in an additional thousand. Although the latter plan was never carried out, the camels already imported proved useful, particularly in the arid districts of California and New Mexico where they often carried water for the mule trains.

In spite of this service the mule skinners and their mules detested the camels, the former because the sturdy beasts from the desert could carry five times as much as their mules and might easily drive them out of business. And the latter? Who knows. Perhaps for the same reason. Common are the accounts of mule and horse teams stampeding if they met a camel train. It is said that on one such occasion a consignment of whisky being drawn by a horse caravan that stampeded at the sight of camels was dumped into the river in the vicinity of Hell Gate and, for the first time in Montana, water was a popular drink.

This is a little ahead of the story. At the end of the war, the camels were put up for sale and one enterprising freighter on the Montana run purchased a train. It was this train that caused the above-mentioned trouble, that gave its name to Camel's Hump, the summit of the little Bitterroot Mountains, and that got the Missourian from Blackfoot City into trouble. The owner of the train had unloaded his beasts and let them loose to graze. The Missourian, out for a little meat for the table, mistook the camel for a moose and, with one lucky shot, brought it down. Triumphantly he went to collect the carcass only to be confronted with a torrent of abuse from the freighter. Poor McNear was forced to part with his watch, all the money he had with him, his gun and ammunition, and the deed to his mining claim in Ophir Gulch before the camel's owner considered himself repaid. As final retribution he was forced to dig a hole big enough to give the "ship of the desert" a decent burial![7]

---

[7] Like most folklore both these tales are found with variations in locale and other details; they remain essentially factual, a humorously different bit from the old West.

The decline of Blackfoot City was nearly as rapid as its rise. For many years after the prospectors of the first rush had left for richer diggings, a few solitary wanderers would drift in and, learning of the vast wealth that once filled the ground, would pan a few ounces of dust and move on. Hunters of a different kind of treasure have found, on the site of Blackfoot City, ox shoes, gold pans, and even an old opium pipe. Many have hoped to find the grave of Calamity Jane's mother who, according to her notorious daughter, died at Blackfoot City.

20

EMERY

EMERY, NINE MILES EAST OF DEER LODGE, HAS HAD ONE
of the longest production lives of any mining camp in
the area.

Largest of all the properties in the district is the Emery mine
itself. Last operated by an English company some twenty years
ago it is credited with a production of $1,500,000. . . .

Best known, perhaps, of all mines in the district is the Blue-
eyed Maggie owned by James E. Higgins of Deer Lodge. For 25
years this property had yielded a consistent tonnage of high grade
ore. Through the lean depression years just ended the Maggie
carried on without stint. Whether in bull or bear metal markets
she never flinched and oldsters will tell you that, like Tennyson's
brook, she will go on forever. There have been days of grave doubt
and fear, just as in any successful career. During such times the
genial Mr. Higgins used to gather his ever-present guests about
the huge open hearth at the cabin and sing a theme song to the
tune of an old favorite:

> "Pretty little Blue-eyed Maggie
> Better times are comin', wait and see."

Even the spirits are mining at Emery. Legend has it that on
Cottonwood creek several men belonging to a certain religious cult
are haunting the pay streak in a strange manner. As the story goes,
they first hold some kind of seance during which a visitation occurs
to one and another. The person so favored by a manifestation from
the spirit world then rises after the manner of somnambulists and
leads the others to a prescribed spot on the hillside as directed by
the guiding spirit. There, without thought to rock or reason, these
spiritists immediately swing pick and shovel in their spooky quest
for the yellow glitter.

So far the spirits have not been willing. . . . Perhaps the ghost of some pioneer will return to reveal the secret of hidden treasure which was buried with him. . . .[1]

---

[1] *Midland Empire Farmer,* May 30, 1935. They were probably seeking the lost Springer or Deadman claim.

21

YELLOWSTONE CITY

ON AUGUST 30, 1864, THREE MEN WERE WORKING THEIR way up one of the wildest and most formidable gulches of Montana. "On all sides deep gorges have been gashed out by aqueous forces cutting through the very core of the mountain, and forming those wonderful gulches which only the hardy and daring miner has ventured to explore."[1]

David Weaver, with four friends, had started west with one yoke of cows, two yoke of oxen, and a wagon. They had joined a 68-wagon emigrant train going to the gold fields and, on arriving at a point 150 miles up from the Yellowstone River crossing, had decided to part company. Weaver, Norris, and Shorthill remained in the Yellowstone country; Owens and Travis went on toward Virginia City. The latter took one yoke of oxen and one cow. Weaver and Norris, taking the wagon, the other yoke of oxen and the other cow, began prospecting up the gulch. They passed through Chico Springs where Curry, the Irish tailor, was having better luck. On past the first and second falls they went, pick, shovel, and pan in constant use. About five miles beyond the third falls, at a place where the waters of the gulch flowed over solid bedrock, Shorthill,

---

[1] U.S. Geological and Geographical Survey of the Territories. Report, 5th, 1871, p. 54.

picking up the shovel, stuck it through the water, under a shelving of rock and brought up two shovelsful of the sand and gravel which were thrown into the pan. It was the work of but a few seconds to "pan" this out, and there in the bottom of the pan lay unmistakably the object of our long journey. There was perhaps a dollar's worth of gold in this first pan. I fancy I can hear yet the yell of delight which Shorthill gave, as well he might, for had we not travelled over two thousand miles and spent four long, weary months at the heels of slow ox-teams, since we first "hitched-up" on the prairies of Iowa?"[2]

This was not "color" but coarse gold with nuggets frequently of twenty to twenty-five cents' worth. The discoverers hastened to send a messenger after their friends who had started for Alder Gulch. He overtook them within sight of Virginia City. They, and others along the way who heard of the strike, turned back, eager to share in the new discovery. The district was named "Shorthill" after the discoverer and the gulch "Emigrant Gulch."

Miners from the Curry district, including Tom Curry himself, moved up; claims were staked; miners' meetings were held to formulate laws, and for seven feverish weeks gold was dug, panned, and sluiced from the rich deposits. By the end of the seven weeks, ice forming in the sluice boxes forced suspension of the activity for the winter. The miners packed their supplies and blankets and moved down the gulch about six miles to Yellowstone City where fifty log cabins had been built to provide shelter during the winter. These cabins had the usual pole, grass and dirt roof, but they were often carpeted with elk skins.

---

[2] D. B. Weaver, "Early Days in Emigrant Gulch," Historical Society of Montana, *Contributions*, VII (1910), 80-81.

That first winter in Yellowstone City was a difficult one. Even the metropolis, Virginia City, was having flour riots. Small wonder that the isolated miners of Yellowstone City should be facing serious shortages. Plug tobacco sold at $5.00 a pound and smoking tobacco was "ounce for ounce"—an ounce of gold on one side of the balance, an ounce of tobacco on the other. With gold at $18.00 an ounce, this made the tobacco nearly $300 a pound in gold or $550 in "greenbacks." More carefully than they emptied their pokes, thrifty miners shook their flour sacks to get out the last spoonful of flour. Weaver tells the following incident concerning the flour famine:

One day in May, 1865, I was going down to Yellowstone City to get supplies to take up the gulch, and as I was passing beneath some trees of the pine or fir variety, I was startled at hearing a scratching and moving sound up in one of the trees. I say startled which expresses it very mildly, for in that region a man instinctively associated such a noise with just one thing—grizzly bears. I wasn't prepared to deal with grizzlies, and was on the point of taking to my heels without waiting for any developments, when I was greeted by a friendly voice from the tree. It was a fellow named George Stukey. He accompanied me to the city and explained that he had been gathering some of the "pitch" or chewing gum from the tree. Their cabin, he said, had been out of flour since March. . . . He had found that chewing this gum relieved the craving for flour foods.[3]

Another miner, trying to work on meat for breakfast, meat for dinner, and meat for supper, angrily threw down his tools declaring that, if the gold could not buy flour, he had no use for the gold.

As soon as spring came, the miners moved back to

---

[3] *Ibid.*, pp. 85-86.

the Shorthill district. A man named Gage, who had
seven donkeys, ran a pack train the six miles from the
"City" to the mines, charging three dollars per hundred for freight.

There were a few women even in this remote area.
One of these, Mrs. William Moore, had brought with
her some garden seeds, and, when the earth warmed
under the summer sun, she carefully chose a spot, well
removed from the mining activities, and planted her
precious seeds. However, when the corn was about a
foot high, the discovery was made that it was growing
in "pay dirt." This was the first and last attempt at
gardening in old Emigrant Gulch.

A variety of trouble dogged the region. Twice the
original or "discovery" claim was buried under thun-
dering avalanches. Before the second slide, one of the
three owners had been posted across the gulch to shout
a warning if the snow mass should begin to move. The
warning was given seconds too late; the other two men,
Gibboney and Skinner, were buried under tons of snow.
Skinner's body was dug up, but not until the sun melted
the snow was Gibboney's body found.

Not only were the wild, relentless forces of nature
to be endured. The Crow Indians, on whose territory
the gulch lay, were a constant menace. Hunting parties
were harassed, and stock was driven off.

In the spring of 1865, the Crows ambushed three
Virginia City men who were camped on Mission Creek
near Yellowstone City. Two of the men were killed
and the third, Hughes, a former resident of Yellowstone
City and a friend of Weaver, escaped into the brush

along the river having no more than an arrow wound in his arm.

The Indians pushed through the brush close behind him, but when they were closing in on him, he wheeled suddenly and with his revolver shot three of them through the bodies. It was the Indians' turn to be surprised, and they lost no time in retreating. Hughes jumped into the creek, and hid himself in some driftwood that had collected against a small tree. He was wearing at the time a light colored hat, which one of the keen-eyed savages quickly detected. A gunshot sounded, and the bullet plowed across Hughes' forehead. He now knew that they had at least one gun in their party and that they knew how to use it. What they didn't know, fortunately for Hughes, was that his revolver was now empty, as all his ammunition was on his riding horse, which the Indians had captured. He quickly got rid of the conspicuous hat, and trusted to the approach of darkness as his only salvation. As it grew darker and his chances of escape thereby improved, the Indians tried to lure him out by calling to him: "Good evening, Charlie." "Come out, Charlie." "Won't hurt Charlie," "How'dy do, Charlie," etc. But Hughes didn't care to be on any closer terms with the redskins just then. He kept concealed until well after dark, then went down the creek in the water for about a mile, turned west and traveled all night. . . . About daylight he reached the Yellowstone canyon, where he was fortunate enough to meet a man on his way to Yellowstone City, and was given a ride in the wagon. Hughes had lost all his property and was pretty well discouraged when I saw him, and was most anxious to get back to his family in Keokuk, Iowa. We raised a purse for him, and he left the next day for Virginia City.[4]

After the Indian scare abated, miners drifted in and out of the gulch, but the heyday of Yellowstone City was past. Some of the men believed that Chico, near the mouth of the gulch, would be a safe spot, and quite a town was established there with about $80,000 in gold being taken out in 1865.

---

[4] *Ibid.*, pp. 88-89.

The many travelers entering Yellowstone Park by way of the Yellowstone Canyon see only a fairly open river valley and may question the reputation for wildness that is attributed to Emigrant Gulch. However, by proceeding only a few miles up the gulch they will find some of the most rugged country in Montana. The site of Yellowstone City was practically wiped out by later dredging, but White City, a camp just above Chico, is being restored, not as a mining camp but as a tourist and hunting resort. For the energetic there is still the steep mountain trail used by the miners and Gage's donkeys that leads the six miles up the gulch to the ruins of the mill whose slag pile, even today, will yield color as a reward for the energy expended in reaching it.

22

CINNABAR

LIVING IN A CABIN IN THE LOWER END OF YELLOWSTONE CITY were two brothers, Charles and James Soule, who had tried unsuccessfully to get down to bedrock in the lower, or Curry district of Emigrant gulch, and who toward summer struck out in the hills prospecting. Following up the river to a point near the northern boundary of Yellowstone park, they found on a mountain-side a red-colored rock which they imagined was cinnabar ore. They kept the discovery to themselves during the summer, but toward winter, after staking claims for themselves, they took samples and struck out on their horses for Virginia City, then the booming metropolis of Alder gulch. There they announced that they had made a great quartz strike and offered to stake out claims for others at $100 apiece. They offered to take pay in gold dust, grub or mining tools and supplies, explaining that it would be necessary to drive a tunnel into the mountain to tap a body of rich ore, in which they expected to find quick silver.

Meanwhile, back in Emigrant gulch the miners had all ceased their work for the season of 1865 in Shorthill's district, as the winter had set in on October 26 with a heavy freeze. They had packed their blankets and cooking outfits down to Yellowstone City, and were settling down to a quiet winter when, on November 1, about dark, the camp was aroused by horsemen riding in. It was the Soule brothers with mail from Virginia City and their pack horses laden with provisions, tools, powder, etc. They explained to the miners that they had during the past summer found a big lode of cinnabar ore up the valley on the west side of the river, and that they had sold seven claims to Virginia City people. They said they were going to drive a tunnel into the mountain.

Their story caused a little excitement, and the next morning an Irish baker, William McDonnell, came to my cabin to ask what I thought about the Soules. I told him I knew nothing about cinnabar ore, but that I did not take any stock in this "strike" as the samples they had showed looked like red rock underlying hard coal formations I had seen in Pennsylvania, and also certain soft coal beds.

"Well," said McDonnell, "They tell me that when they get their tunnel in where the ore is rich, the quick-silver will seep through the rock, and by forming a basin at the bottom of the tunnel, it will collect so that they can dip it out with a cup."[1]

I told McDonnell that I would want to see this before I believed it, and he said that if I didn't stake a claim on the cinnabar lode, he didn't want any either.

There was a good deal of fun in Yellowstone City over the Soule's mining enterprise and I don't think any of the boys there took claims. The Soules went along up to their mountain to drive the tunnel. A few days later Charlie Soule came back to get one of the miners, Richard Owens, to help them put their tunnel through, for they had run into a snag. They seemed to be better promoters than they were miners, but in those days promoters did not get very far. When Owens reached their diggings, he inquired: "What are those things that look like rat tails?"

"Those," replied Charlie Soule, "are the fuses that we put in. They failed to fire the blast in the holes where we put the powder. We want you to help dig them out."

"Don't you know," said Owens, "that if you try to dig them out with your pick that the steel will strike fire, set off the blast and blow you up?"

"Sure, we know that," Soule said. "That's why we hired you to help."

Owens shrugged his shoulders and didn't answer, but by using water to soften the tamping, and working with a wooden stick, he soon got the holes cleaned out. Then after showing the Soules where to dig new holes, he took a walk a few miles up the river and was rewarded by finding the coal outcroppings that I had expected might be there. He returned and told the Soule brothers, and they were quite pleased, for they said they would now be able to roast out the quicksilver with coal instead of wood.

They worked away at the tunnel till the spring of 1865, ate their grub, burned their powder, and failed to reach the place where

---

[1] Quicksilver, used in the reduction process, was scarce and much in demand.

they could find quicksilver. Finally, they packed their outfits and started for the diggings at Last Chance.

That was the last heard of Cinnabar until 1872, when Professor F. V. Hayden made his interesting geological survey of Montana. He went to the "cinnabar mine" to get samples, but on inspecting the so-called ore, he pronounced it red-colored rock, which it most certainly was. However, to commemorate the "strike" of the Soule brothers, they called the mountain Cinnabar Mountain, with the Devil's Slide as one of the features.[2]

Just before Cinnabar faded from the maps and the postal guides, it was the capital of the United States for 16 days. Over the telegraph wires from its humble railway station pulsed the messages which guided the ship of state and kept the world informed of White House decisions.

Old Cinnabar was established in 1883 as the terminus of the Yellowstone park branch of the railroad. It was for nearly 20 years the jumping off place for Yellowstone park via the picturesque old stagecoaches. Its location was the oldest industrial spot in southern Montana. The area was the scene of the first coal development in the state—the Red Streak Mountain Coal Co. so named because of the famous dike known as the Devil's Slide, was granted a corporation charter by the Bannack legislature of 1864. Across its flat meadow land passed Washburn, Langford, Doane, Hayden and the others who explored the area that is now the nation's Wonderland.

For reasons best known to its engineers, the Northern Pacific chose this spot, four miles from the north entrance to the park, as the end of its branch road. Until 1902 the town served the tourist trade and the mining and coke communities of Aldridge and Horr. The latter is now called Electric. The coke ovens are crumbling ruins, and the Aldridge mines have long since ceased to produce coal.

In 1902 the Northern Pacific extended its road to Gardiner, with its station 100 yards from the park line. But in early 1903 it had not completed its station and other service facilities.

So Cinnabar drew the honor of being the nation's temporary capital while President Theodore Roosevelt, in April and early May,

---

[2] David Weaver in the *Dillon Examiner,* February 22, 1922.

1903, made a pre-season tour of Yellowstone park, prior to his dedication of the huge stone entrance arch.

A string of Pullmans and parlor cars and a diner were the temporary White House from which Presidential Secretary William Loeb, Jr., conducted affairs of state in the name of his former cowboy-Rough Rider chief. A string of messengers maintained communications between the White House on Wheels and the president, no matter where he might be within the park.

Cinnabar was perhaps as novel to the presidential cortege of officials, secret service men and news writers as the visitors were to the pioneers who peopled the community.

Composed of a few hundred people, rather mean, often shabby structures housing frontier homes and business houses, Cinnabar offered little or none of the refinements and luxuries of the Capital City in the District of Columbia.

Harry Colman, day manager of the Washington bureau of the Associated Press, remarked: "Well, thank goodness, this blooming town will be wiped off the map when we leave. It's a mystery to me how it got on in the first place. . . ."[3]

---

[3] *Silver State Post* (Deer Lodge), June 30, 1938.

23

COOKE CITY

HIGH ON THE GREAT MOUNTAINS NORTH OF YELLOW-
stone Park a little group of buildings constitutes the
town of Cooke City. Strangers may wonder amusedly
at the term "City," not knowing that this town dates
back to the mining days when all camps aspired to be
cities, when all inhabitants shared Joaquin Miller's vision
of unlimited development.

More than 15,000 feet of shafts, tunnels and levels have been
run in exploring the 300 mining claims in the seven mineral mountains around Cook City. Imperial Rome sat on her seven hills of
common dirt on the Yellow Tiber, but Cook City reposes on seven
mountains filled with gold, silver, lead and iron. It took a thousand years for the palaces of imperial Rome to take the place of
the dug-outs where Romulus and Remus were nursed by a vulpine
mother; but palaces will replace the log cabins of Cook City in
a hundredth part of that time.[1]

In 1869 four trappers Adam Miller, J. H. Moore, Bert Henderson and James Gourley . . . were robbed of their horses by Indians
who had discovered and looted their cache on Cache creek. These
four men in escaping from the Indians fled north of Cache creek
and crossed the divide that separates its headwaters from Republic
creek. They discovered the manganese-stained outcrop on the property which was later developed into the Republic mine, panned a
small amount of gold from the streams and pushed on to Stillwater,
later Columbus. . . .[2]

[1] Joaquin Miller, *An Illustrated History of the State of Montana* (Chicago:
Lewis Publishing Company, 1894), pp. 798-99.
[2] *Cascade Courier,* June 17, 1937.

Miller and Moore made the first location, naming it the Shoofly.
It was also in '69 that a husky young trapper, named Jack Crandall with his partner, an Irishman named Daugherty, came out
of the unmapped, unknown country between Yellowstone park and
the Clark's Fork to Bozeman with placer gold to fire the imagination of those as adventurous as themselves. They met the four
trappers in Bozeman and agreed that they should meet the next
July on the headwaters of the Clark's Fork and prospect together.

The four men from Bozeman kept the rendezvous, found the
Clark's Fork but no sign of the men who were to meet and guide
them. Their search failed to reveal the missing prospectors and
what happened to them remained a mystery until '71 when "Hank"
Bottler, another prospector, and his partner, came upon a grue-
some sight on the bank of a tributary of the river. They found
the heads of the two prospectors sticking on their picks in their
camp where they had been killed by Indians. Each head had a
tin cup in front of it, a sign telling other Indians that their victims
had been surprised while eating. That's how Crandall Creek was
first named.[3]

Jay Cooke, Jr., son of the financial backer of the Northern
Pacific shortly before, became interested in the Cooke area even
before the Crow reservation was moved and the camp was named
after him.

After 1882 there was little activity until 1885 when the Great
Republic smelter ran for 100 days. Some 440 tons of silver-lead
bullion was sold for [$] 95,000 but the cost of coke and transporta-
tion destroyed all profits.

After 1886 a number of attempts were made to infuse new
activity into the camp, and more than 100,000 tons of ore were
put on mine dumps over the years. Some of the ores were good
under average conditions, but isolation rendered them worthless.

For 40 years there were periodic attempts to get a railroad into
Cooke, for with rails believed claim owners and speculators, Cooke
would become a bonanza. Bills were frequently introduced in
congress to secure a railroad right-of-way through Yellowstone
park or to remove from the park the area north of the Lamar river
and east of the Yellowstone.

One of the few comedies connected with the Cooke story occurred

---

[3] *Ibid.*

in 1885 when a bill was in congress to remove the area in question from the park. Speculators at Gardiner and Livingston were watching the legislation. One day a telegram came to Livingston that the bill had passed the house. The recipient of the wire became flustered and thought it had become law. He passed the information to associates in Gardiner, giving the signal for an intendedly quiet safari in late winter into the Soda springs area to stake mining claims.

Outsiders found out something was happening, and set a watch upon the movements of certain individuals. When the "insiders" greeted daylight on Soda butte after a hurried night ride, they found the camp followers were numerous and coveted claims were snapped up before the original clique could get their stakes down.

Then came the sad news that it was all a mistake.

Meantime, many of the 1882 pioneers settled down on their Cooke claims to await the "million dollar" deals that were to come pretty soon. Within recent years old men have died who spent their mature lives on the slopes of Henderson mountain or in other parts of the mountains around Cooke. Mostly they eked out a precarious existence. Occasionally one of them would decide that a coin in the pocket was worth more than gold in the mountain and would sell their claims for what might be offered. Not all of them, though.

Fresh in the minds of Park county people is the memory of one old couple who wasted their lives waiting for that "million dollar" claim. They were at various times offered as much as $50,000 by someone who wanted to take a flier at mining. But——

"No, Sir, this mine is worth a million dollars. Why! Just look at that ore; see the gold running through it. We're going to have a million dollars out of this claim."

The couple, foreigners, had gone to the Horr-Aldridge coal and coke properties north of Gardiner. They were not in the vanguard, but several years later they took their stake of [$]1,200, bought a claim at Cooke and settled down to develop their fortune.

The man grew old before his time. He kept drilling away at a tunnel. A man-sized tunnel meant a lot of work. A small tunnel would move forward faster and reveal quicker the mother lode he was sure was there. The years went by and the stooping in his rat-hole tunnel bent his body until he was hopelessly deformed. In this condition he kept pecking away at the face of his tunnel.

County charges in their last years, the man finally died, and it was not long until his wife was taken to the state hospital, a veil of mercy enshrouding her last days.[4]

---

[4] *Kalispell Times,* February 1, 1940.

24

NYE CITY

AS EARLY AS 1864 PROSPECTORS HAD BEEN IN THE Beartooth region but had found little of the gold they sought. Then, in 1868, the area was, through chicanery or error, included in the Crow Indian Reservation and any prospectors who were there were forced out.

Fifteen years later, several prospectors, including some of those who had originally explored the area, returned to the region seeking silver and copper as well as gold. Several of them had already won fame in the Territory: Uncle Billy Hamilton, mountain man and Indian fighter, "Skookum Joe" Anderson, discoverer of the Spotted Horse mine at Maiden, and Jack Nye, after whom the town was to be named, and his cousin James Hedges. Bud McAdow, famous in Maiden and Coulson grubstaked "Skookum Joe" for the trip.

It was to these formidable frontiersmen that Mr. Armstrong, Crow Indian agent, issued stern warnings. They were on Indian land and were to get off immediately. When they didn't comply, he dispatched his Indian chief-of-police and a number of the Indian policemen to the scene of the claims with instructions to arrest the miners and burn "one little cabin." Although the lawmen couldn't find the miners to arrest them, they did burn the cabin, thereby kindling a flame that blazed throughout southern Montana. The miners under the leadership of Hamilton, sent their side of the controversy to the *Billings Gazette;* the next week Armstrong answered in the same paper, stating that, if the cabins were not on the reservation, he was willing to forfeit one hundred dollars and rebuild the burned cabin.

In his reply Uncle Billy stated:

We did not return until the line had been surveyed and were assured our property was off the reservation. Firmly convinced that we are right, we will defend our rights, until legally convinced that we are wrong, any orders emanating from the Crow agency to the contrary notwithstanding.

Mr. Armstrong's methods of legalizing his official acts by fire may account in a great measure for the numerous fires that have originated so mysteriously at the agency during the last 15 months under his fiery administration, to the detriment of the Indian service.[1]

A map was secured from the surveyors to prove that the prospectors were right. Armstrong declared the map was a fake, but inexplicably he dropped his action against the miners and Nye City was free to begin its short life as a mining camp.[2]

In 1885 the cabins were built right in Nye City by permanent prospectors. My brother Jonas and I built several of these cabins and received $100 each for them. We could build one in a day. We built two cabins for ourselves at the Ohio mine, high on the mountain almost at the edge of the snow line. . . .

The Minneapolis company had to have passable roads for the transportation of all the heavy smelting machinery they sent to Nye City. John Turco and Fred Fristicator were the company

---

[1] *Hardin Tribune Herald,* June 7, 1929.

[2] In later litigation over the location of a ranch it was found that the surveyors' maps were wrong and that Armstrong had been right all along. A suspicion of collusion between the miners and the surveyors was even hinted by some.

freighters; in muddy weather they had to use six horses to a wagon to get through the mud.

In 1885-86 Nye City was a booming mining camp. There were between three and four hundred people working. Wages of $4 a day and board were paid miners, the road workers receiving $2. The men were paid in cash that came directly from Minneapolis, this money was always brought in by the sheriff on pay day. . . .

The intention was to smelt the ore on location to get the pure ore. A large smelter of lumber and rock was constructed. Other company buildings were the assay office, mess hall and living quarters for company men. The huge smelter was built, machinery was in place and ready for operation, and a fire was never built in that roaster . . . that huge smelter was never used. The machinery was torn out and sold to other mining interests, the buildings were gradually torn down and hauled away.[3]

Nye's decline was rapid. In 1888, Anderson's diary notes,

"Go to Nye on a visit. See Bill Hamilton and a few other men. It is one of the most dead towns I ever saw."

A year or two later he speaks of going to Nye so that he can put his horses in some of the empty sheds away from the flies. A few of the miners hung on until the early part of the next decade, awaiting a new turn of the wheel of fortune.

In 1895, while in that section of the country, Fred Mashaw of Billings, with several other men, were driven by a storm to find shelter at old Nye. Of the 50 or 60 cabins which had been there in the days of the smelter, only a few were then in sufficient repair to furnish any shelter.[4]

The old town of Nye City has completely disappeared. A new little town, population 225, serves the trade needs of the scattered inhabitants, summer visitors, and sportsmen who come to hunt and fish in the beautiful wilderness. Chromium deposits in the area may replace to some extent the wealth of gold, silver, and copper on which the prosperity of old Nye was built.

---

[3] Hedges diary, as quoted in the Montana News Association, April 26, 1937.

[4] *Hardin Tribune Herald*, June 7, 1929.

25

CEDAR CREEK, LOUISVILLE, FOREST CITY, MAYVILLE

LOUIS BARRETTE WAS A FRENCH CANADIAN, ONE OF those who, during a lifetime of prospecting from Canada to California, was wise in the ways by which nature revealed her treasures to those who had learned to interpret her signs. After prospecting in California he had traveled north, lured by word of a strike on the St. Joe in Idaho. Like many other such rumors, this one had little foundation, and, strapping his grub and blankets on his horse, Barrette moved on over the Coeur d'Alene Mountains that separate Montana from Idaho. At the summit his practiced eye swept the vast terrain below him and noted a basin that, to his prospector's mind, meant gold.

However, his provisions were short and winter was close so he moved on to Frenchtown where he spent the winter of 1868-69. In the spring one thing and another delayed his return to the basin, but the memory of it stayed with him. In the fall of 1869, with his friend, Lanthier, he finally packed up his horses and started back. With an unerring memory for terrain he followed up the Clark Fork River, then past the Lozeau ranch on the north shore near the confluence with Cedar Creek and, crossing the river, proceeded up Cedar Creek. Arriving at Cayuse Creek, a little tributary of the Cedar, the two made camp for the night, and, as was the custom of prospectors, as Lanthier cooked supper, Barrette "tried his luck" in the stream. Before supper was ready he had panned out four dollars in gold.

Bedrock was only four feet down, and the pair took $370 from various spots along the creek during their first three weeks there. Staking their "Discovery" claim about four miles from the original site, they made their way back to Lozeau's ranch and outlined not one but two ways to get rich: first, of course, was the gold. In Barrette's own words, "I knew we had diggings." Second, the trio, knowing that there would be a great influx of miners who would have to cross the river, planned to install a ferry with a sufficient toll to bring in thousands of dollars.

All this was to be kept secret until spring. If the news leaked out so close to winter in this region of deep snows and, at times, bitter cold, it could create a stampede that, like the Sun River stampede, would bring the bitterest suffering to the participants. Furthermore, lumber wasn't yet whipsawed for the ferry.

Craftily they sent Lozeau to Frenchtown to lay in supplies. Since he was a permanent resident such purchases would go unnoticed; if Barrette or Lanthier acquired a grubstake, suspicions of their having made a strike would be aroused.

Lozeau, unfortunately for secret-keeping, had his failings. He was a sociable Frenchman who loved people and whisky. Frenchtown had both. As he moved from one convivial group to another, confidences came more and more easily.

The stampede was on. Little did it matter that win-

ter was near and that there was no ferry across the
Clark Fork. Typical of the stampeders were J. R. Latimer and his partner, Hank Froach.

Returning from a trip to Moose Creek, Idaho, [they] passed
through Frenchtown just as the news leaked out. They came on
to Grass Valley and Tyler Woodward's ranch; turned around, went
back to Frenchtown from where at 7 o'clock that evening a party
consisting of T. J. Demers, Harry Hamel, Hank Froach, J. R. Latimer and seven others started on horseback, carrying with them
no provisions whatever. Riding without a stop until 4 o'clock in
the morning they reached Lozeau's, where they expected to get
their breakfast. There they joined an excited horde of men, so many
that there was standing room only in the Lozeau's house. Hastily
a breakfast of boiled beans straight was gulped down and before
daylight the ranch was deserted by the hundred men or more off
for their "New El Dorado."
The Clark's Fork river was forded a short distance below Lozeau's
about five miles above the mouth of Cedar. Up the creek rode the
excited stampeders, until those in the lead at the mouth of "Oregon"
gulch concluded the going from that point was too rough for the
practical use of their horses and each tied his mount securely to
a tree, continuing the remaining distance up the creek on foot. Old
"Louis Brown No. 2" took the lead for a time but Latimer, being
younger, eventually passed Brown and was the first one to reach
the ground where Barrette and Lanthier had found their gold. By
evening, one by one, all the stampeders had come and a meeting
was called by Joseph E. Marion, who made a brief talk in which
he declared that the proper procedure would be to start at the
"Discovery," then to survey and record 200 feet claims running
each way, up and down the creek. Marion's suggestion met with
unanimous approval, he being elected recorder of the district. By
night of the following day almost the entire gulch had been staked
off in claims. . . .
By morning of the third day the miners began to realize quite
vividly that it was an absolute necessity that each and everyone
must soon find some means of appeasing a rapidly growing hunger.
. . . Nearly everyone then went back where for two days and nights
his horse had been left tied and saddled and began a return ride,

each with the very definite idea in mind to first connect up with a square meal somewhere, then to procure provisions for the winter on his mining claim.

Though the greater part of the gulch was located by these first miners, yet the real stampede was only begun. News of the strike was broadcast the length and breadth of the land. Parties from every mining camp or other point where men were living in Montana, and beyond our border, especially from Salt Lake City, Utah, set out and traveled day and night, each individual urged on by the dream of sudden wealth as well as by the deadly fear that someone else might reach the mines before he would himself. On foot, on horseback, muleback, by wagon, cart and stage coach; with provisions, without; any way to get there, they came. Three thousand miners from all quarters wintered in the gulch, while hundreds went in, remained but a day or two and went away. Over 10,000 men visited the creek before a year had passed from the date of discovery....[1]

The first town that was built was Louisville. Onto a narrow "shelf" that would seem to hold no more than a few hundred, between three thousand and seven thousand people crowded into the town. They were predominately Frenchmen and Irishmen, and an international ruckus threatened to develop over the provisions of a law adopted by the miners of the district. This provision stated that the discoverer could stake a claim for an absent friend. Barrette located No. 1 above discovery for his friend Dubien of Frenchtown. The claim was rich and the other miners, particularly the Irish, eyed it with longing. As time went by and the claim went unrepresented, those who coveted it wanted it declared "jumpable." The French decided to defend it for their countryman. Feeling ran high but before any violence occurred a meeting was called.

---

[1] Will Cave in the *Mineral Independent* (Superior), December 21, 1933.

A crowd gathered at the meeting, which was held in the open. There was hot debate over the question, the division being such that it seemed the anticipated fight which could have resulted in fatalities, was about to begin, when Hugh O'Neill, professional pugilist who at that time was undoubtedly the "champion" of the squared circle west of the Mississippi river . . . and who was recognized as the one whose influence was of the greatest weight with the Irish, got up and took sides with the French. Speaking calmly but forcibly, he maintained that the debated section had been adopted at a representative miners' meeting, without particular objection, that it had worked to the disadvantage of no one miner more than to another, that it had been recognized as the law of the camp; in short, that it was as fair to one as to another, it was only just and right that it should be upheld. This stand of the leader mollified the opposition to the end that the section in dispute was retained. There was an exception: One whose name is unknown, but who went by the nickname of "Cayuse Larry," an irresponsible sort of fellow, with a very considerable "gift of gab" jumped up on a stump and started in violently denouncing the course above agreed upon. At this juncture a miner named Joseph Young picked up a chip about the size of a dinner plate, hurled it with such force that, striking Cayuse Larry full in the face, knocked him off the stump, completely "squelching" him and effectually putting an end to further objections, though two "strangers" became involved in an altercation over the situation and, coming to blows, both fell into a prospect hole. A big Frenchman ran to the hole, but, the man on top in the scrap called out in French: "Leave us alone. I'll take care of this fellow. . . ."[2]

As mining activity moved up and down the creek, two other towns flourished. The largest of these, Forest City, boasted stores, a blacksmith shop, a post office, a Wells, Fargo office, and an undetermined number of saloons. Sixty mule pack trains brought supplies in from Missoula.

Once when Pat McGrath's packtrain was going in, loaded, when

[2] *Ibid.*

passing over the point, one of the mules on the back of which was packed two 20-gallon kegs of whisky, got to bucking, bucked off the road, plunged over a cliff down to the river below. Of course, that was the end of both mule and pack. When the rest of the train reached McGrath's store in Forest, he was appraised of the mishap, and was heard to say, "I don't give a damn for the mule, he was a damned outlaw anyway, but I sure do hate to lose that whisky."

There was little of excitement in Forest City during the winter of '71-'72. Each hardworking miner pursued pretty consistently the even tenor of his way. There were drinking and gambling in the saloons, of course. While there were a few who might have been styled professional gamblers, those who sat around the green cloth were as a rule miners playing one against another; therefore, the games were pretty generally "on the level," and, consequently, no fatalities. A raid by four toughs led by one Jack Harrigan upon a house kept by Rafael Acosta, a notorious Spanish woman, resulting in the burning of the building and in one of the toughs being put out of commission for several hours from the effect of a blow on the head by a flat iron thrown by the irate woman was about the only case which would have brought the principals into court under present-day conditions. . . .

Guns were seldom "toted." Many miners possessed six shooters, but these were generally hung up in the cabins. Not precisely along these lines but akin thereto I might mention one David Graham, who perhaps deserves at least passing notice. He was a typical son of the "ould sod," had been a sailor, was as kind-hearted as a child, when sober, but when loaded with a few shots of whisky became a veritable little demon, spoiling for a ruction. He would sally forth giving vent to his battle cry: "I'm the onion from Scullion Hill; I can whip any damned ——— ——— ——— in the camp," following up anyone against whom his disjointed fancy happened to take a turn (often one of his best friends) using the vilest language, making things extremely annoying for the object of his venom. Most everyone had learned his traits and usually managed to overlook them but now and then there would be a scrap with the "Onion" invariably coming out second best. . . . On one occasion John Slowey had dodged the "Onion" the better part of a day until finally his patience became exhausted. When the fray was ended Dave was a sorry sight. Between the booze and batter he was laid out on the sidewalk in front of a saloon, oblivious and bloody. . . . Poor old "Onion"; he never had a dollar ahead; yet for more than 40 years he managed to live in or about the old camp becoming as it were part and parcel of his beloved hills until he heard the final call to cross the great divide. . . .

On a night in July, 1872, the store of Caplice, Smith & Co. was broken into and a small iron safe, weighing about 75 pounds was carried away. It contained several thousand dollars in gold. It was found with the door broken off at the head of the street, near the mouth of Marion gulch. . . . The alarm spread and it soon appeared that four Chinamen were missing from their cabin. Naturally suspicion fell immediately in their direction and search was begun for them. There was a Chinaman and Chinawoman in another part of town who had a washhouse. A number of hotheaded miners jumped at the conclusion that these two must have been in league with their countrymen; . . . Ropes were procured and hangman's knots placed about the necks of the totally defenseless "Chinks," who could only protest, "No sabe!   No sabe!" The ropes were thrown over a beam running out from the roof of their cabin and the Chinese were pulled up and down in a vain effort to secure some sort of confession or information. This method not being attended with success, the more than half-choked unfortunates were finally released. . . . Next morning a posse was sent out on each possible trail leading from the creek. . . . the posse consisting of Pat McGrath, Billy Buck and Ed Warren did not return for several days. They had found the trail which led to Marion gulch across the divide to Oregon gulch thence over the mountains to the St. Regis river. There they had located the objects of their pursuit and—well, anyway the posse brought back the stolen gold. With boyish curiosity I was eager to learn the details, listening with excited ears to Ed Warren telling the story, which was: that they had discovered the Chinamen just after the latter, having waded the St. Regis, had taken off their wet clothes and were drying them before the fire. When ordered to "throw up their hands," the Chinese without waiting for clothing, loot or anything else, plunged into the chaparral and disappeared. The posse having secured the plunder paid no further attention to the Chinamen. No one believed the story but as no one was particularly interested in the fate of the Chinamen, it was accepted as satisfactory. It developed afterward that the story was true up to the call of "Hands up," which was followed by a little shooting to the end that even dead Chinamen tell no tales. An attempt was made to dispose of the bodies by burning over a big camp fire, but this was not entirely successful; what remained being discovered by other parties and buried.[3]

Feeling against the "Celestials" ran particularly high in the Missoula and Cedar Creek area. On September 22, 1870, the *Missoula and Cedar Creek Pioneer* noted:

ADVENT OF CELESTIAL CYPRIANS

Several almond-eyed damsels of the Chinese persuasion passed through town last week on their way to Cedar Creek. They were, we believe, the first Johnesses who have yet made their unwelcome appearance on this side of the range and it were a consummation devoutly to be wished that they may be the last.

A trail leading between Cedar and Quartz creeks was repaired, and Chinamen were charged twenty-five cents per head to use it; if they didn't have the money, their blankets were confiscated.

During the one year of 1871, Chinamen in and around Cedar Creek lost $30,000 in the purchase of "salted" mines sold to them by whites. Little wonder that one remarked sadly, "Melican man b'long too muchee all same thief."

The hey-day of the Cedar creek placers was over by 1873. Forest City was deserted and the miners moved up the stream to Mayville, a new location. This mining camp, deep in the mountains, boomed for a short period and then it, too, became a ghost town. Because of the great difficulty of transporting goods over mountain trails on mules, Mayville was left intact when the miners departed. Furniture was left in hotels and cabins, billiard balls and

---

[3] *Ibid.*

cues lay where they had been dropped on the pool tables of the saloons, and miners' tools lay beside the diggins, just where the owners had dropped them. For a short time after the desertion of Mayville the Cedar creek gold district was taken over by the "Heathen Chinee." The Chinese worked over the old diggings. Returns were small but the Chinese were diligent and some of them returned to China with small fortunes.

Louis Barrette made another attempt at mining in Cedar creek in 1884. With a group of men from Frenchtown he formed the Cedar Creek Placer Mining Co. The hey-days, the gay-days of the '70's were gone forever, but with the improved machinery the Cedar Creek Placer Mining Co. operated successfully until 1906.[4]

Interest in the Cedar Creek mines has never completely died. Today the Gildersleeve mines on the upper creek are active; throughout the length of the canyon there are ruins of later mining enterprises but little remains of the original towns. A diligent search may reveal rotted foundation logs or relics left behind by the first stampeders. One mine operator who worked the gulch years after the first wealth had been taken, found so many interesting relics of the Chinese occupation that his attention became devoted more to the recovery of such mementos than to the recovery of gold. To the casual traveler or fisherman in the canyon, however, only the piles of tailings in the creek bed would indicate the great mining activity that was once carried on there.

---

[4] *Silver State Post* (Deer Lodge), August 6, 1936.

AMADOR, CAYUSE, PARDEE, SILVER CITY

AS EARLY AS 1872 COPPER WAS DISCOVERED IN CEDAR Creek at the Amador Mine site. Since the expense of mining copper was great, and the value of the ore could not be compared to the value of gold, little was done at the Amador until 1900. Then active production was started; Amador City was built to house the Amador railway workers and the miners. The Amador railway, eleven miles in length, served only to transport the ore from the mine and the supplies and equipment to the mine. A smelter was built at the mouth of Cedar Creek Canyon and, by 1907, the operation was ready to go into full production. However, late the same year, the mining panic closed the Amador as well as many other mines.

Sporadic attempts have been made since, one as late as 1952, to recover the wealth that is still there, but today, at the site, there are only the ruins of the early activities, one shack of later construction, and the gaping hole leading back into the tunnels of the Amador.

Not even this much remains of other "towns" spawned by the Cedar Creek stampede. Old Superior, forerunner of the present town and a few miles up the river from the present site, is completely gone except, perhaps, for a few rotting foundations. There are neither buildings nor the ferry to recall what was an important stop on the freight routes to the mining center.

The same is true of The Junction, Carter (later known as Keystone), and Cayuse. At the latter place the Chinese Cayuse Flume Company recovered thousands —some say millions—of dollars' worth of gold after the Irish had "worked out" the diggings.

Across the river and far up the mountain behind the present town of Superior, Pardee grew up around the great Iron Mountain Mine where pay dirt was found at the grass roots.

Silver was $1.25 an ounce and there were tons of it to be had at Pardee. The crude was hauled down the mountain to the Clark Fork, loaded on flatboats and floated to the nearest railhead. Pardee, whose only access was by the tortuous road up the mountain, mushroomed with cabins, stores, saloons, and dance halls, all built from rough logs hewn from the surrounding forest. Being completely isolated, it became a law unto itself, and the reputation of Pardee rivaled that of Butte and Beartown.

There were important mines in the immediate vicinity of Silver City a little farther west near the Idaho border: the Hemlock, the Last Chance, the Ben Hur, the Silver Cable, and others. These, combined with the traffic to the larger mines both east and west, created a very lively town out of Silver City. It was another whose funerals became famous.

. . . If accounts can be believed, those early-day funerals were jolly affairs, indeed. The mourners tossed coins at the casket to see who would have to go to the saloon and get the next bucket of beer. If the clothes on the corpse were in good condition they were removed to be given to some less fortunate brother among the living. Among those who lie in Boot Hill cemetery is the lovely Katy Dillingham. There are the makings of a first rate ballad in Katy's story. She killed herself for love of a traveling dentist who did not return her affection. The dentist, who is remembered only as "Fat," is said to have played the piano much better than he pulled teeth, and it was his piano playing in a local saloon that charmed the ill-starred Kate.[1]

When the Coeur d'Alene branch of the Northern Pacific was built, the population shifted to the railroad, and the new town of Saltese, named in honor of a Nez Perce Indian chief, attracted the population from Silver City.

Much of the early construction in this area was wiped out by the great fire of 1910. This fire, one of the worst ever to sweep the Western forests, started in the Idaho panhandle on July 8, 1910. In spite of the efforts of five hundred fire fighters, it continued burning and spreading until, on August 20, fanned by a terrific wind, it went completely out of control. Racing through eastern Idaho it roared into western Montana. The towns of DeBorgia, Saltese, and St. Regis were evacuated. Some residents of the area found refuge in mine shafts, lakes, or rivers, but most fled on boxcars through walls of flame to Missoula. When they returned to their homes it was to find that one man had perished at Saltese and several near Taft had been suffocated by smoke. Sixty-eight buildings, valued at $40,000, had been destroyed at DeBorgia, and many of the old landmarks of the region were smoldering under the ashes of the devastating fire.

---

[1] William West in the *Silver State Post* (Deer Lodge), August 6, 1936.

Courtesy Historical Society of Montana, Helena

GRANITE MOUNTAIN
About 1890

PLATE I

Courtesy Historical Society of Montana, Helena

DISCOVERY OF GOLD AT GOLD CREEK, MONTANA

Courtesy Historical Society of Montana, Helena

PIONEER CITY, 1883

PLATE III

A ROCKER

AN ARRASTRA

PLATE IV

CHINESE WOMAN AND HOME
Virginia City, 1899

FIRST MASONIC BUILDING IN MONTANA
At Virginia City

PLATE V

Courtesy Historical Society of Montana, Helena

DISCOVERY OF GOLD AT LAST CHANCE
From a mural in the State Capitol

Courtesy Historical Society of Montana, Helena
HANGING TREE, LAST CHANCE

PLATE VII

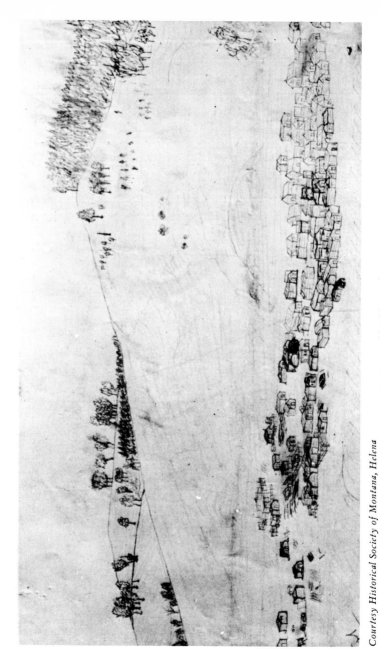

Courtesy Historical Society of Montana, Helena

BLACKFOOT CITY, 1865
Sketch by Granville Stuart

I have struck it at last. I am rich!
Whether silver or gold, I hardly know which;
But see, 't is gold as sure as I am born.
It sticks out of this quartz like grains of corn.
A trip to Europe I shall surely take.
I have struck it at last. I am sure of a stake.
No more will I live on bacon and beans,
But wine and dine with bonanza queens.

THE STORY OF A PROSPECTOR'S LIFE
The verse was penciled on the back of the photograph

PLATE IX

     Photo by Dan Dutro, 1897

The mine has pinched up and all played out;
I feel badly used up and not very stout.
When I first struck this I thought it rich;
Now it is played out and I am in the ditch.
Flat broke—not a dollar—no bacon in camp,
I think I will pack up and go on a tramp.
I have tramped from California to the Black
    Hill mines;
Have been to the Klondike a number of times.
This is the poorest I ever have found—
It is no better than the commonest rock
    on the ground.

THE STORY OF A PROSPECTOR'S LIFE
The verse was penciled on the back of the photograph

PLATE X

Courtesy Historical Society of Montana, Helena

STREET SCENE AT GRANITE, MONTANA
Fourth-of-July parade, 1900

PLATE XI

Courtesy Historical Society of Montana, Helena
RUINS OF THE OPERA HOUSE AND LABOR HALL, GRANITE

PLATE XII

Courtesy Historical Society of Montana, Helena

FIRST FUNERAL, MAIDEN, MONTANA, 1883

PLATE XIII

Courtesy Historical Society of Montana, Helena

LAST BULL TEAMS AT MAIDEN, MONTANA, 1884

HELL GATE

Judge Woody in front of the Worden & Co. store

PLATE XV

OPHIR, 1865
Sketch by Granville Stuart

Courtesy Historical Society of Montana, Helena

27

QUARTZ

AFTER THE STRIKE IN CEDAR CANYON, PAY DIRT WAS found in numerous nearby spots. East of the canyon, Quartz Creek became the center of a mining area. Here the gold was coarse and nuggets running as high as $126 in value were common. A post office was established and the usual stores and saloons catered to miners and travelers. Near Quartz Creek occurred one of the heroic feats of the era. Elie Ritchott, one of the many miners in the area who had come from eastern Canada, began to work a claim at Quartz in 1880.

He had sunk a shaft 42 feet below surface and was drifting on bedrock. Perhaps it might be well for us to follow him from the beginning of the shaft. At the top of this he built a framework upon which he constructed a windlass, to which was attached a sufficient length of heavy rope so that when unwound it would reach to the bottom of the shaft when finished. At the loose end of the rope was a hook for the bucket used in hoisting the dirt and gravel taken, first from the shaft as it was being sunk, then from the drift driven along the bedrock from the bottom of the shaft. The shaft was four feet by six feet in size, timbered to prevent caving. The drift or tunnel was four feet wide and nearly five feet high. The posts, round and peeled, usually fir or cedar, were three feet and eight inches in height, eight inches in diameter, upon which rested caps four feet long and one foot in diameter, made along similar lines to the posts. . . . It will be readily noted that the miner could neither stand nor walk upright, but must ever be in a stooping position when at work. As Ritchott was alone his method of removing dirt from the tunnel was to shovel it into the bucket or tub, which rested on the "car" as it stood on the track at the bottom of the drift. When the bucket was filled, he pushed car and bucket to the shaft, there he attached the bucket handle to the hook at the end of the windlass rope; then he would climb a ladder to the surface, where he could operate the windlass, turning it by a crank, until the bucket reached the top of the shaft, where was another car which he pushed under the bucket. Then unhooking the bucket, he would push this car along a track to where he would dump the contents of the bucket into the sluice boxes through which the dirt and gravel were washed by a sluice head of water. When the bucket was emptied Ritchott would push the car back with it to the shaft, hook it to the rope, push the car back out of the way, lower the bucket to the bottom, climb down, loosen the bucket from the hook, push it on the car back again to the face of the drift, where he would begin again the process, painfully slow. . . . Heart-breaking, back-breaking work in such a place, especially so because of the fact that a miner there may never stand erect. The reason why in placer mining the tunnel is not made with top higher from the floor is that the pay dirt is usually right on or very near the bedrock. The labor and expense involved in removing the dirt is such that no more is moved than is actually necessary. . . .

Ritchott had run his drift about 200 feet in from the shaft. About 8 o'clock one morning he had just raised his pick to begin work at the face of the drift, when he was horrified by the fearful rumble "like thunder" betokening that the dirt had caved and filled in the tunnel behind him. As soon as there was quiet he went back about 60 feet and found the drift filled solid. He was caught like the proverbial rat in a trap. It would be difficult to devise a situation more horrible than that in which he was placed. . . . (His nearest neighbor was a half mile away and it might be days before the accident was discovered). . . . He decided to dig at least until he could dig no more rather than just giving up. Thinking that the tunnel might be filled for its entire length he decided to dig upward at a slant since he was about 38 feet below the surface. He had only three candles which he figured would last him probably 15 to 18 hours. After about 14 hours of digging he broke through into a chamber left by the cave-in. When he got up into this cavity he found it to be the width of the drift, about 20 feet long and seven feet high, its roof being held up by great boulders. He then realized that the drift was filled in for but little greater than that of the open space in which he then was and decided to dig downward into the unblocked section of the drift. He had only three inches of candle left; this lasted him for only about two more feet of digging, then he dug in the darkness, loosening the dirt with his crowbar and shoveling it aside with his hands, fearing always that another cave-in might bury him. Finally he reached the lagging on top of the drift. He worked at the lagging with his crowbar in his cramped quarters and was finally rewarded by the breaking of the lagging and the inrush of fresh air. "Better than anything to eat; better than anything to drink; better than anything in the world. And then I knew I was going to get out." The air in his burrow had evidently become so foul that he had been working for some time in a dazed condition. The fresh air immediately revived him. After breaking the first lagging, he succeeded in enlarging the space in which to handle himself because the dirt could now sift downward, but even then it took him hours to cut three more laggings so that he could squeeze through, push the dirt away, which by that time almost filled the drift beneath him and crawl out to safety. He sat down and rested for five minutes, then went to the shaft and out. It was but 300 feet to the cabin.

When he reached it it was 7:30 p.m. of the second day since leaving it. He had been 35½ hours in digging his way out of the tunnel. He made and drank a cup of coffee, then crawled into his blankets, where he remained until near noon the following day.

"Though I worked my claim for nearly two years after, I never again went into that tunnel. I had had enough."[1]

The old Quartz Creek store was burned many years ago but was roughly rebuilt on the original site. Ruins of some of the cabins still remain, but the economy of the region is now based on agriculture and lumbering rather than on mining although a day's panning in almost any of the streams in the area will still turn up the gleam of gold.

---

[1] Will Cave in the *Mineral Independent* (Superior), December 21, 1933.

28

QUIGLEY

PICTURESQUE IN ITS DESOLATION AND DESERTION, THE ONCE POPU-
lous and bustling city of Quigley, with its blasted hopes and material
ruins, is one of the most historic might-have-beens of the lost cities
of Montana.

It was the lure of gold, back in the early 90's which attracted
fortune seekers. Quigley was transformed from a scenic spot in
a pretty valley to a hustling, eager city of many buildings and
several thousand persons almost overnight. One and a half million
dollars were invested in buildings and other improvements.

Then the bubble burst. Gold was not there. Quigley was abandoned with dramatic suddenness. One day it was full of hope and
activity; the next day the buildings stood as monuments to lost
hope. Like rats deserting a sinking ship, the population was gone.
Quigley was no more.

The final touch to the city which vanished was added last week
when Joe Daigle, who, with his family, are the only inhabitants,
plowed up Broadway, the main street, which once was the nightly
scene of excitement when the saloons and gaming houses were
flourishing, when men would drink and shoot and fight, when gal-
loping cayuses brought in their joyous riders for a night of dancing
and hilarity. Broadway is going to grow spuds next year, and ambitious ones they ought to be.

Grover Cleveland, then president of the United States, is said
to be one of the persons who invested considerable money in Quigley. Colgate, founder of the Colgate company, is also declared to
have been a heavy investor. Few Montanans lost much besides their
time and expectations. The city was named Quigley after Senator
Quigley and it was established in 1895 and deserted in 1896.

More than $1,500,000 invested. Not a cent produced!

A carload of ore sent from Quigley to Denver was assayed and
reported to contain gold in unprecedented quantities. The Golden

Scepter Mining company had the bonanza of the century, it was declared.

A stamp mill was erected at the cost of hundreds of thousands of dollars and the best machinery obtainable installed. A roadbed for a 12-mile railroad was prepared, the ties laid, the equipment ordered. Hotels, saloons, pool halls, residences, clubhouses and other structures grew up like mushrooms.

Quigley boomed and boomed. The prairie schooners brought out the pioneers with their families and all their possessions. Those who carried all their worldly goods on the saddle of a fleet of horses arrived in the city. Steers lumbered along with other loads. Those who did not have any other means of conveyance hiked with packs on their backs, with just a grubstake until they could become rich.

Hammers hammered, saws sawed and shovels shoveled. Materials brought to Quigley netted the Northern Pacific railroad about $300,000 in freight charges alone. Then there was still 12 miles to transport the material from Bonita to Quigley.

If the census taker had come to Quigley the day before the information was given out that gold was not there, he could have counted 2,500, possibly 2,750 noses of men, women and children. The census taker of 1920 found five human beings there.

George Babcock, who was declared to have been penniless when he died in Butte a few years ago, was the promoter of the Golden Scepter Mining company.

Babcock was the hero of the day. Wherever he went, he was wined and dined. Every one knew of Babcock. Babcock, the magic name, which meant fortune. In Missoula, he was carried around on the shoulders of the rejoicing residents. Few persons even today question Babcock's sincerity. His faith was boundless. He also had everything to gain.

But just one little mistake was made. Just the fact that the gold was not there had been overlooked.

Not a wheel was turned in the expensive stamp mill. Not a train rumbled or whistled over the railroad track. The Jumbo, Brewster and Golden Scepter mines produced no ore. Only the gamblers, picking up the spare change around the faro tables or at the great national indoor sport of poker, made any money. The saloons sold drinks on faith. The hotels and rooming houses gave credit.

Quigley was all ready for the clean-up. Then the Golden Scepter became the Golden Specter. Only the ghost of the town was left.

How completely and thoroughly Quigley was abandoned is testified to by a number of Butte citizens. A. T. Morgan, of Butte, several years afterward rode on horseback into the desolate city. The mirrors in the saloons—mirrors which were more expensive then than even now—were there and the doors were open. Pool tables were still standing, the balls buried in dust. Fixtures and furniture in most of the buildings were untouched. Moss flourished, bats made the places eerie, spiders wove their artistic webs, dust accumulated and moths bit and chewed, while man seldom disturbed them.

One of the buildings of which Quigley was most proud in its days of enthusiasm was the residence of George Babcock. The inside woodwork was elaborate and artistic, fireplaces were installed, the mantels were works of art, the bath tubs still have the reputation of being the largest in the state, the place was intended as a real mansion for a gold king.

Today the residence is the clubhouse of the Bonita club, composed of Missoula sportsmen and some of Butte and Anaconda.

A few years ago the buildings in Quigley were sold because of non-payment of taxes. Homesteaders in the vicinity were the only bidders and the average sale price of the buildings was $4.50. The buyers hauled the lumber away. The stamp mill was burned five years ago.

Joe Daigle and his family occupy the only residence in the city with the exception of the clubhouse. A few other buildings are used as barns and sheds. Otherwise, Quigley is no more.[1]

---

[1] Eilef Rue in the *Dillon Examiner*, November 17, 1920.

29

CABLE

South from Drummond lies one of Montana's most beautiful valleys. Through it flows Flint Creek, tumbling wildly at first through its rocky channel from Georgetown Lake, then flowing placidly through the lush pasturelands brilliant with the magenta of marsh flowers. To the south rise the white peaks of the Anaconda Range, to the west the Sapphires, and to the east the Flint Range.

In this area occured some of the state's busiest mining activity, activity that is marked today by the picturesque ruins of the mining camps. As early as 1866 gold was discovered in the mountains sixteen miles from Philipsburg by three men, Pearson, Caldwell, and Aitken, who found gold at the grass roots. It is told that two of these men were formerly sailors working on the laying of the Atlantic cable, and, for this reason, they called the mine the Atlantic Cable Mine and the camp Cable City.

Here were mines so rich that single pieces of gold valued from ten to several thousand dollars were found. A cigar box of samples assayed $1,000 and a single nugget, supposedly the world's largest, was worth $19,000. In order to prevent heavy losses from smuggled gold, the mineowners found it necessary to set up a system of searching the miners as they left the mine.

The thriving town had a school, a Protestant Sunday school, two stores, two boardinghouses, a saloon, a blacksmith shop, and other business establishments. Freight was shipped by steamer from St. Louis to Benton, then hauled by ox and mule teams up the precipitous trail to the city that clung to the mountain high above Georgetown.

Approximately three thousand people lived at Cable, and it had the reputation of being one of the most orderly of the mining camps.

You could not ask for a better town to live in than Cable was in the early days. The mining men were there to work. They did not want to molest anyone and every man was a law unto himself. We had a justice of the peace and a constable, but neither had much to do. It was uncommon to hear of offenses. One could leave his valuables in a poorly secured cabin and they would never be bothered. The men who came west to mine were a good, sturdy class of men. They wanted peace to work and they got it.[1]

Although the Cable Mine, employing about 150 men, was the major producer, other diggings swelled the wealth of the area. About one hundred Chinamen were engaged in placer mining in the vicinity. Many of these were employees of white owners and, when asked how much they made, invariably answered, "Fo' bittee day," a meager share of the millions produced by the Cable mines!

Today a sign near the site of Southern Cross[2] indicates the crumbling ruins of Cable City. A bit of

---

[1] *Anaconda Standard*, October 9, 1921.

[2] Southern Cross, itself an interesting ghost town, was abandoned in spite of its rich ore, when operators found it almost impossible to control seepage in the tunnels.

searching or digging may turn up a rust-encrusted shoe
that served to protect the feet of the oxen as they lumbered up the rocky trail to the once busy town,[3] but
for the most part the site is again wrapped in the silence
of the mountains, and the town that bustled with thousands of miners and their families is gradually being
taken over by the forest growth.

---

[3] Today ox shoes are museum pieces, but in the days when oxen were used for
much of the freight hauling, shoeing them was often more profitable than
mining. The ox was put into a frame of stocks, and the split shoe was applied
by the smith. The going price for shoeing was six dollars per ox, and a good
smith could shoe eight oxen and still have most of the day to himself.

30

GRANITE

THE MOST OUTSTANDING GHOST TOWN SOUTH OF DRUM-mond is Granite, site of the richest silver strike the world has ever known. These ruins are strikingly different from those of most of the other camps as this was no placer operation that fell rather quickly into decay. Here sturdier brick was used to build huge furnaces and mills whose red ruins still stand, vivid against the blue sky. Although the ceiling of the vast miners' hall has fallen in, the walls stand dominating the mountaintop where raucous jays fly through glassless windows, and marmots burrow under the cold furnaces. The heavy metal doorposts and lintel of the hall have escaped the theft and souvenir hunting that has obliterated every trace of some of the great mining camps.

Here in 1872 silver was discovered by a prospector named Holland. One day, while trailing a moose he had shot, he noticed that the animal's hoofs kicked up what looked like rich specimens of float. After getting and taking care of his meat, he gathered some of the ore. The assay was encouraging, and for the first time the great Granite Mountain Mine was staked. For the next eight years halfhearted attempts were made to work the mine, and in 1880 it was sold to Charles McClure, a seasoned and energetic mining man.

It was a vast undertaking. . . . The location was remote and inaccessible. Capital was shy of quartz-mine investment. Dollars were not easily coaxed for mine development in Montana. But McClure got together enough to start work. Miners began the attack upon the great ledge on the summit of the divide. It was hard mining; steadily the capital dwindled, but McClure was positive and his confidence was unshaken, though the hoped-for results seemed as far away as when the work was started. But he knew that, somewhere ahead in that solid granite mass there was rich ore. He was determined to find it. And the miners drilled on and on.

But even the infectious confidence of McClure had its limits as a persuasive influence, and there came a day when there was no more money available or in prospect. McClure counted up and found that he had just enough to pay the men for that shift. . . .

There had been no values discovered in the work that had been done. It was the last shift, but the miners worked doggedly on. Through the day there had been no change in the conditions underground. The last shot was tamped home, the fuse was lighted and the miners prepared to leave the work which they had pushed so persistently under the determined driving of the man at the head of the work. That last shot was fired. It threw bonanza ore upon the muckers' planks . . . and Charles D. McClure became in that moment one of the greatest mining men of his time.[1]

Joaquin Miller describes the mining activity that developed from the rich strike:

The Granite mine with all its products, good management and care for its workmen, has made Granite a paradise for good miners. . . . The underground working is very great. The map of them looks like the plat of a city. The Ruby shaft commenced 300 feet below the upper slopes, was down some 1,200 feet at the close of last year and is expected to reach a depth of 2000 feet in the near future.

There are three first class mills on the property, two at the mine and one at Rumsey, connected with the mine by a wire tramway. Mill B has 50 stamps and 16 pans. Mill C has 90 stamps

---

[1] Arthur Stone, *Following Old Trails* (Missoula: Morton John Elrod, 1913), pp. 274-75.

and 32 pans. The mine employs from 510 to 530 men. They mined and worked in 1890, 53,529,053 tons of ore, which yielded in silver 3,930,329.69 ounces and 8,583.48 ounces of pure gold. . . .

All the work is first class; the mine is kept dry and well ventilated. The company provided a reading room, commodious and well supplied with periodical literature of the day, a plunge bath, and a good hospital with medical attendance and nurses free to all sick and disabled miners, who pay only $1.25 a month for its support. Everything is done to secure the safety and health and comfort and intelligence of the workmen. As might be expected, the miners appeared to be picked men from all nationalities which produce experts in mining.[2]

Since the money invested in Granite came from St. Louis, the returns went back there, and much of the city's early growth received its financial stimulus from the Granite Mountain Mine whose outpouring of silver formed the basis of the first great real estate boom in St. Louis. Both the Merchants' Bridge and the Terminal Railway Building were monuments to the seemingly unlimited wealth of Granite Mountain.

While a faraway city boomed with the wealth from Granite, so also did the "city" that grew up around the mine. Although it was a much more stable town than the placer camps, it still attracted enough miners from Butte to keep things lively. One of the most famous buggy races in old Montana occurred when Denny Hynes and Billy Ryan broke the speed record down Granite Mountain.

Hynes was formerly a member of the Quartz street fire station in Butte and shortly after he came to Granite, which was then one of Montana's busiest mining towns, he and Billy Ryan, a Gran-

[2] Joaquin Miller, *An Illustrated History of the State of Montana* (Chicago: Lewis Publishing Company, 1894), pp. 711-12.

ite county native, hired a two-horse rig from "Dutch" Fred's stable
and started for Philipsburg, three miles away.

Both men had been celebrating Denny's birthday and after the
last round in Con People's place, they climbed into the buggy and
started for the "burg." The road had about as many turns and S's
as Harding way, but was somewhat steeper.

As they passed the Bi-Metallic mine at the lower end of Granite,
Hynes asked to drive.

"You are too drunk," Ryan answered.

"I ain't as drunk as you are," replied Hynes. "And what's more,
I drove better in the Butte fire department when I had a few shots,
than when I was cold sober."

The former driver of a Butte fire team continued to ask for
the reins, but Ryan would not let him drive.

After a mile of the steep and crooked grade had been traversed,
Hynes said: "Say, Bill, do you know that I hold the world's record
for driving? I drove down Main street in Butte from Quartz to
Mercury in 20 seconds. But, of course, it was a bad fire and we
had to make it."

"Well, we are not in Butte now and we are not going to a fire,"
said Ryan, who by this time had become greatly peeved.

"I tell you, it took guts to ride with me in Butte," continued
Hynes. "When I mounted the seat and grabbed the reins, we let
the whole damn world know that Butte had a fire department."

"Have you got the idea that no one has guts but a Butte fireman?" asked Ryan.

"Let me drive and I'll try you out," replied Hynes.

"Well, if you've got guts, now is the time to show it," said
Ryan and, like a flash, he threw both reins to the ground and, yank-
ing the whip from the socket, lashed both spirited horses.

In those busy days this steep grade had considerable traffic, but
fortunately no driver was coming toward them. Within a few
seconds both horses were running like mad.

Hynes grabbed both hands onto the seat.

"Let go," shouted Ryan, "and show your guts."

At the terrific pace the horses tore down the crooked, steep
mountain grade. It was but a matter of a minute until the crash
came. Unable to make a turn at the wild pace, both horses ran
off the road, the grade at this point descending more than a hundred feet on the steep mountain side.

Both animals were killed, and the buggy looked like it had been sent to a toothpick factory. Hynes and Ryan were both lying seriously injured in the ravine.

When picked up by some men who had witnessed the accident, both were unconscious. They were hurried to a Philipsburg hospital and after their injuries had been dressed they were placed in adjoining beds.

When the attending physician announced that both would live, Hynes, looking through his bandaged face, said to Ryan: "Bill, I tell you now, you gave me some ride, and you have guts enough to be a Butte fireman."[3]

But Granite's work and hilarity came to an abrupt end with the panic of 1893.

The city of Granite . . . which had a population of 5000 . . . was completely "wiped out" by the drop in the price of silver in 1893-4. Two of Montana's leading mines of the day, the Bi-Metallic and the Granite Mountain, which employed about 3000 miners and which were working levels as low as 1,500 feet, closed down without even a day's notice to employees.

The closing of the mines caused the entire population of Granite to seek new homes. They each packed up a few articles of personal property and trudged down the hill—to Philipsburg, Anaconda, Butte, Helena and other nearby towns. . . .

Mr. Scheers reviewed the effects of the "panic of 1893" in a manner that indicated an intimate knowledge of the "Cleveland depression"—of the hundreds that lay about the beer saloons for warmth in the day time and who made beds of newspapers on the saloon floors at night. Of the thousands of idle men who fought their way back east away from the closed mines and smelters— fought their way against hostile deputy sheriffs and even federal troops.

He referred to "General Hogan's division of Coxey's army" a group of Butte men who had the sympathy and support of the communities—Butte, Bozeman, Livingston and Billings, and also of the railworkers, but who were pursued by a posse of deputies under United States Marshal William McDermott and were finally

---

[3] *Mineral Independent* (Superior), January 19, 1928.

stopped by the troops from Fort Keogh. . . . The hostility of the federal government toward the Butte contingent of Coxey's army, it appears, was due to the report sent to Washington that they "had a boxcar of ammunition and firearms and were coming to Washington to make trouble."[4]

---

[4] *Geraldine Review*, May 9, 1938. Mr. Scheers was an editor in Granite during its heyday.

SUNRISE

IN 1933, IN RESPONSE TO THE NEED CREATED BY THE great depression, Montana's ghosts hitched up their winding sheets in an endeavor to regain some of their former vigor and produce again some of the wealth that was so desperately needed. Pioneer prepared for large-scale dredging; the Waseca claim, first patented mine in Montana, reopened. At Sunrise and Granite work was resumed for a short time. Sunrise had been deserted overnight when the price of silver broke; when interest was revived almost half a century later, returning miners found that furniture still remained in cabins, engineers' charts were scattered on the mess hall floor, and the old dinner bell still hung outside the door. Thousands of dollars' worth of mining machinery had been left to rust away in the mill.

Not far from the main camp the newcomers found a marker which warned against disturbing the ground within a radius of sixty feet since, somewhere within that area, six Chinamen, victims of an early-day tragedy had been buried. How or why they met their death was not stated.

Neither at Sunrise nor at any of the other camps that attempted a come back was mining really successful again; in a more complex economy characterized by mass production, far more wealth than that of a single vein was needed to make a paying operation.

BUTTE CITY, SILVER BOW

THE STORY OF BUTTE IS PRIMARILY THE STORY OF BIG-business copper mining. There is no intention here of including Butte in the category of ghost towns, but before Butte, the copper capital, there were other towns now lost to the world, ghostly names on old maps: Butte City, Silver Bow, Rocker, Farlin.

Captain Mills writes poetically of the discovery of Silver Bow:

Never prettier name was coined, and it came of this. On the evening of a cloudy day in January, 1864, Bud Barker, P. Allison, Joe and Jim Ester, on a prospecting trip, reached the vicinity of the creek near Butte, and a discussion arose as to its name. As the argument went on, the clouds rolled from the sun, its bright glance fell on the waters sweeping in a graceful curve around the base of the mountains, burnished them to brilliancy as they clasped the vale in a bow of silver. And so they named the farthest southeast waters that flow through Columbia to the sea. To them it was a land of beauty, of promise and profit. G. O. Humphreys, Denis Leary and Alex Scott followed in May. They were the discoverers of the camp, where every pan prospects and every sluice pays; a camp nearly twelve miles square, almost every gulch, bar, sag and hill yielding pay; with fifty-three miles of public ditches; where the best ground is on the hills, and good pay on their very summits.[1]

This isn't the way "Seven-up" Pete tells it. "Seven-

---

[1] M. A. Leeson, *History of Montana, 1738-1885* (Chicago: Warner, Beers, 1885), p. 900.

up," long a familiar figure on the streets of Butte, recounts his discovery and the naming of Silver Bow:

"Oi and two others, a Scotchman and an Englishman, crossed the Main Range with our pack critters through the Pipestone Pass; we were upon a prospectin' tower for placer diggins; we traveled down and westerly along this crick that runs down the valley for sivin or eight moiles, and as it was near sundown, we halted and camped a few rods from the crick. Whoile me pards made the camp and were a-preparin' the supper, Oi unpacked my Saratogy thrunk, which boi the way, wuz a flour sack, to get me gum boots.

"Oi put on me boots 'nd wid me pick and shovel 'nd gold pan in hand, Oi made for the crick bottom, where Oi set about to dig a found after goin' through sivin or eight feet o' wash 'nd gravel. Oi panned some uv the dirrt Oi had scraped from the bed rawck 'nd it was rich in gold. Yez mebbe shure Oi wurrked harrd to git through before darrk but th' days wuz long thin—it wuz in the month of June. Boi this time it wuz too darrk to worrk furder. Whin Oi got back to camp Oi showed me pards the results uv one pan uv dirt. There wuz about sivinity-five cints wurrth uv gold. Av coorse we wuz all excoited over the foind.

"Airly nixt mornin' afther we had berakfast swallowed, we all started fur th' crick to investigate furder. Whin near the banks uv the crick the sun come sthreamin' over th' mountains, and its rays a-glancin' along the sthream. Ye see, th' sthream runs wesht so the sun's rays run with the coorse. The crick wuz full uv curves or bends, and the sun a-glancin' along its wathers made these curves, as we looked easthward to look like so many silver bows. One of me pardners sez 'Oh! Look at the silver bows.' Oi noticed them and sez, 'Silver Bow goes. That's a good name, anyhow,' 'nd then wuz the way these diggin's wuz discovered and named."[2]

Allison made his camp in Baboon Gulch and, in exploring the area, discovered that mysterious hole known later as the "Original Lode." Here someone, long before, had sunk a prospect hole using elk antlers, which

---

[2] *Montana Standard* (Butte), January 26, 1958.

still lay nearby, as his tools. Allison and Humphreys located the Missoula Lode also; soon other strikes were made in the vicinity, and that fall Butte City was founded in Town Gulch. About this same time placer bars were discovered on Silver Bow Creek, and in a few weeks the lusty, exciting drama of Alder, Grasshopper, and Last Chance was being re-enacted.

The advance of civilization and progress has largely wiped from the thinking of Montanans the spirit of the early towns just as it has wiped those early towns from the hills and valleys of the state. Only in Butte does the spirit live: the laughter, the acceptance of the bad with the good, the generosity toward all unfortunates. And you have to live in Butte to gain the spirit and know its history back to its Butte City days to understand the origins of its unusual psychology.

Butte City started and lived with unrivaled zest. Races called forth wild excitement whether organized or impromptu. On one occasion, following a funeral, thirteen miners lined up at the Five Mile House in livery rigs and put five dollars each in a hat, the first driver to reach the Three Mile House to get the purse of $65. With the hubs of the carriages touching, the word to go was given, and before the first one hundred yards were covered, five of the buggies were minus wheels. Two complete upsets resulted within a quarter of a mile and the remaining six rigs dashed down the old dirt road like a modern Ben Hur chariot race.

"If we only had two fips fer this harse we'd win," yelled one driver to the man seated with him. Hardly had the words been spoken when a wheel of his buggy locked with the wheel of another racer and both rigs went into the "also rans."

Persons driving toward the Five Mile House saw the wild race covering the entire road coming toward them and, whipping their horses, they dashed out into the prairie. But one of the thirteen drivers made the Three Mile House on his one-horsepower vehicle.[3]

When it came to organized racing all of Butte would declare a month's holiday when the racing season opened. Thousands of dollars would pass through the betting ring every day. Not content with what the local scene could offer, race-track bettors organized a race poolroom. In these institutions were received by wire, direct from tracks all over the United States, the results of the racing. As reports came in bets would rise higher and higher, and the chant of the operator would grow more and more rapid.

Along with horse racing, other gambling kept the faro banks operating day and night. The town at three in the morning was as wide awake as at noon. One game, in the old Combination, ran twenty-four hours a day without closing for two years, and closed then for only a few days because the star dealer was ill.

These dealers were the Beau Brummels of Butte City. Immaculate, imperturbable, they sat enthroned, and with dignity and determination, after the bets were placed, would slip the cards from the deal box. On the turn of every card large sums of money were won and lost. After two cards were slipped from the box the dealer would first take the bank's winnings,

---

[3] *Mineral Independent* (Superior), January 19, 1928.

then he would pay the bets the bank had lost. This done, he would wait until the players had placed their bets and repeat the process. When two cards of the same denomination came out of the box on one turn, it was a split and the bank was entitled to one half of the money that had been bet on those particular cards.[4]

All-night vaudeville or variety shows were open to male patrons only. These would start at eight and close about four in the morning. Although the artists were often quite talented imports from the East, no admission was charged. Profits were made from drinks that were served by barmaids who passed among the crowds of miners.

Hurdy-gurdies, those social centers of the mining camps, offered their gaiety to the lonely men from the gulches. Dimsdale, though disapproving of such iniquity, describes them vividly:

One "institution" offering a shadowy and dangerous substitute for more legitimate female association, deserves a more peculiar notice. This is the hurdy-gurdy house. As soon as the men have left off work, these places are opened and dancing commences. Let the reader picture to himself a large room, furnished with a bar at one end—where champagne at $12 a bottle, and drinks at 25 to 50 cents are wholesaled, correctly speaking—and divided at the end of this bar, by a railing running from side to side.

The outer enclosure is densely crowded, and on particular occasions, the inner one also, with men in every variety of garb that can be seen on the continent. Beyond the barrier sit the dancing women, called "hurdy-gurdies," sometimes dressed in uniform, but more generally habited according to the dictates of individual caprice, in the finest clothes money can buy, and which are fashioned in the most attractive styles that fancy can suggest.

On one side is a raised orchestra. The music suddenly strikes

---

[4] Dan Conway in the *Scobey Sentinel,* February 4, 1927.

up, and the summons, "Take your partners for the next dance," is promptly answered by some of the male spectators, who, paying one dollar in gold dust for a ticket, approach the ladies' bench and—in style polite, or otherwise, according to antecedents—invite one of the ladies to dance.

The number being complete, the partners take their places, as in any other dancing establishment, and pause for the performance of the introductory notes of the air.

Let us describe the first class dancer—"sure of a partner every time"—and her companion. There she stands at the head of the set. She is of middle height, of rather full and rounded form; her complexion as pure as alabaster, a pair of dangerous looking hazel eyes, a slightly Roman nose, and a small but prettily formed mouth. Her auburn hair is neatly banded, and gathered in a tasteful, ornamental net, with a roll and gold tassels at the side. How sedate she looks during the first figure, never smiling till the termination of "promenade eight," when she shows her little white hands in fixing her handsome brooch in its place, and settling her glistening earrings. See how nicely her scarlet dress, with the broad black band around the skirt, and its black edging, sets off her dainty figure. No wonder that a wild mountaineer, with leather breeches, would be willing to pay—not one dollar, but all he has in his purse—for a dance and an approving smile from so handsome a woman.

Her cavalier stands six feet in his boots, which come to the knee and are garnished with a pair of Spanish spurs, with rowels and bells like young water wheels. His buckskin leggings are fringed at the seams, and gathered at the waist with a U. S. belt, from which hangs his loaded revolver and his sheath knife. His neck is bare, muscular and embrowned by exposure, as is also his bearded face, whose sombre expression is relieved by a pair of piercing eyes. His long black hair hangs down beneath his wide felt hat, and in the corner of his mouth is a cigar which rolls like the lever of an eccentric as he chews the end in his mouth.

After an amazingly grave salute, "all hands round" is shouted by the prompter, and off bounds the buckskin hero, rising and falling to the rhythm of the dance, with a clumsy agility and a growing enthusiasm testifying his huge delight. His fair partner, with practiced foot and easy grace, keeps time to the music like a clock, and rounds to her place as smoothly and gracefully as a swan.

As the dance progresses, he of the buckskins get excited, and nothing but long practice prevents his partner from being swept off her feet, at the conclusion of the miner's delight, "set your partners" or "gents to the right." An Irish tune, or a horn-pipe generally finishes the set, and then the thunder of heel and toe, and some amazing demivoltes are brought to an end by the aforesaid "gents to the right" and "promenade to the bar," which last closes the dance. After a treat, the bartender mechanically raps his blower as a hint to "weigh out," all transactions being in gold dust, the ladies sit down, and with scarcely an interval, a waltz, polka, schottische, mazurka, varsovienne, or rather quadrille commences.

All varieties of costumes, physique, and demeanor can be noticed among the dancers, from the gayest colors to the loudest styles of dress and manner, to the snugly fitted black silk and plain white collar which sets off the neat figure of the blue-eyes, modest-looking Anglo-Saxon. Yonder, beside the tall and tastily clad German brunette you see the short curls, rounded tournure, and smiling face of an Irish girl; indeed, representatives of almost every dancing nation of white folks may be seen on the floor of the hurdy-gurdy house.

The earnings of the dancers are very different in amount. The dancer in the low-necked dress with the scarlet "waist," a great favorite and a really good dancer, counted fifty tickets into her lap before "The last dance, gentlemen," followed by "Only this one before the girls go home," which wound up the performance. Twenty-six dollars is a great deal of money to earn in such a fashion, but fifty sets of quadrilles and four waltzes, two of them for the love of the thing, is very hard work.

As a rule, however, the professional "hurdies" are Teutons, and though first-rate dancers, they are with some few exceptions the reverse of good looking.

The dance which is most attended is one in which ladies to whom pleasure is dearer than fame represent the female element, and, as may be supposed, the evil only *commences* at the dance house. It is not uncommon to see one of these sirens with an "outfit" worth from seven to eight hundred dollars, and many of them invest with merchants and bankers thousands of dollars in gold, the rewards and presents they receive, especially the more highly favored ones, being more in a week than a well-educated girl would earn in two years in an Eastern City.[5]

Prize fighting took its place with horse racing as a favored sport, and that famous 105-round fight took place in Butte in December, 1889, between Ward and Gallagher. Ward was a carpenter and Gallagher a miner. Both were big, broad-shouldered men, and both were strong in the conviction that right was on his side in the dispute, the origin of which is still vague. It was decided that they would settle the matter by fighting a finish battle for a side bet. Since this was illegal, great secrecy attended the preparations.

At eight o'clock in the evening everything was in readiness. Ward seemed to be superior to his opponent and for a long time had him at his mercy. Gallagher was the first to fall, ending the first round. In the forty-eighth round Gallagher's left arm was broken between the wrist and elbow. For 49 rounds more, suffering inconceivable pain, Gallagher fought on, his body becoming a mere mass of bruises and each round, 97 straight, ending with him being knocked to the floor.

In the 98th round Gallagher caught Ward off his guard and delivered a terrific right-hander. Ward fell senseless, but partially revived and fought seven rounds in a half dazed condition, receiving terrible punishment from Gallagher's right hand, Gallagher's left dangling helpless at his side. In the 105th round Ward went down for keeps. He was brought back to town and taken to his room where he died the next day.

Gallagher's friends spirited him out of town, and, although a reward of $100 was offered for his arrest, he was never apprehended. The charges against the principals of the fight were later lessened to "unlawfully attending a prize fight" and there is no record that anyone was ever convicted in connection with the affair.[6]

Even the nicknames richly revealed the characters to whom they were attached. "Callahan the Bum" knew fifty-seven different ways of bumming a drink which was accompanied by a free lunch; "Buckets" filled buckets at the Maryland boardinghouse; "Gamblers' Ghost" hung about gamblers as a shadow, probably the first kibitzer. Then there were Dandy Jim, Fred the Rattler, Three-finger Jack, Bloody Knife, Dog-eating Jack, Eat-em-up Jake, Fatty the Gambler, Scarface Charlie, Old Poison, Neet Oil Bill (a "smooth" gentleman), Gros Ventre (Fat Belly) Johnnie, Old Evil Eye, and Stink-foot Charley.

Among those bearing colorful nicknames were two ladies of the shadows who were reputed to be the world's slickest "dips." The first of these, Jew Jess, lived in Butte for many years. An old newspaper account tells of her prowess.

Frank Hickman had a sandwich shop. A sheepherder stopped and bought a sandwich. He started east on Galena Street and a few yards from Hickman's place he was stopped by a frail dark woman, holding a cigarette in one hand, who asked him for a match.

As the sheepherder handed her the match, she lifted a pocketbook from the inside pocket of his coat. With a movement so deft and yet so swift as to defy observation, the woman, who was Jew Jess, slipped the wallet to a Negro woman. The latter, however, was a bungler and the sheepherder got a flash of his wallet.

<hr>

[6] Dan Conway in the *Scobey Sentinel*, February 4, 1927.

He pulled a revolver and shot near the Negro woman's feet. With a scream of terror she dropped the wallet and ran. The stranger picked up his pocketbook and, stepping to Hickman's door, counted the contents. It contained $999. "It's all here," he said. "I came into town with a thousand dollars, and I spent one dollar."

Meanwhile Jew Jess had disappeared as completely as though the sidewalk had swallowed her.

"I wonder how in h—— that nigger wench got my wallet?" the rube said to Hickman. "She must have got it when I gave that little woman the match."

One day the champion's standing was challenged by an immigrant from the Idaho mines of the Coeur d'Alenes. This was the "Virgin." Back in Gem, Idaho, a big Irishman by the name of Murphy bet he could buy her a drink without having his pocket picked. He went to her room and bought her the drink. As he reached in his pocket for money for the second round, he found his pocket empty.

As the Virgin dashed for the door, Murphy seized her by the hair. "I don't give a damn for the money," he yelled, whipping out his gun, "but it's me pride. You'll never frisk another guy." But the Virgin's luck held; she jerked her head aside and Murphy blasted off three of his fingers. In the ensuing excitement the Virgin escaped and hitched a ride on a handcar to Wallace. From there she made her way to Butte. She was too much even for Butte and was floated out of the city within two weeks.

Like all the other mining camps, Butte and Silver Bow had their share of Chinese. One of the old tales concerns one of these, Sin Louie, whose story is re-

counted still among the old legends of Silver Bow
Creek.

Sin Louie was an inoffensive little laundryman who
had wandered into the gulch to wash a lot of clothes
and pan a little gold. While he was there, a series of
thefts had aroused the camp to a frenzied pitch, and
Rick Walsh, a virtual giant from Indiana, was chosen
as head of a vigilance committee determined to bring
the thief to justice. Six-guns, long left hanging on
cabin walls, made their appearance on the hips of prospectors; as the thefts continued, even Rick Walsh's
poke was reported stolen.

One day as he, La Pierre (who had lost more than a
thousand dollars in dust and nuggets), and other vigilantes were discussing the situation, Sin Louie approached
them, a buckskin pouch in his hand and an incredible
tale on his lips.

"Alle same found 'um over by Lob's place, light on
ground."

No one was likely to credit such a tale, and Walsh
immediately arrested the little yellow man, accusing
him of all the thieving that had been going on. Poor
Sin was dragged, followed by an ever-increasing crowd
of angry miners, to Pulpit Rock, a huge boulder on
the side of the canyon. Here, on its flat top, the trial
took place. Sin was forthwith found guilty and sentenced to be hung on the spot. While Walsh was preparing the rope, Heaven took a hand in saving the
Celestial one. A storm that had been brewing all morning, suddenly broke and the great rock, loosened apparently by the pouring rain, went crashing to the bottom
of the canyon scattering the vigilantes and their vic-

tim in all directions. Walsh, when he picked himself up from the mud, feared his prisoner had escaped, but Sin Louie was too paralyzed to do more than lie in an abject heap on the soaked earth.

"Give me a gun, and I'll finish the Chink myself!" shouted Walsh, but the miners, always superstitious, believed that Providence had acted. A young Irishman, recently arrived, declared that Walsh would have to fight him first if he wanted to touch Sin Louie. Even La Pierre agreed to let the matter drop, and was somewhat puzzled at Walsh's insistence that he would "get that Chink." La Pierre befriended Sin Louie to the point of letting him sleep in his cabin, and it was there that the climax of the matter took place four days later. In the middle of the night, a gun blast shook the little cabin. Leaping to his feet, La Pierre saw Sin Louie standing in the door, a six-shooter still smoking in his hand. Outside someone was groaning in pain.

"What's going on here? Who's doing the shooting?" asked La Pierre.

"Lick," answered the Chinaman. "He come cleeping, cleeping to cabin, tly stick knife in my libs. I shoot 'um, then Lick yell, lun out door."

Walsh was seized and bound, not so much for trying to kill a Chinaman, as for going against the decision made by the group. Before he was tried, however, he worked loose from his bonds and escaped. The miners, having no great interest in the matter, were about to forget the whole incident when, several weeks later, some prospectors came upon Walsh's body. He had been trapped in a rockslide, and whether killed outright or pinned to the ground so that he died of thirst and starvation will never be known. An examination of his pack revealed the pokes of gold dust stolen from the camp. In one was the identical azurite nugget taken from La Pierre.

Little Sin Louie was "adopted" by La Pierre's family, with whom he lived for fourteen years. Then he returned to his homeland where he lived out his days in comparative comfort bought by the gold from Montana.[7]

Around the fringes of Butte City other camps were developed that today have been swallowed up in the city or live on as suburbs of the Copper Capital. Rocker was a mining camp with business houses and families when Butte was a log cabin, but it declined steadily after 1871. During these years, hydraulics were operated during the season when there was sufficient water in the gulch for mining, but the rich owners of the land and equipment chose to live in places more attractive than Butte's barren hills.

During the summer of 1875 William Farlin installed a ten-stamp quartz mill below Butte, but by December his funds were exhausted and work was suspended. The Farlin brothers of Butte were legends in the territory. Their schemes were vast, their energy boundless. It was they who located the great Indian Queen and Greenstone lodes where another town of Farlin was founded only to join the ranks of other lost and forgotten camps. Although the Farlins never amassed a great personal fortune, the success of Butte is sometimes attributed to their unfaltering faith in Montana's mineral wealth.

---

[7] Sid Stoddard in the *Rocky Mountain Husbandman,* August 6, 1931.

Burlington, four miles west of Butte, was first established in 1885; a large mill attracted a population of six hundred to seven hundred people. There were frame houses, a post office, a schoolhouse and lodge rooms. Van Zandt, the mine superintendent, built a fine brick house and started a free public library in it with reading and writing rooms that were always filled. Other forms of wholesome recreation were offered and the place became a popular community center. After its mainstay, the Bluebird Mine, was abandoned because of the low price of silver, the town was saved by a thriving dairy industry that furnished milk and butter to a fast-growing Butte.

Among all these towns clustered around the richest hill on earth, population was extremely fluid. Typical of this mobility was the shift from Butte to Silver Bow in 1868. During the preceding year the placers around Butte City began to play out after having produced almost unbelievable wealth. Many of the miners were moving on to other diggings, unmindful of the riches in copper that they were leaving behind.

In the fall of 1868 Barnard & Company, working near Silver Bow, brought a ditch in to wash the gravel of Pioneer Gulch. They uncovered not only dust but sizable nuggets. The excitement in Silver Bow and Butte City was intense and the whole town of Butte moved to Silver Bow. Many of the less substantially built buildings were torn down and re-erected at the site of the new bonanza. Butte was deserted while in Silver Bow the population skyrocketed to over a thousand. Now, it was believed, Silver Bow would again enjoy its old prestige, temporarily dimmed by the brief growth of Butte.

However, with the first hard frosts, the water supply, essential to the mining operation, froze. No longer did the precious stream flow down the flume to wash gold from the gravel. All mining operations ceased; those who had moved their buildings from Butte moved them back to Butte, thus ending, at least for the time, Silver Bow's hope of becoming a metropolis.

33

WOODVILLE

NINE MILES NORTH OF BUTTE CAN BE SEEN THE TRACES of one of the most interesting activities of the early days. Here, at old Woodville or Elk Park, the timber represents a second growth, the first growth having been stripped from the hills to keep the mines of Butte, Meaderville, Anaconda, and Philipsburg supplied with fuel.

The source of heat and power in those days was mainly dependent upon the efforts of the humble woodchopper, supplemented in a small measure by costly coke shipped from the Pennsylvania coal fields. But cordwood was the main and most dependable resource. The chopper appeared in thousands and he did this job so well that the hills and mountains surrounding Butte for a radius of many miles were completely stripped of their forest growth during the years preceding the utilization of coal and hydro-electric power. Everything that would burn was cut and fed into the mouths of the boilers and smelting furnaces and much of the natural beauty of hill and mountain was changed into desolation. . . .

Cordwood was a staple product and poured into Butte and Anaconda in thousands of cords daily by wagons, sleighs, pack trains and flumes, and went up in smoke from mine hoists, smelters, 'heap' roasting of ores and stamp mills, to say nothing of the base-burner and kitchen stove, for wood was the only resource in which to keep the "home fires" burning.

In the cruder methods of those days in reducing ores, the sulphur content was disposed of by resorting to "heap roasting." Long ricks of cordwood were piled upon the ground; thousands of tons of ore were piled upon the great ricks which were then fired. The addition of this dense and sulphurous smoke to that of the regular output of the mine hoists and busy smelters, made the atmosphere of Butte at times anything but pleasant. Often in a still morning, especially after a rain, a dense pall of smoke and fog would settle over the city, often so thick that a pedestrian could scarcely discern the sidewalk upon which he walked, while the querulous voice of some bewildered teamster would penetrate the gloom with impatient vehemence:

"Where the h—— are we now?"

Indeed the story is told of one ore hauler who, during one of these impenetrable blankets of fog and smoke came down the hill with his horses and seven or eight tons of ore, headed for the Meaderville smelter, and when the sun finally broke through the dismal darkness, found himself at the foot of Montana street with his load backed up to the imposing structure of the old Silver Bow brewery. He consoled himself with a liberal allowance of the product of the malt factory and made a new start toward his rightful destination. . . .

In the rugged mountainous sections there was much good timber located on the higher slopes where the cost of constructing a wagon or sleigh road would be prohibitive, but this did not deter the optimistic carver of cordwood. Sometimes he was able to build a chute of poles and slide his wood down the steep mountain side where it could be loaded upon wagons or sleighs, and also there were pack trains of mules available. Jimmy MacDougall cut wood all winter and in the spring would round up his bunch of a half dozen moth-eaten and skinny mules, and proceed to pack the result of his winter's work to a location where it was salable. The whole countryside was made aware of Jimmy's summer activity by a steady stream of the most lurid, blasphemous and fluent profanity, absolutely startling in its originality and force as it shattered the atmosphere of a still calm and beautiful summer morning. Jimmy's pack mules appeared to require pungent and compelling argument.

Old man Johnson and his two sons had cut quite a lot of wood high up on the mountain just west of Woodville, seemingly without much thought as to the problem of getting it to market. None of the wagon haulers would buy it until it was moved to a place where it could be loaded on their wagons, so the Johnsons began to study schemes to land it at the foot of the mountain. One of the boys was struck with a bright idea and put it into effect by securing a couple of discarded wagon tires. A half cord or so of wood was placed inside the tires, and when completely filled, wedges were driven in to hold the load firmly. The loaded contraption resembled a huge barrel with the tires serving as hoops. When ready the thing was heaved over the brink of the mountain side and started on its wild career, but the inventor had miscalculated the strength of the old tires, and as it landed about half way down the steep slope after a leap of several hundred feet, the tires burst in a cloud of dust and the load was hopelessly scattered over the mountainside.

Inventive genius was not disheartened, however. Heavier and stronger tires were secured and another attempt made. The results proved that the idea was sound basically, though possibly impractical as a business venture. As before the load was wedged solidly within the encircling hoops and started on its way. It held together this time and reached the foot of the mountain intact, but, unfortunately, it failed to stop there. It had gained terrific momentum and continued its wild career until it collided with the cabin of "French Pete" on the outskirts of Woodville where it burst with a startling crash, raining shrapnel in the shape of splintered cordwood over the peaceful little village. No casualties were reported, though a wild-eyed Pete emerged from the wreck of his cabin grasping an old Sharps buffalo gun, and convincingly stated his attitude toward any further bombardment of his domicile. He was finally placated by the promise of the inventors to repair the damage. The Johnson product ultimately reached a market as a burden of the patient mule.[1]

In 1883 Woodville had a population of 170 and was considered a "modern settlement" with a post office, general store, a saloon and other business establishments including a barbershop operated by Mrs. A. Than, reputed to be the first woman barber of Montana.

[1] R. H. Bemis in the *Mineral Independent* (Superior), August 5, 1926.

34

HIGHLAND CITY AND RED MOUNTAIN CITY

NEAR BUTTE IS THE TOWERING RANGE KNOWN AS THE Highlands. Here were located two of the area's richest camps, Highland City and Red Mountain City.

Gold was first discovered on Fish Creek on July 25, 1866, in a gulch that lay at the foot of Red Mountain. A stampede followed and Highland City boasted a population of five thousand, greater than that of Butte. Its life was wild and short. Dances often lasted two days and two nights and attracted miners from many miles around. There were three hundred houses, ten saloons, five dance halls and not one church. Only for one year did the gold of Highland last. Then, with the gold gone, the population of the camp went, too, all except one.

John Kern still had faith in the diggings. He was among the first there and he was still there a few seasons later, when he saw the last of his prospector friends load his belongings upon his wagon and with his wife and family start down the trail.

Year after year he had labored, and on occasions, in the summer of 1908, he was partially rewarded for his efforts when he uncovered what he declares was the third largest nugget ever discovered in Montana. The lump of gold weighed 61 ounces and was sold for $1,228. Only two larger nuggets were ever discovered in the history of the state.[1]

---

[1] *Bynum Herald*, March 13, 1922.

John Kern died in 1923. His frozen body was found in his cabin when a friend, Fred Stanton and his sons, snowshoed into the town to see how Johnny was. Unable to bury him in the deep snows and frozen soil of Highland, his friends took him to Butte where he was buried with the reverence due a true pioneer. Some old-timers, reminiscing about his long, lonely life in the Highlands, connected his name with that of Shot-gun Liz, who lies buried in Highland City. Liz, or Lulu as she was called when she first came to Highland, was a beautiful Russian girl. No one knows what her life was before she appeared as a hurdy-gurdy in Montana. John Kern, then a handsome youth of nineteen or twenty, found favor in her eyes and they planned to marry. One night a drunken miner tried to force his attentions on Lulu who, seizing a shotgun, blasted him to eternity. From then on she was "Shot-gun Liz." Whether it was the shock of this incident, the severity of the climate (one of the worst in Montana), or some other cause, the following year Liz's body was found in her dingy room above the dance hall. Perhaps, even though his other friends left one by one, John Kern remained in Highland to be near the grave of the one who was dearest to him.

Today at the site of Highland City, now accessible by road, there remains the ruins of the blacksmith shop and the brewery. Perhaps a few barrel staves and hoops could be found, and in spite of the years of rain, snow, and wind, the smell of mash can be detected by any sensitive nose.

Also in Highland Gulch was Red Mountain City. Many of those who had stampeded to Butte were idle because of the shortage of water. Although plans were to bring a ditch in from Silver Bow Creek, many of the miners were too impatient to wait for it and went off to prospect other ground.

Early in the summer of 1866 J. H. S. and E. B. Coleman and William Crawford went to Charlie Carver, who had a store down "in the diggings" and asked him to grubstake them so that they could go out into the hills to prospect. This he did and they started out accompanied by Tom Rutter, Dan Parker and J. B. Dunlap. The next thing that was heard from them was that they had struck it rich in the Highlands.

Immediately there was a stampede for the new discovery, about 150 men going out from Butte. Soon the gulch was taken up for its whole length and operations were begun at once. The result was marvelous. The gold was found to be the richest of any in Deer Lodge county, being worth $20 an ounce. In a very short time the fame of the discovery spread and there was a general stampede from all the camps around. . . .

When the stampede was proven to be something more than a wild dash, the men began building cabins and sawmills and blacksmith shops and stores, and soon there was a thriving little town, which they named Red Mountain City. At the first county election there were a thousand voters. The principal store keepers were Charlie Wunderlich and Rod Leggat and E. S. Stackpole. Wunderlich had a blacksmith shop in connection with his store, and Leggat and Stackpole had a two-story log building. The upper floor was used as a lodge room for the Masons. There were, of course, a number of saloons and dance halls. . . . One of the best loved characters in the district was Dr. Seymour Day. He doctored the whole country around. Unfortunately he was given to hard drinking, and eventually drank himself to death. He would never go near a sick person when he was drunk. He would say, "No, you will have to wait until I am sober." He had a song that he sang on all occasions, which amused his hearers very much. Each verse ended with the refrain, "In the chilly winds of December." He spent his last days at Divide, dying there about 1883 at Charlie Wunderlich's boarding house.

The town boasted a system of waterworks, with hydrants. The

piping was made of green logs about ten feet long and six or eight inches in diameter, with a hole bored through the center. The boring was done in a machine of home construction, turned by hand. The auger was made by Charlie Wunderlich in his blacksmith shop. . . .

Bill Owsley told me that he and his partner took out $3,100 a day from their claim, but they only worked three or four days a week in digging. They spent the rest of the week sluicing. Their neighbor, Mansfield, spent his money lavishly, even foolishly. His extravagances were a marvel to all onlookers. It was true in his case that willful waste makes woeful want, for he died in the poor house. Uncle Jimmie Murphy spent his money in a different way. When he had collected as much as he needed he turned his claim over to his friends and allowed them to go down and pan out as much as they wanted. . . .

While the "gum-booters" were busy washing out the yellow sand, there was another class of prospectors none the less busy. These were the ones who were after quartz. They scoured the hills around Red Mountain City searching for something more enduring than the fleeting placer claims. With only two exceptions, none of the quartz discoveries amounted to anything. The claims on the Ballarat lode gave food for thought and speculation for many months and those on Nevin's Hill paid well for a number of years. . . .

The Ballarat mine was a typical wildcat proposition, and it is surprising how men of discernment and knowledge of mining could be so deceived. There were four men who discovered this mine. They had great hopes for it and really thought they had a good thing. These men were William Smith, William Baldwin, Daniel McKiever and E. B. Watson. They lived in a cabin close to their prospect. It stands today, but in a fallen condition.

They worked for some months taking out ore and storing it until they could have a cleanup. They built an arrastra near their cabin which also stands today. It was a crushing machine run by horse power. The men, whenever they came down into the town, would tell of the richness of the Ballarat mine. The Deer Lodge and Virginia City newspapers had much to say about it, and all visitors to the camp went back home with glowing tales of this mine which promised to make a permanent thing of Red Mountain City.

One day they started to crush the ore and after it was all pulverized they panned it out. Great was their chagrin to find that there was scarcely any gold in it. They dreaded to face the ridicule of their fellows, and so they gathered together what dust there was and melted it into a piece of gold about the size of an assayer's button. This they took to town and displayed as a sample of their ore. The people of Red Mountain City were amazed at this wonderful product of their mine. Everyone was talking of it. Professor Swallow of Deer Lodge heard of it, and he at once saw that such a rich property should be developed, and he succeeded in interesting two St. Louis capitalists in the property. They bought it and some adjoining claims for $15,000 and proceeded to build a 24-stamp mill. Professor Swallow was put in charge of the whole plant.

Cabins for the men employed were built not far from the mill, and one fine one with an up-to-date fireplace was occupied by Professor Swallow and his family. Everything was booming. Ore was brought to the mill from all the neighboring quartz claims to be crushed. They had a whistle that could be heard in Butte.

After a while the St. Louis men began to wonder why there were no reports of dividends. They waited a while then they sent Professor Philip Knabe out to investigate the property. He stayed a year, and not only investigated the Ballarat claims, but every one in the Highlands. He sent back his report saying that in his judgment the whole gulch was not worth two bits. Everything was shut down at once. The mill machinery was sold to Jim Talbot of Butte, who installed it in the old Silver Bow mill. The whistle did service at the Parrot smelter. . . .

Somewhere on the old townsite lies buried a large fortune. It was the property of a man known as Beastly Butler. He was so called because of his extreme carelessness in dress and of his person. This was all the more noted and criticized because of the fact that he was a man of unusual mind and education. He worked diligently upon a placer claim and made a lot of money, which he put into tin cans and buried somewhere near his cabin, it was supposed. One day he was killed by a fall of earth on his claim. His fellow citizens searched in vain. They never found the gold. And it is still there somewhere. It is one of the secrets of the Highlands. Perhaps some day it will be found, and it will be as great a find as Captain Kidd's treasure. . . .

When the placers were worked out and the town began to

dwindle, many of the claims were bought up by Rod Leggat, others were turned over to him on debts, and eventually he owned the whole gulch. For a number of years he stayed out there and placer mined a couple of miles down the gulch, but with no success whatever. Whatever he may have lost in this mining in Highland Gulch was made up to him at a later day when the Butte Water company approached him to find out what his price would be for the water right of all the Highland water. His price was $160,000. And he got it.[2]

---

[2] *Fergus County Argus*, October 8, 1920. The Leggats are an important Butte family today.

35

CONFEDERATE GULCH

(Diamond, New York, Brooklyn, Cavetown)

CONFEDERATE GULCH[1] WAS DISCOVERED IN 1864 AND DURING THE fall of that year and the spring of 1865 prospectors thronged there and the vicinity was extensively mined by men who had come up from the Idaho and California placers. The richness of the pay dirt in Confederate Gulch was the sensation of the Montana gold camps. As high as $180 in gold to a pan was obtained. Montana bar, situated above Confederate gulch, and consisting of a foothill of two acres, was richer than the main gulch. When the first cleanup was made on that bar the flumes were found to be clogged with gold by the hundredweight. When bedrock on the famous bar was reached the enormous yield of $180 to the pan in Confederate was forgotten in astonishment at the wonderful yield of $1,000 to the pan.

Confederate Gulch was not so large as Alder, Last Chance or Oro Fino but it was the richest in proportion of all Montana gulches that yielded gold. The best informed miners of that day declared that, in proportion to the area of the surface worked, Confederate Gulch and Montana Bar produced more gold than any other spot in the world.[2]

One day in the sixties a heavily laden freight outfit pulled away from the streets of Diamond City,[3] center of the fourteen rich gulches, with two and one-quarter tons of gold dust, valued at $900,000, the cleanup of

---

[1] So called because the discoverers were former soldiers of the Confederate army in Missouri under General Price.

[2] *Mineral Independent* (Superior), June 10, 1920.

[3] So called because the first four cabins at the site of the strike happened to be placed in such a way that the paths from one to another formed a diamond in the snow, with the cabins at the corners.

one short season's work of three or four men on the rich bar. Naturally, the transport of such a sum through country infested with road agents required only the most brave and the most honest escort. Naturally, too, the choice fell on X. Beidler who later described the trip:

I was at Diamond City a couple of weeks previous to this shipment, and William Fredericks asked me to guard this gold from Helena to Fort Benton, to which place they had concluded to ship it and then load it on boats for the states. I agreed to go along. He told me to consider myself employed and to keep a lookout for toughs in the meantime.

I had known this man, Fredericks, before either of us came to Montana. In the winter of 1861 Fredericks was prospecting in Colorado in the Gunnison country and was snowed in for the winter. He had to eat his pack animals to live. I met him in the spring as he was coming out near Twin Lakes. He came to my camp nearly starved to death. I fed him and his party some good substantial grub, which they had not seen for six months. Fredericks never forgot that square meal, and the next time I saw him was at Diamond City, where he employed me, after he had made a cleanup from his rich strike on Montana bar. After we shook hands he brought out a pan of dust and set it on the table and told me to help myself to a nugget. I picked out a large one. He said, "X., there are larger ones there—take a big piece." Several weighed over four hundred dollars, but I was too modest and kept the first one.

Well, we started from Helena to Benton with the dust loaded on three two-mule wagons, the dust in three safes, and fourteen men armed and on horseback. Job Travis went along to bring the horses back. While in the bank on Budge Street in Helena, getting the money ready, one of the men interested in the money let his double-barreled shotgun go off accidentally and the charge went into the ceiling which raised quite a commotion.

When we left Helena we were ready for almost any emergency and camped the first night in Prickly Pear canyon. While we were in camp an outsider came to me with a proposition to steal the dust and whack it up. He said I could fix the guns in our party so they could be stolen, and then no one need be killed on either side. He said when I was ready I could whistle. Then he would have his gang take the treasure and I would get my whack.

I told him I didn't want to hear any more plans—I knew the man well, and told him that if I heard any whistling I would kill him if I could. I reported the proposition to Fredericks and it alarmed the outfit and the men put a heavy guard—no whistling and no money taken.

The next night we camped at the Dearborn. Had no trouble till we got to Bull's Head, 12 miles this side of Benton. While riding on a walk my horse broke his right forward leg just below the knee through no apparent cause—no holes, rocks or anything else to cause it, and how it was done none of us could find out. It just snapped off. We shot him right there and I rode on in the wagon to Benton.

While we were there we fixed the safes ready for shipping them down the river in mackinaw boats, no steamers being there. We fastened ten-gallon casks with long ropes to each safe in case the boats might upset, when the casks would act as buoys and the safes could be located. They got through to the states all right. I got eleven ounces for my trip.[4]

The miners of Diamond and its surrounding gulches drew up their own miners' code:

Resolved, that this district shall be called Confederate Gulch, and that a claim shall be 100 feet long in the creek, 200 feet long in a gulch and 50 feet front on the bank, and that a man may hold one of each.

Resolved, secondly, that no more Chinamen shall take up claims.

Resolved, thirdly, that a white man must stick up a notice at each end of his claim when he takes it up.

Resolved, fourthly, that a man may lay over his claim a month by posting a notice and paying the receiver one dollar.

Resolved, fifthly, that all disputes about claims shall be settled by a miners meeting and no lawyers.[5]

---

[4] *Mineral Independent* (Superior), June 10, 1920.

[5] *Big Timber Pioneer*, June 7, 1920.

Discoveries in New York Gulch in 1866 led to the establishment of the town of New York on one side of the gulch and Brooklyn on the other. "Thus," says Leeson, "in the heart of the mountains, history was repeated so far as nomenclature was concerned." During the three years from 1866 to 1869 thousands of miners were in the New York-Brooklyn area.

Cavetown, also in the Diamond City trade area, was the scene of the most famous claim-jumping episode in Montana.

A party of claim jumpers had been organized in Idaho and Nevada. These men, with knowledge of the fact that no set of laws existed in the territory, and that possession alone was evidence of ownership of a claim, decided to come to Montana, steal claims from their owners, and to hold them by sheer strength of numbers. They chose the Diamond City region and went to Cave gulch because that area was the most accessible and had good gold prospects.

These claim jumpers were a sinister, desperate band of frontier desperados, as may be judged from their plan of action. They established their camp and served notice on two miners who were working on a good looking bar, to leave their diggings and make themselves scarce by sunset of the following day or take the consequences which they declared would be sudden death.

In alarm these miners consulted with their neighbor prospectors, and word was sent out quietly to five or six other camps in the neighborhood. That night a score of miners had gathered with ample provisions for a prolonged seige, and well armed. They portholed one of the cabins not far from the claim of the two men who had been threatened, and secluded themselves therein. They spent the day playing cards, not showing themselves outside of the cabin. At dusk a dozen of the claim jumpers appeared prepared to take possession of the diggings which they believed had been abandoned in accordance with orders.

No sooner had the leader of the claim jumpers set foot beside the flume than a shot rang out from the cabin and the desperado fell dead. The followers of the slain man at once opened up a fusilade of shots at the cabin, and the shooting for a few minutes was general. Then a party of the miners rushed from the cabin and took a stand in the open. Three of the claim jumpers fell mortally wounded, and in a few seconds the rest broke and ran into the timber. As far as is known this is the only attempt of organized claim jumpers to ply their operations in Montana Territory.

. . . This episode was the beginning of what was known as the fight between the Irish and the Missourians, which in later months and years resulted in much prejudice and many a bloody and some- times tragic quarrel.[6]

For three years, when Diamond City was at its best between 1865 and 1868, it was in every sense one of the best boom towns of the West. Stores, saloons, gambling houses, hurdy-gurdy houses and hundreds of log cabins grew like mushrooms up and down the gulch. . . . Roads were hewn to other camps in all directions and soon rumbling stages began to arrive daily from Last Chance Gulch. Along the trails walked and rode weather beaten, booted men with wiry bodies and strong faces, some with pack horses and many carrying blankets on their backs as they strode along. Soon ox and mule trains began to drag into the gulch, hauling stores of goods for trade with the miners.[7]

Crews worked night and day bringing water seven miles for the hydraulic work. Double shifts worked on the bedrock drains and these methods kept the sluice boxes working almost constantly until Diamond City itself was almost buried beneath the avalanche of tailings that poured down the gulch. Houses had to be raised 15 feet to save them from burial beneath the debris.[8]

Even after its decline began, Charlie Russell considered it to be one of the most perfect types of the old mining camps.

As quickly as it had grown, Diamond City waned. Ten years after its founding the population had dwin-

[6] *Roundup Record-Tribune*, November 26, 1942.

[7] *Mineral Independent* (Superior), June 10, 1920.

[8] *Kalispell Times*, August 4, 1938.

dled from five thousand to forty-nine. In 1883 Judge
Hedges wrote:

Diamond City is desolate, deserted and dreary to behold in the
shreds of its departed glory. . . . Its very site will soon go down the
flume, which is already within the borders of the old town and glean-
ing a rich harvest—probably the last. There are only four families
left of all the hundreds that have dwelt here since the glorious
days of '66. If the goose that laid the nestfull of golden eggs can
only be found in the shape of a prolific mother vein, of gold bearing quartz, the days of Diamond's departed glory may return.[9]

The hope that this vein would be found persisted
for many years, but one by one the old-timers who kept
faith with the dream died. "Chinee" George, the first
and last Chinaman in the camp, became too helpless to
care for himself in his cabin at Diamond. The county
had supplied his meager needs for several years, and
finally, at the age of eighty-two, he consented to live
out his days at the county farm, abandoning the life
he had known at Diamond where, since 1865, he had
been respected for his industry and honesty and loved
for his quaint speech and kindly nature.

In 1920-21 Felix White, too, agreed to go to the
county farm rather than spend another winter in the
deep snows of the gulch where for many years his aging
hands had tried to sift a livelihood from his dry washer
on the steep hillside where the shortage of water had
left some gold-producing gravel.

Finally, in March, 1959, the last inhabitant of Diamond City was buried in the Deep Creek Cemetery.
His death was noted in the *Townsend Star* of March 5:

[9] M. A. Leeson, *History of Montana, 1739-1885* (Chicago: Warner, Beers, 1885),
p. 808.

Funeral services were held this morning for E. F. "Robbie" Robison. . . .

Ernest Blair Robison was born in Blair county, Pennsylvania, April 26, 1881. He came to Montana over 40 years ago, locating at Diamond City where he has since made his home, devoting all his time to gold mining.

Last November his home was destroyed by fire and he was severely burned, and has been in the Broadwater hospital since that time. . . .

"Robbie" as he was affectionately known by most of his friends, was one of Broadwater county's most colorful residents. When he came to Diamond City it was quite a mining town, but in later years Robbie was the only permanent resident, and was hailed far and wide as the "Mayor of Diamond City." He made very infrequent trips to town, but people who passed through Confederate Gulch always stopped for a visit with him, and he has shown many a tenderfoot the art of gold panning.

One lone cabin, long unoccupied, stands in Confederate Gulch, a shed and the blackened ruins of Robbie's home close by. The cabin consists of a low, debris-filled room with an attached lean-to. The sheet-iron stove is tipped awry; bedding rots on the built-in bunks, and the neatly sawed wood that was to keep Robbie warm for another winter is stacked against the outer wall. A three-wheeled barrow, filled with gravel, stands near an inclined screen, the last testimony of an old prospector's faith.

36

CASTLE

CASTLE IS A MINING CAMP BUILT IN A BEAUTIFUL SHELTERED valley near the southeast base of Castle mountain. This mountain received its name from the castellated rocks which form the very attractive features of its crests and peaks. The principle mines are on a series of rounded mountain spurs from one to six miles from the town. The mountains are limestone, porphyries, granites and various eruptive rocks, flanked by more recent formations containing veins, crevice veins, blanket veins of segregation. . . .[1]

The first men to locate mines in this camp were the four Hensley brothers who came here in 1885. The next year these same men made the first carbonate discoveries in that district. . . . Quickly following this discovery 1,800 claims were taken up in the same district. . . .

When at its best Castle was one of the richest mining camps in the state. Buildings were substantial, a $5,000 school was built, two smelters operated and it is claimed that $3,000,000 worth of ore was taken from the Cumberland alone. Marcus Daly was a heavy investor; the Jawbone[2] ran within a mile of the town bringing in mail and freight and hauling out precious metals.[3]

[Rooming houses and hotels were crowded.] When all beds were

---

[1] Joaquin Miller, *An Illustrated History of the State of Montana* (Chicago: Lewis Publishing Company, 1894), pp. 761-62.

[2] It gained its name from the slang expression, "Jawbone" (big talk and promises by its promoters of a big future). The Northern Pacific is said to have asked its president, Richard Harlow, for a timetable. Harlow said ". . . there were no towns on the line, nor any provocation for any. But I drew up a schedule and located plenty of them. Two young ladies (Fan and Lulu) were visiting at my house. On the timetable as a result you will find Fanalulu just below Ringling." "Know Montana: The Jawbone Railroad," by H. G. Stearns, *Dillon Daily Tribune*, June 1, 1953.

[3] Martha Plassman in the *Roundup Tribune*, September 29, 1927.

full, guests were allowed to unroll their blankets on the floor [at the prevailing rate for beds]. The hotel guest chamber had one guest room as a sort of ram pasture where guests were given some sort of bed at $1.00 per night—no meals—room about 40 feet by 20 ft.[4]

Castle was a wide open town. Its poker games were no place for a piker in the old days. . . . There were accidents whose horror seemed greater in the intimate associations of a small and isolated community. Two deaths are recorded from dynamite explosions. Jack Nesbitt was killed while delivering a box of dynamite to a mine. It is supposed that he slipped, dropping the dynamite which exploded. Another miner was killed at Robinson by a charge he had set.

One shooting occurred in which Bill Rader, a deputy sheriff lost his life. Two suspicious characters, Bill Gay and his companion, one Gross, had come to Castle shortly before the camp closed down. They were suspected of being implicated in robberies in the state and elsewhere. A warrant was issued for their arrest, and Fred Lewis, deputy sheriff, went to their cabin to serve the papers. Both men and their wives were at the cabin. They submitted peaceably to arrest and even engaged Lewis in a friendly game of cards. The upshot of this social evening was that Lewis was thrown off his guard, and the two men made their escape. They hid in the timber near town, and since the charge against them was minor rumor was current that they intended to give themselves up. However, when Radar came on them in their hiding place, barricaded behind logs, they ordered him back, and drawing their guns threatened to shoot if he came nearer. Rader was a fearless man, and with the words, "Boys, I have to take you," started forward. Both fired and Rader fell.

Gay and Gross made their escape down the river to Merino (The site of Harlowtown). A posse was hastily gathered and started in pursuit. The outlaws had all the advantage since they were concealed in heavy underbrush, and the sheriff's force was not large enough to entirely surround the timber where they were hidden. One member of the posse, a man named McKay, came onto Gay and was shot down. George Williams narrowly escaped death when he walked onto Gay's hiding place. Williams drew his gun but it

---

[4] *Great Falls Tribune,* April 14, 1957.

jammed and missed fire; by coincidence Gay's gun snapped without exploding the shell and Williams escaped.

Both Gay and Gross evaded the posse at this time, but the reward offered for their capture kept men on their trail. Gay was tracked to Needles, California, and captured there. He was pinioned from behind as he entered a blacksmith shop. He was returned to Montana.

Gross was trailed to St. Louis, Missouri. Two deputies approached him as he was walking on the St. Charles bridge. He eyed them, smiling until they were within a few feet of him, then suddenly pulled two guns, ordered them off and backed from the bridge into the underbrush at the river's edge. He was never captured.[5]

The old Castle Road was an institution in southern Montana. It began at the Northern Pacific railroad in Lewistown, winding northward through the hills west of the Shields river, past the general vicinity of the Higgins ranch east of Ringling, then along the present Martinsdale-Ringling road to near Lennep, where it turned up the creek for a water grade to the mines.

At all times Castle was jammed with huge freight wagons and string teams, as was a feed yard in Livingston, maintained especially for the Castle traffic. The road was always alive with teams—silver bars coming from the mines, and supplies going in. . . .

There was the "Cayuse Kid"—Jim Benson—who was so nicknamed because of the fact that his freight outfit was made up of cayuse ponies, a type of horse seldom used for draft purposes. "The Cayuse Kid," says Mr. Sumner (rancher and freighter of Castle) "never mended his harness except with bailing wire. It finally reached the point where there was more bailing wire than leather in the rigging of the cayuses". . . .

There were a number of bull teams on the road, many of them traveling all the way from Ogden, Utah, to Castle, for some of the Castle silver went to Utah smelters for its final refinement. . . .

Mr. Sumner recalls that on one trip out of Castle he had a passenger. A gambler had cleaned out the camp and dared not linger there for fear of reprisals by others of his profession and revenge by his victims. He dared not take the regular stage to Livingston for fear of being waylaid. . . .

During that night ride the gambler talked much of the tricks of his profession, and described the sharpers' methods of fleecing

---

[5] Grace Stone Coates in the *Roundup Tribune,* April 26, 1928.

the sheepherders—and then continuing to hold their friendship. It was a popular pastime of the gamblers to compare notes on how many sheepherders were "working for them."

The herders stayed out with their flocks all season—some of them would come to town only once in two or three years. They always showed up with an accumulated pay for a long period. A gambler would tell a herder of a game where he could "make a pile" with the gambler's help. At the table a confederate would deal the game while the coaching sharp gave signals to his victim. The gambler always matched the herder's cash with money of his own, "so we both can cash in." At a signal from his mentor, the herder would bet the pile—and lose. Afterward the gambler would mildly berate the herder for having misinterpreted his signal. The herder, broke and very contrite, looked and felt like one of his wooly charges.

"Oh, well," the gambler would end, "better luck next time. Here, John," turning to the bartender, "lend me $10. My friend has had hard luck, and he needs money for some overalls and grub."

The herder would return to his flock thinking the gambler was a swell fellow not to treat him rough, since both had lost their roll on the herder's fool play. Next time he was in town the herder's first duty to himself was to look up his gambler friend and repay the ten spot.

After such games, of course, the sharpers got together and split the "take."[6]

Sharing the thrills and dangers of old Castle was a beautiful girl who later became a belle of international society. When Anna Robinson was seventeen her father came out from Minneapolis and started a boardinghouse in Castle. Here Anna waited on tables and in the evenings often sang to the miners in her unusually clear, beautiful voice.

Three years after leaving Castle she was famous as an actress and musical comedy star. Men flocked to pay tribute to her charm and beauty. In 1905, after

[6] *Midland Empire Farmer,* September 1, 1938.

winning a place in the best of Europe's social circles, she was married to the Earl of Rosslyn but divorced him two years later. The Duke of Manchester offered marriage, and King Leopold of Belgium was supposed to have showered her with jewels.

But like many of the prospectors in her father's boardinghouse in Castle, she squandered her gold. Returning to New York, she lived quietly with her sister until, shortly after the European War, she died, poverty-stricken and wasted by disease, in a New York state hospital for the insane.

The decline of the town was as rapid as its rise. In the early 1890's the exodus of people was almost complete. Most of them left by the covered wagon route, never to return and claim the homes and household goods many of them left behind. The log structures fell rapidly into decay, and of all the residents of Castle's palmy days, only two believed that the town would some day "come back"—that mining operations would once again be undertaken on as large a scale as in the early days. The two were Joseph Hooker Kidd and Joseph Martino.

Martino, now well over 70, said the winter of 1936 was the snowiest and most severe he had ever seen. On the level, the snow was four feet deep and in drifts it sometimes reached 40 feet. For weeks no one had entered or left the ghost town. Finally Kidd decided to go to Lennep, eight miles distant, to stock up on groceries and to get the mail. The supplies in the cabins of the two men were almost exhausted.

After battling the drifts for an entire day, Kidd had driven his team and cutter only three miles. He stayed for the night at the Moore sheep camp. The next day he reached the A. C. Grande ranch with some difficulty, but from there to Lennep the roads were in fair condition. Kidd purchased the necessary food and returned as far as the Grande ranch where he spent the night.

He shoveled snow and fought the drifts the next day and got within a mile of Castle when his tired team refused to go any farther. He turned the horses loose and pressed on afoot. At 9 p.m., he reached Martino's cabin and drank some hot coffee. Kidd's cabin was only 500 yards down the road and he soon attempted to reach it.

Martino lighted a lantern to direct Kidd on his way. In a few minutes he heard Kidd calling, "Joe, Joe." Rushing into the street, Martino saw Kidd staggering, then his knees buckled under him and he collapsed into the snow. When Martino reached him, Joseph Hooker Kidd was dead. Martino, too weak to carry the body, covered it with a blanket.

Traveling on skis, Martino notified the herder at the Moore sheep camp of what had happened. Three days later the sheriff and coroner from White Sulphur Springs, themselves on skis, pulled Kidd's body away on a toboggan.

Only one old man was left to dream of the days of Castle's greatness—when the mines poured an "unending"—so they thought —stream of gold into the pockets of the people, when the streets rang with the sounds of revelry at night. Only one old man lived to hope that a great strike might again be made and that Castle might relive the days of its youth.[7]

The fascinating thing about poking around abandoned towns is that you never know what treasure you may unearth. According to the *Scobey Sentinel*, Castle, years after its abandonment, was the site of one of the richest strikes ever recorded in Montana.

Some of the engineering force of the Brophy interests at Castle uncovered a rich deposit in the town proper in the rear of an old saloon at that place.

The day was a rainy one, and due to the fact that they could not work in the timber, they came down to the old town, to find a piece of wide, white pine lumber, with which to make a draughting board. Moving rubbish in the back end of the building, they exposed one of the richest pay streaks yet reported.

The discovery consisted of 10 gallons of Three Star Hennessey brandy in a barrel, where it had reposed since the closing of the saloon some time shortly after 1893. It is claimed that one of the discovery party tried to keep the find secret, and maintained it

---

[7] George Marsh in the *Silver State Post* (Deer Lodge), March 14, 1940.

should be used for strictly medicinal purposes. The others, however, refused to be mislead a second time by that companion, and stood unanimously for a division of the resources.

After a long and voluble meeting it was decided to divvy with every man in camp, and that Whispering Johnson could keep his for medicinal or social purposes as he saw fit. . . .

The camp usually boasts a dozen men, counting in the entire population of Castle mountains. However, 20 gathered for the division, one man coming in from the hills, a fellow who hadn't been seen for years and reported lost in the blizzard of 1911. The division resulted in an equal share of one-half gallon each, with a few "shots" over, which were not left for long.

The following resolutions were adopted by the meeting:

"Whereas, the world has forgotten Castle for a long time, and

"Whereas, the unfounded rumor has been circulated that no more pay streaks can ever again be uncovered in the old camp, therefore, be it

"Resolved, that Saturday night shall be declared a holiday, to celebrate the coming prosperity of Castle, to again use the old tables and paraphernalia found in the old building, to consult again the spots on divers pasteboard, and in other ways and means, duly have a party."

They did.

It is understood that the Brophy interests will take a lease and bond on the property and thoroughly prospect all back rooms.[8]

Out of the thousands of buildings that made up the town of Castle only a few remain: the old blacksmith shop with its hand-hewn logs, portions of stone walls that were once part of fine buildings, a few homes, drear reminders of their former elegance, and here and there holes that mark the site of caved-in wells.

---

[8] *Scobey Sentinel*, October 8, 1926.

37

COPPEROPOLIS

HALFWAY BETWEEN MARTINSDALE AND WHITE SULPHUR SPRINGS, the Electric highway swings over the divide that separates the head waters of Smith River from the North Fork of the Musselshell. Approaching from the west, one sees the hills on either side of the road pocked and pitted with innumerable prospect holes. These "gopher-holes" spill their red and yellow or oxidized black rubble, bearing witness to the energy with which prospectors dug these barren hills for copper.

Conspicuous to the left is the hoist and dump of the old Northern Pacific shaft, and immediately below it is a log cabin that marks the site of the original Copperopolis stage station. Passing this, one must look quickly backward and to the right to catch a glimpse of the deserted "new" Copperopolis whose heyday began in 1900. The town lies in a swampy depression a quarter of a mile from the road, hidden from it by intervening knolls.

The mines of Copperopolis were located by J. E. Hall and his partner, Hawkins, in 1866. They took out some very rich ore, and sent it by pack mules to the Missouri river, to be shipped to Swansea, Wales, for smelting. This was the year before the townsite of Butte was laid out to accommodate its 500 inhabitants. Hall made money on the copper he shipped. How much is a question, but enough to make him hold his claims until 1900, when he sold them for $1800.

Up to 1900 there had been plenty of prospecting, and occasional shipping of ore, but little significant development. A John Blewitt worked for a year or two in the late '90's finding rich ore. But Copperopolis was a thriving stage station and little more. In July, 1884, there was sufficient stir in Copperopolis to justify Mary Holliday in buying Eliza Scott's hotel and stage station and paying $2000 for it. . . . But the cost of hauling ore from Copperopolis was prohibitive until the "Jawbone" was built into Martinsdale.

Then, in 1900 after Marcus Daly had acquired the property, W.

W. McDowell, thirty-three years old and energetic, arrived with a bang to put Copperopolis on the map.

He was a good promoter. . . . He located a townsite and offered a fine lot in the center of town to anyone who would start building at once. By the end of October, 1900, there were five 6-horse teams hauling ore from "Copper town."

The town boomed; there were side walks using 15,000 feet of lumber and sewers, a novelty for a mining town. But a month later Marcus Daly died, and, although the work went on vigorously, ill luck dogged the copper industry. In 1901 an economic crisis in Germany cut copper exports to that country in half. The price could not be stabilized. The Daly estate was in litigation with the federal government over timber rights; the Anaconda was in a fight with Clark and Heinze, and the Amalgamated was on the verge of being outlawed by Judge Clancy's famous Minnie Healy decision. With these adverse prospects operations at Copperopolis were restricted to cleaning up the ore in sight. . . . There were three patented claims in the camp, the Northern Pacific, the Darling Fraction and one other. The deepest shaft was only 550 feet, at the Northern Pacific. Much of the ore lay "under the grass roots" and some of it ran 80 per cent copper.

The superintendent of the mines, a Mr. Gallagher, is authority for the statement that the mines yielded a quarter of a million dollars, gross, during the first nine months of operation. A total of approximately half a million dollars was taken from the mines.

With the closing of the mines in 1903, the miners scurried out of camp and the more foot-free residents followed as soon as they could adjust their affairs. Families left as soon as places were provided for them elsewhere, and the camp was dead. Two old men remained—to tramp the "15,000 feet" of deserted sidewalks—and their story is curiously sad. They were old George Dinsmore and Jack Norris, who was so invariably referred to as "Dog-eating Jack" that old-timers have to stop and think to recall his real name. Norris was not an educated man, perhaps, but he had native wit. He had been given his nickname from an incident in his earlier life, when, lost in the mountains without food, and finding no game, he killed his dog to provide himself with meat. . . . These two men, Dinsmore and Norris, for some reason became implacable enemies. For years they lived in the deserted camp, each avoiding the other, never speaking when they met by accident. Each had his own hour for going to their common spring for water, and neither trespassed on the time of the other. To their utter physical isolation they added the spiritual isolation of hatred, and died unreconciled.

There was a flare-up of excitement in 1907, when the Meagher Enterprise of May 21 announced a rich strike of copper by Ed Laundt at Red Butte, with gold-bearing ore, sapphires, rubies and what-not. But nothing came of it. . . .

The ghost camp remained comparatively unmolested until the great influx of dry landers that began in 1915. As claims were taken up in the vicinity of Red Butte, homesteaders descended eagerly upon the building materials of the old camp. They ripped up sidewalks, and ripped down log walls; they tore out window sashes and lifted doors. They did a new kind of "mining" in the camp, and neighborhood feuds started over the possession of the more handsome and substantial of McDowell's "sewers."

Farming the "Copper" hills was a sadder mistake than prospecting them for ore. The empty cabins and fallen roofs that Red Butte looks down on suggest greater finality of failure than do the caving prospect holes.[1]

---

[1] *Rocky Mountain Husbandman*, January 8, 1931.

38

MAIDEN

IN 1883 MAIDEN[1] WAS THE QUEEN OF THE JUDITH Basin. In the three years since "Skookum Joe" Anderson and Dave Jones had discovered gold in Maiden Gulch, the camp had grown until it boasted three general stores, a drugstore, a clothing store, two hardware stores, a bakery, meat market, a restaurant, a blacksmith shop, a news depot, two barbershops, a livery stable, a newspaper, and thirteen saloons. Joaquin Miller wrote glowingly of it:

> In some respects Maiden is one of the most remarkable mining camps in the world. Maiden is in the midst of, and claims for its mineral kingdom all the peaks and ridges and foothills of the Judith mountains; for nearly all of them are literally covered with vast quantities of gold float and must be intersected with numerous veins of rich ores. . . . The Judith mountains must have been, are now and must continue to be the paradise of prospectors. In many places I saw large bodies of iron ores so charged with gold as to make them most desirable fluxing ores. And above all the valleys and gulches and mountain slopes were strewn with fragments, great and small, rich in gold and silver. So abundant is the float from the veins of these mountains that it will be gathered up with great profit at no distant day.[2]

Although it was far from the beaten paths and the

---

[1] Only one explanation of the name was found, "It was called Maiden because it was so inaccessible."

[2] Joaquin Miller, *An Illustrated History of the State of Montana* (Chicago: Lewis Publishing Company, 1894), p. 706.

gleaming rails that were bringing civilization to Montana, its needs were supplied by mule and bull teams.

HOWLING BILL HITS TOWN

Bill McClain, alias "Howling Bill" was in town this week. He understands the handling of a bull team to perfection. Bill is blessed with a large pair of lungs and the echo of his "H-o-o-o" is still ringing from the hillsides.[3]

Several factors combined to give Maiden a slightly more orderly development than that of other mining camps. First of these was the date of its discovery. Being established as late as it was, it enjoyed the law and order that had so grimly been won by the vigilance committees. Now and then there might be a little trouble but nothing serious.

One fellow, under the influence of liquor, essayed to take a shot into a window of a building where Bishop Brewer was holding services but his arm was struck and the bullet deflected to the lower part of the building. When told of the incident, the good bishop remarked: "I don't think the fellow had anything against me." That was true. When not drinking he was one of the best men in the camp.

One of the bad men, at times, was Tom Newcomb, who killed a man at Deadwood, in the Black Hills. One other noted character was "Kicking George" Gantz; although a gambler, he was not a "bad man" but good natured and gentlemanly. He was a bad loser. He did not like to be bluffed on two deuces. When he roared he could be heard a block away. . . .[4]

Due credit for Maiden's order should be given to her first justice of the peace and his court.

---

[3] *Mineral Argus,* August 9, 1883.

[4] John Vrooman in the *Lewistown Daily News,* January 5, 1950.

... A quaint character, known in camp as "Pony" McPartland, was appointed Maiden's first justice in 1881 or '82. This being before our arrival in camp we do not feel able to do the jurist justice. "Pony" was all his name implies, a jolly wholehearted fellow always in for fun and ready to go "fifty-fifty" with a friend in need. He had probably spent the most of his life on the western prairies and in mining camps. His dress was that of a hunter and trapper.

When installed as justice his jurisdiction knew no bounds. When he called court to order, he would lay his revolver on the table and say, "Now, children, be good," and everyone present obeyed the injunction.[5]

One day a prominent cattleman of the area, having imbibed too much, was hailed into court for using obscene language and disturbing the peace. Since he was known to be wealthy, the court imposed a fine of $250. To this the cattleman objected, declaring that there wasn't that much money in the whole town.

"How much you got?" asked the accommodating justice. The defendant frisked himself and announced the results.

"Well," commented the judge, "we'll let it go at that, but be d——n careful it don't happen again."

Finally Maiden was given stability by the fact that for the first three years of its existence it was located on the Fort Maginnis Military Reservation. Although this protected it to a great extent from outlaws and Indians, it created problems that did not exist in other towns. Being on federal property, the citizens of Maiden could not establish title to land and, whereas other towns had claim jumpers, Maiden had to contend with

---

[5] *Scobey Sentinel*, December 30, 1921.

lot jumpers. An early-day newspaper account continues:

A fence around your holdings constituted possession, but if this evidence was allowed to deteriorate, it could be jumped. Mrs. Otto Anderson had two lots near the Frank Sage livery stable and her fencing needed repair so she asked Pat Skinner, a big, gruff Irishman, to fix it. He began, when a very dignified white man known as "Hungry Wolf" appeared with a shotgun and ordered Pat to desist, with dire but very polite threats. Pat finally let out a roar, gave a jump and, grabbing the gun, broke it and threw the pieces in the brush, while "Hungry Wolf" retreated up the gulch.

The attempts to discourage jumping, however, were carried so far as the publication in the Mineral Argus of the Vigilante committee's warning bearing the fateful signature in figures that all knew.[6]

The worst blow from Maiden's military status came in 1883 with the publication of the following directive from the post commander:

Order No. 134. In obedience to general order No. 26 from headquarters of the army, dated Washington, D. C., April 13, 1883, and subsequent instructions from headquarters department of Dakota, all persons now residing on the military reservation of Fort Maginnis, M. T., or working any mines, or prospecting for mines or carrying on any other kind of business, or who may hereafter come on said reservation, without proper authority, I hereby warn that they must leave the reservation and remove therefrom all property that they may have brought with them or acquired since coming on the reservation. Sixty days from this date will be granted for the completion of this removal herein ordered, at the end of which time those remaining without proper authority will be forcibly ejected. By order of Captain Cass Durham, F. W. Kingsbury, post adjutant.[7]

---

[6] Ibid.
[7] Ibid.

A period of feverish activity followed. Town meetings were held. Committees were appointed. Petitions were presented. With great relief and bold headlines, the *Mineral Argus* of August 30 announced:

GLORY TO GOD

Stay of the Execution of
Order No. 134 Until
Next July

The reservation was remapped so that Maiden would no longer be included.

Having saved their town, the residents of Maiden, when talk of the creation of Fergus County was started the following year, were determined to have Maiden selected as the county seat. A local committee was appointed to go to Helena to lobby for Maiden when the enacting law was framed.

But the stockmen of Judith Basin were more powerful, individually and collectively, than the miners, and Lewistown was named as county seat in the bill creating the county.

Along with all the other mining camps, Maiden declined as its ores were depleted. The great Spotted Horse mine, discovered by Skookum Joe, is a tumbled-down ruin. The town of Canyon just below the junction of the Spotted Horse and Maiden canyons has been nearly obliterated by new growth of grass and timber.

As late as 1949, however, some of the old prospectors still lurked in the mountains but found it necessary to defend the very fact of their existence as is

borne out by the following letter that appeared in the
Lewistown Daily News on February 6, 1949.

MAIDEN, MONT.
Feb. 3, 1949

DEAR EDITOR:

Even though I have lived in these parts for over half a century,
there are people around here who seem to doubt my authenticity,
just because I don't show up for a lot of social gatherings and
things like that and because I live back here in the mountains
and mind my own business most of the time.

This being the case, and because of those letters in the Daily
News showing that people are curious who I am, I have decided
to tell some of the story of my life, and send you a picture, both
of which I hope will muzzle the Doubting Thomases.

My name is Randolph R. E. L. Culpepper, and you will see what
the "R. E. L." stands for if you read on.

I was born with a silver spoon in my mouth on the Culpepper
plantation, which had been in our family since before the Revo-
lutionary War and is in Culpepper county near Culpepper Courthouse, Va., on the eastern slope of the Blue Ridge Mountains.

Robert E. Lee and Stonewall Jackson both marched through our
place many times in the War Between the States—which North-
erners call the "Civil War"—and were good friends of my father,
Jefferson Calhoun Culpepper. So when I was named, it was natural
they put in the "R. E. L.," which stands for that great general and
Southern gentleman, Robert E. Lee. The "Randolph" is for John
Randolph, of Roanoke, Va., who was a descendant of Pocahontas
and served with great honor in Congress for many years.

Even though the Yankees took our slaves away from us, my
father held things together, and we were almost as prosperous as
we were proud; so I had almost anything I wanted when a kid,
though, being independent and fiery in nature, I didn't seem to
appreciate it.

When I was 18 father took me out of Staunton Military Acad-
emy and sent me to Washington & Lee University, at Lexington,
Va.—which didn't appeal to me much, but I put up with it until
Thanksgiving vacation, when I got mixed up with a girl from a
proud family, and it seemed best that I depart from Virginia—
which I did rather hurriedly, heading for Texas.

I worked a while at a roller-skating rink in Waco, Tex., but this was too tame, so I soon went to Pecos, in western Texas, where Judge Roy Bean ruled with an iron hand from the court he set up in his saloon. But I soon got itchy feet; so tied up with a cattle outfit which was running about 1,000 head up the old Chisholm trail to the Powder river country in Wyoming, where I arrived just in time to get involved in the Johnson county war between the big cattle barons and the settlers.

This was a good war, but some of them got to taking too much of an interest in me, and I had heard about the Maiden strike in the Judith Mountains and decided it was for me.

When I was paid off by the cattle outfit, I was smart enough to save some of my money and to win some more in a poker game at Miles City on my way up here, so was flushed when I fell in with a fellow named Cuff Collar at Maiden, who had drifted in from the Neihart country.

Anyway, Cuff told me he was a prospector; so I grubstaked him, and he hit a big pocket at Bear Cave, in Spotted Horse Gulch above the Spotted Horse Mine.

In the picture I am sending you, Cuff and I are standing before Bear Cave. I am the one on the left, and by looking close I am sure a lot of these Doubting Thomases around here will recognize me and be sorry about their questioning my authenticity.

Well, Cuff took $59,000 out of that pocket and split it 50-50 with me. E. W. King, of the Gold Reef, who was later Speaker of the Montana House of Representatives, took a bond and option to buy the claim for $200,000, but it was a dud after the one pocket, so we never got anything else out of it.

Well, I had almost $30,000, which put me on my feet, but was getting itchy feet again, so went to the Klondike, which was busting wide open then; but when I got up there I heard about the strike at Kendall and came right back.

I had been pretty lucky and still had most of my money; so when I ran into Cap Darrow I let him talk me into going to Goldfield, Nev., and opening a gambling house with him, which was right next to Tex Rickard's place there. He is the fellow who later made Jack Dempsey famous.

But I didn't last long in Nevada, as there were too many rattlesnakes and women there; and before long I was broke, so drifted back to Central Montana and decided to stay away from the dig-

gin's for a while, so took a job breaking horses for the Fergus outfit for a couple of years.

Just then the Boer War broke out in South Africa, and I took a
contract furnishing horses for the British, using Miles City as my
roundup and shipping point.

It was said that Winston Churchill, who was a young war correspondent, rode one of my horses into the relief of Ladysmith.
The Boers had surrounded Ladysmith, which was a town of about
15,000 people, and almost starved them out in a six months' siege.

Anyway, I must have made $100,000 selling horses to the British,
though I never did keep much check, as Uncle Sam wasn't after
his cut so much in those days.

But all that money was my undoing, as I got to chasing pretty
girls again, and they sure skinned me for everything I had. To
keep ahead I got to gambling, and when my luck went bad I got
to drinking to forget my losses in poker. I got to be a real bum,
and it was several years before I straightened out and became a
gentleman again.

Cuff Collar had faded out of the picture years before, and I
heard that my old partner had gone over into the Little Rockies,
where they say he misjudged some dynamite and got blowed up.
Anyway, I figured I'd follow Cuff's trail over there, so did and
prospected around a bit.

For the next few years I prospected around a lot, but never
did have much luck in the Little and Big Rockies, around old Yogo
in the Little Belts, and I even got all excited about that iron ore
along the Great Northern near Stanford. I went down in the Yellowstone country for a while after agates and got quite a few, but
they were so pretty I hung onto them instead of selling, except for
a few I gave to women, and I guess I've got one of the biggest col-
lections of agates in the world today.

Along about 1930 I came back to the Judith Mountains and have
been here ever since, as it kind of seems like home to me. I haven't
had much luck since, but I have my cabin in Blind Breed Gulch,
and peace, and contentment.

Girls haven't gotten me into trouble for a long time now. I still
like them real well, but somehow I don't seem to appeal to them
no more—and maybe it is just as well.

I'm still doing a little prospecting, and it looks like I got something real good that will pay off big. I'd like to make one more

strike, as I figure that the trouble I had with that girl during the Thanksgiving vacation at Washington & Lee University during my freshman year has blowed over now, and I could go back to Virginia for a visit. I would like to see Culpepper Courthouse and the old place again, and would then be real satisfied to sit out the rest of my days in these diggings.

So this is the story of my life, and I hope those Doubting Thomases will keep their noses out of my business, after having my story like this and seeing my picture.

39

PONY
(FERGUS COUNTY)

THE SAME PONY MCPARTLAND (MCPHARTLAND IN THE following account) had his own trading post and post office in Fergus County.

Long before the present postoffice of Pony, in Madison county, was established, there was a postoffice of that name in Fergus county. Long before the present postoffice of Pony in Madison county was established, too, the postoffice which was called Pony, in Fergus county, was discontinued. The story of its establishment and of its discontinuance is a tradition among the old-timers of central Montana.

The Fergus county postoffice of Pony, was named after "Pony" McPhartland, in whose trading post it was located, and who conducted it for the convenience of his customers and the residents of the region, and not for any financial return, for, as a matter of fact, there was very little financial return.

The commission that Pony McPhartland received on the postage stamps he sold during any one year, averaged about $6, and Pony wouldn't have bothered with the postoffice even for a day for $6 if it hadn't been that the people who lived round and about needed a postoffice.

So he enacted the role of postmaster for the accommodation of his friends, nor did he set himself above his fellows because he was the sole federal official within a wide stretch of territory. Nor did he consider himself beholden to the United States government for his job.

One day a stranger rode up in front of the store, alighted from his cayuse and tied it to the hitch pole.

Pony, seated on a bench just outside the door, greeted the newcomer with the simple hospitality of the west. The fellow immediately developed an attitude of inquisitiveness, however, that jarred upon Pony's aesthetic sensibilities.

"Where's the postoffice?" he asked abruptly.

"That's it," said Pony, pointing to a five-gallon kerosene can with the top cut out of it that stood on a shelf just inside the door.

Just then a resident of the neighborhood rode up, dismounted, dropped the reins of his horse, and with a brief greeting to Pony and the stranger, stepped through the door and helped himself to the contents of the can.

He examined each letter attentively.

Outside, where sat Pony and the stranger, an ominous silence pervaded the atmosphere.

Only the man who was examining the mail spoke.

"Bud Wright's getting a letter from his wife in the east," he muttered, half to himself and half to the two who were seated just outside the door.

"It's a wonder he wouldn't go back to her and quit that Cree squaw he's taken up with," he continued. Then:

"Hm! Jim Gallagher's old father is writin' to him again. Wonder if he sent him any money.

"Hullo! Here's a letter to Paddy McGee from his lawyer in Helena. Wonder what kind of devilment Paddy's up to now."

He ran on through the pile of letters, showing an intimate knowledge of the affairs of everyone to whom a missive was addressed, and even reading all of the postal cards.

When he had finished he mounted his bronco and rode away. Neither Pony nor the stranger knew whether he had found anything for himself or whether he had taken any mail with him. It was customary for whoever got there first to take the mail to everyone who lived along his route when he started for home, without saying anything about it.

Pony, of course, knew that.

By this time the stranger probably suspected it.

Pony said afterwards he could see the man swelling little by little until he looked like he "was agoin' tuh bust."

Pony must have been doing a little swelling himself, judging from the conversation which followed.

"I am a United States postal inspector," said the stranger, trembling with rage, "and I want to know if that is the way you conduct the business of this United States postoffice."

Pony stared at him in silence. Then he arose, also in silence. The stranger arose also.

Pony, without a word, lifted the "United States postoffice" from its resting place on the shelf, and walked to the creek a few yards from the door.

"That," he said, "is the way I conduct the business of this United States postoffice and if you don't like the way I conduct the business of this United States postoffice, you and the United States postoffice can both go to h———"

With that he dropped the can, caught it on the toe of his boot and kicked it across the creek, scattering its contents far and wide.

And that is why the postoffice called Pony, Montana, is now in Madison county, instead of in Fergus county, for that was the end of Pony McPhartland's postoffice.[1]

---

[1] *Hardin Tribune Herald,* February 13, 1937.

40

KENDALL

NOT FAR FROM MAIDEN, ADOLPH HARMON LOCATED the Horse Shoe and Mule Shoe claims in 1896, and two years later J. T. Winderstein and M. L. Woodmen located the Discovery and Passaic claims.

In the same year . . . Messrs. Draper and Waldorf located a number of claims now comprising a portion of the Santiago and Kendall group. However, when they came to stake it off, they abandoned the claims on the present Kendall ground. Thus was the Kendall ground, worth millions, cast aside. Shortly after this, however, Charlie Allen located some claims, which at present are among the most valuable of the Kendall group. He gave Tom Resir a half interest for digging a ten foot hole in one of them. Tom Resir's half interest was bought for $150 cash, and a six months bond was taken on Allen's half interest for $500 by Harry T. Kendall. . . . As early as possible in 1901 the big Kendall cyanide mill was erected, and started to grind out gold bricks in the fall of the same year. The mill at present handles from 200 to 300 tons per day. The returns in dividends to the stockholders is $25,000 per month for ten months and $50,000 for two months. From the beginning of its operation until 1905 the output of the Kendall mine in bullion was $25,000,000. . . .[1]

This wealth was matched by the Barnes-King mines, and the town that grew up around these mining districts aspired to have all the advantages of a city. Several hotels were built, including the Shaules, a forty-

---

[1] Josephine Lily in the *Dillon Examiner*, May 12, 1909.

room stone structure of impressive architecture. The
Kendall Miner printed the news; two stages ran daily
to and from Lewistown; almost four hundred students were enrolled in the schools; there was a post
office; Jones' Opera House offered cultural entertainment; and two churches, Catholic and Protestant, served
the orderly little community. The completion of the
Protestant church, costing about $3,500, was an event
in Kendall.

. . . The laying of the corner stone was very picturesque and
extremely interesting to the many who witnessed it. It was a beautiful October afternoon when the exercises took place. The Sunday
School children marched to the church singing, "I am a stranger
here within a foreign land, My home is far away." After the appropriate exercises the stone was put in place and a tin box sealed in
it, which contained all sorts of things such as copies of newspapers,
money, letters, advertisements, lists of names of the Sunday school
scholars, members of the board of trustees and other things. Altogether it was a unique experience. The present Sunday school is
said to be the largest in Fergus county. It certainly is a splendid
one.[2]

As a group probably the most interesting men in Kendall were
the freighters. Freighting into Kendall was a comparatively short
and easy haul. These men were old hands at the game and could
tell of places where the work was not so easy. There was a certain
technique about handling a dozen horses or oxen. Freighting in the
old days was a dangerous and responsible job.

As I listened to one old Kendallite tell of "wheelers," "pointers"
and "jumping the chain," I became much bewildered and asked for
explanations. The old timer, gravely taking out pencil and paper,
drew a diagram, a long rectangle which, he said, represented the
wagon, and circles for the horses.

"Now," he said, "these first two horses next to the wagon were
called wheelers and the next two were pointers. Before the pointers
were the swing team and those in front were called the leads. The

---

[2] *Ibid.*

left hand lead horse was the brains of the whole outfit and, next to the leaders, the pointers had to be the best trained horses. They were at the end of the wagon tongue and, on rounding a sharp curve on the trail, they would step outside the chain, which connected the swing and lead teams to the wagon, and hold it steady while the other horses pulled it around in position."

"What if you had more than eight horses?" I asked. "I've heard you tell of 12 and 14 horse teams. What were the other teams called?"

"All the horses between the pointers and the leads were usually called swing teams," answered the old-timer.

"Makes me think of the fellow from Gilt Edge who went back to Missouri and told an old feller there that they used 12 horses on the freight teams out here. The old feller answered that he wasn't that big a fool to believe such stuff. He knew there wasn't any wagon tongue long enough for six teams of horses."

". . . Did they always use horses? I thought cattle were sometimes driven."

"Cattle were used to a great extent in the earlier days before there were many horses in the country. They were very intelligent but much slower than horses. Cattle didn't even need the jerk line, which was used on horses from the wheelers to the leads to give directions. They turned when the driver yelled 'gee' or 'haw' but one thing the cattle freighter had to be careful about was in stopping the cattle a mile or more from water. If they smelled it, they would stampede as sure as fate and run to the water, dragging their wagons behind them. . . . They used cattle a good deal at McGinnis, Maiden and Gilt Edge but the most interesting form of freighting at Fort McGinnis, I think, was with old Red river carts from Rocky point. These carts were put together without a single nail—just mortising and rawhide straps. They were two-wheeled and each cart was driven by a squaw or Indian child. The old buck just rode along on horseback to 'boss the job.' The more children an Indian had, the more freight he could haul, with one papoose to a cart."[3]

During the great years at Kendall $18,000,000 was produced by the Kendall-Maiden-Gilt Edge mines. To-

---

[3] *Great Falls Tribune*, July 14, 1935.

day there is little left at Kendall. Some of the buildings, or parts of them, still stand, but many have been removed to be used on nearby farms. The bandstand became a granary at Joe Peter's ranch and faced stone from Kendall's finest structures has gone into the foundations of many a sturdy chicken house in the Judith Basin.

41

GILT EDGE

ALSO IN THE JUDITH MOUNTAINS WAS THE TOWN OF
Gilt Edge that grew up around the Gilt Edge Mill.
There were more than fifty dwellings; the business district was three blocks long and boasted two hotels, a
restaurant, several grocery stores and clothing stores,
a livery stable, an assay office, two or three blacksmith
shops, and thirteen saloons. An up-to-date school enrolled ninety pupils.

By 1894 the financial backers of the Gilt Edge were
becoming concerned over the mine's failure to pay dividends. The manager, Robert Ammon, kept assuring
them that all was well, that the mine was producing
and the money was safely deposited in Great Falls.
However, they decided to send a young lawyer, Mess-
more Kendall, out to investigate the situation.

"I arrived in Montana in midsummer [of 1894].
"It took 24 hours in a stagecoach with six horses to go from
Great Falls to Lewistown, the county seat of Fergus county where
the Gilt Edge mine was located."
In Lewistown (Kendall) met Judge Dudley DuBose, the district
judge. Judge DuBose told Kendall Ammon had taken all the gold
from the Gilt Edge mill and was then in California. Ammon had
not paid the miners. DuBose advised Kendall to go to Gilt Edge
and await Ammon's return.
Kendall found everything at a standstill at Gilt Edge. He visited
the neighboring mining camps of Maiden and Spotted Horse; hunted

antelope; went to country dances with the daughters of Granville Stuart; killed a mountain lion; wrote a report to the Gilt Edge Mining Co., and paid off the miners with money sent from New York. While waiting for Ammon, he stayed at the Lazy Z ranch for four months and met Charles M. Russell, the cowboy artist.

In December Judge DuBose sent for Kendall and advised him that he had heard Ammon was returning in a day or so. The judge advised Kendall to try to recover the missing gold without bringing suit. Kendall agreed, but had papers prepared to serve in case Ammon failed to come through.

Ammon arrived at the Gilt Edge mill a few days before Christmas. He was extremely polite and friendly. He arrived in a buckboard which he had driven from Great Falls. While Kendall was frying venison steak and making baking powder biscuits for supper, he heard Ammon prowling through desks and cupboards in the mining company office. Kendall called him to supper.

Ammon said he had seen Judge DuBose and knew why Kendall had come to Gilt Edge. He said there was nothing to worry about; the money was in a safe-deposit box in Great Falls and they would drive there to get it. The next morning Kendall drove with Ammon to Lewistown.

Judge DuBose told Kendall privately he believed Ammon would do as promised, but advised him to be watchful. The following day was Dec. 24. About noon Kendall and Ammon started for Great Falls in the buckboard.

That night, Christmas eve, they planned to stay at the ranch where stagecoach horses were changed. About two hours out of Lewistown, a light snow began to fall and it got very cold.

Finally the snow obscured the road and the buckboard struck a chuck hole. The front axle snapped and caused the horses to run away. They ran for about a mile before Ammon got them under control. Then they tied up the broken axle as best they could and proceeded toward Great Falls. By nightfall they were hopelessly lost in Judith Basin.

Ammon wore a buffalo coat while Kendall had on a sheep-lined overcoat. They had lost one of their robes and had only a wolf skin left for covering. They made a bed in the snow with their one blanket.

Exhausted, Kendall fell asleep at once but woke up a few hours later, every bone aching. He was terribly cold and decided to get up, but a sudden lethargy seized him. Then he began to feel warm, dreaming of glowing coals. Ammon awoke and asked, "Are you cold?"

"No," Kendall replied. "Can't you feel that grate fire?"

Ammon jumped out of the bedroll, seized Kendall by the collar and tried to stand him on his feet. Kendall collapsed. Ammon then kicked him. "Get up!" he shouted.

Then Ammon ran to the buckboard and got the blacksnake whip from its socket. He tore off Kendall's overcoat and began to belabor him with the whip. It was several minutes before Kendall realized Ammon was doing his utmost to keep the young lawyer from freezing to death.

At dawn, as they were hitching the horses to the buckboard, they heard the bark of a dog and heading in the direction of the bark, found a sheepherder in his shack. Delighted to have company on Christmas day, the herder made coffee and biscuits, and fried chops from a freshly killed lamb.

By 10 a.m. the delinquent mine manager and the young attorney resumed their journey. Before they reached the next ranch, both became violently ill as the result of overeating the fresh-killed lamb. They remained at the ranch, which they reached at 11 o'clock Christmas night, for two days.

"I should like to record," Kendall wrote, "that after the saving of my life from freezing, and our horrible joint experience with the hot lamb, Ammon and I became great friends to the day of his death, but, unfortunately, such was not the case. It was soon evident to me in Great Falls that his promise to make good the company's money was not to be fulfilled. The safe-deposit box did not materialize, and in answer to my demands, he laughingly put me off. I went to every bank and found he had no safe-deposit box and no money on deposit. When I confronted him with these facts and told him the sole object of my trip to Montana was to obtain a return of the company's gold, he grinned:

" 'You write those dodos and tell them you couldn't get it.'

" 'What are you going to do?' I asked.

" 'I am off to California.'

" 'How about your promise to me that you would make good when we got to Great Falls?'

" 'Well, I had to get out of Fergus county, didn't I?' "

Before Ammon could board a train for California, Kendall had a warrant served on him and a summons in a civil suit as well.

Ammon was soon out on bail. Fearful lest he jump his small bail, Kendall pressed for trial of the civil suit. The trial resulted in a verdict for the plaintiff in the full amount owing—an empty victory, since Ammon had no seizable resources.

As Ammon left the Cascade county courthouse, he "cussed out" Kendall who was standing on the courthouse steps with another lawyer named Parks.

"Don't you talk to me like that," said Kendall, giving Ammon a push. Caught off balance, Ammon slipped and rolled down the whole flight of 20 steps. He picked himself up and fled. That night he jumped his bail. Kendall saw him no more until six years later when he encountered Ammon on Nassau street in New York city. Ammon then offered to pay in full the amount of the judgment awarded the stockholders of the Gilt Edge Mining Co., in Cascade county. But by that time the mining company was no longer in existence.

A short time later Ammon was sent to Sing Sing prison for his part in a big stock swindle.

"I have never been clear in my mind as to what part Judge Du-Bose played in the Montana career of Ammon," Kendall wrote. "After a year or so he disappeared from Montana and, I understand, about the time gold was discovered in Alaska went there where he lived the life brilliantly depicted by Rex Beach in 'The Spoilers.' "[1]

The most recent map of the Montana State Highway Commission shows Gilt Edge but does not index it as a town. In 1950 three or four of the buildings were inhabited and the old jail, in which Calamity Jane was now and then locked up to restrict her more violent outbursts, was still standing.

---

[1] *Great Falls Tribune,* Sunday morning October 29, 1950. Based on Kendall's autobiography, *Never Let Weather Interfere* (1947).

42

LANDUSKY, ZORTMAN

POWELL LANDUSKY WAS ONLY EIGHTEEN WHEN HE heaved his gear off the steamer at Fort Benton, but, even before he got out of town, he became involved in one of the incidents that were to mark his trail of violence through the territory. One day on the levee his anger was aroused by a steamer roustabout. Furiously he set upon the man and only the intervention of some of the onlookers prevented his killing his antagonist.

Arriving in Last Chance in 1864 he was soon the butt of miners' jokes because of his "greenness" and his loose-jointed, awkward body. Sometimes the teasing was good-natured, and the "Tenderfoot" grinned even as the angry color rose in his face. There was one miner, however, a cruel bully, who kept taunting the boy mercilessly, jeering at his inexperience or at his slow, slightly Southern speech. One day he sneered, "Where be ya from ennyhow, Kid?" The "Kid" had taken enough. With a vicious swing of his long arm he knocked his tormentor down. "From Pike County, Missouri, by ———," he answered. From then on he was "Pike" Landusky, a man not to be baited.

By the time of his arrival in Last Chance, most of the valuable ground had been staked, and Pike went to work for the Diamond R as a freighter. He was a good, steady worker and held the job until 1868. By that time he was seasoned in the ways of the frontier. His bony frame had filled out to the proportions of a lithe but powerful adult. He feared nothing, particularly when seized by one of his blind rages. Self-assured and competent, he decided to break with the Diamond R and launch on an independent career that would offer more freedom and, possibly, more wealth.

Forming a partnership with another soldier of fortune in the wilderness—John Wirt—he went down the Missouri river to the vicinity of the mouth of the Musselshell and engaged in trapping and wolfing. Wirt was a well known pioneer of the gold camps and in the Indian infested country of eastern central Montana. Level-headed, cool and fearless, he was quite the opposite type to the impulsive, reckless Landusky.

This new occupation furnished the youthful "Pike" with ample excitement from the very start. Hostile Sioux Indians were continuous in their raids upon the camps of white trappers and woodhawks at the mouth of the Musselshell, and trapping operations were ever attended by dangers of the most adventurous brand. By the late fall of 1868, Landusky and Wirt had accumulated fur worth more than $800 at the current prices and these they placed in a "cache" on Holly Flat, near the mouth of the Musselshell on the Missouri while they made a trip to the new town of Carroll to secure supplies. With their furs and pelts they also hid their camp outfits and most of their other possessions.

During their absence a war party of 18 Brule Sioux discovered the "cache," seized the camp outfit and cut the furs up for their own personal use as leggings, etc. Upon their return, as Landusky and Wirt approached the cache on Holly Flat, they were met by the Sioux war party. The Indians were all painted and stripped for fight, and they surrounded the trapper pair, escorting them across the river, the chief designating a place for Landusky and Wirt to camp. They were prisoners, but on their refusal to give up their guns, the matter was not vigorously pressed by the Sioux. The white men were given some buffalo meat, and Landusky cooked it for supper for himself and Wirt. As it was frying in the pan, a Sioux reached over Pike's shoulder and seized the meat for himself. Thereupon Landusky flew into one of his uncontrollable fits of passion. Seizing the heavy frying pan, he struck the Indian over the head with it, splattering him with grease. Then grabbing his gun, he poked it into the Indian's stomach and knocked him down. He then seized the Indian by the breechcloth, pulled it off and whipped him over the head and face with it. This was the worst insult he could offer an Indian warrior.

At once Wirt concluded that the end for both of them had arrived, but he resolved to die gamely; and while the fight was in progress, he stood by cool and determined, with his rifle cocked and lying over his arm. The Sioux chief rushed over and told him to make Landusky stop at once. "My young men's hearts are bad and they will kill you both," he said.

Wirt merely pointed to Landusky who was still punishing the warrior, and said "wha-sta" meaning, "It is good."

At this moment, while the Sioux were hurrying over from their camp, one of the warriors pointed to Landusky and made the sign for "crazy man." He believed (and very reasonably so) that only a man without his senses would take such chances. This explanation of "Pike's" ungovernable rage was accepted by the remainder of the Sioux; and as all plains Indians were possessed of a superstitious fear regarding a crazy person, and as it is against their medicine and religious beliefs to harm a person so afflicted, they immediately caught up their horses and fled.[1]

After this incident Pike remained a passionate enemy of the Sioux with whom he had several other encounters during the next few years while he was trapping, hunting, and woodhawking. Always his violent temper and complete fearlessness combined to rescue him from seemingly hopeless situations.

In 1880, in partnership with Joe Hamilton, he built the trading post of Lucky Fort on Flatwillow Creek with the intention of trading with the Piegans. After a particularly long and exasperating session of parley-

---

[1] *Kalispell Times*, September 23, 1920.

ing, Pike's patience began wearing thin and trouble arose with a young brave who, according to Pike, tried to stab him in the back.

. . . he knocked the young Indian down, and in the throes of one of his typical fits of rage, hurled chunks of wood at him. The Indian escaped into the brush. Immediately pandemonium broke loose. Healy made a flying run for Hamilton and Boucher, who were eating breakfast in the kitchen which was housed in a separate building. When Hamilton arrived at the store, White Calf and a subchief named Running Rabbit were coming out and he noticed that the two Indians were bleeding from cuts about the head. Pike shouted loudly and seemed transformed into a veritable demon. Joe closed the door and shouted to Pike: "Now keep that door locked and your mouth shut, and this thing will blow over in a little while."

Leaving Pike alone in the store to cool off, Healy went to the kitchen while Hamilton proceeded to try out his diplomatic powers with the Indians. He was apparently succeeding very well when White Calf appeared upon the scene and announced his intention to go to the store. Joe protested, but immediately a number of Indians picked him up bodily and carried him to a wagon that was standing between the kitchen and the creek. There they laid him down. He immediately got to his feet and fled to the kitchen.

About this time White Calf secured a small tree and started to parade up and down in front of the store. The sapling was about 12 feet long and White Calf was dragging it by the small end. Suddenly he stopped beside the door and crashed the stick through the small window which furnished light for the room.

This was evidently too much for Pike. He snatched a Winchester from the gun rack and advanced to the window which was so small that he was able to get only his head and one shoulder through. In this position, however, he opened a lively fusillade in the vicinity. He shot three times at White Calf, who ran dodging, and was not hit. At this moment, the young Indian who had been a party in the first altercation, and who had been awaiting his opportunity, shot at Pike from cover of the brush. The bullet struck Landusky on the chin, shattering the right jawbone.

Pike jumped back into the trade room, and when Healy and

Hamilton, who had heard the shooting, rushed into the post, they found Pike sitting on the floor loading his Winchester.

"Are you hurt, Pike?" asked Joe.

The answer was something that sounded like "Yes." Then both Pike and Hamilton opened fire upon the Piegans. The first shot from Pike's gun dropped an Indian and this unfortunate happened to be White Calf's squaw; but that was his last shot in this "Battle of Flatwillow" for before he could reload his weapon, another Indian bullet found a mark in his body.

"Joe, I'm gone!" he said, as he grabbed the counter for support. His companions then assisted him to a bunk. Just after this had been accomplished, Pike flew into another of his fits of rage over his condition. Clutching his mouth with his fingers, he gave a yank and then threw something hard upon the floor. It developed that he had torn from its place in his jaw, a piece of shattered bone, to which were attached four teeth.[2]

With Pike dying, the camp under siege, and the horses driven off, the situation was desperate. It was decided that Healy should try to slip through to the half-breed camp of Louis Riel, there to get help in contacting Fort Maginnis. Dangerous as this mission was, Healy carried it out. On the best army mounts he and the doctor from Fort Maginnis rushed back to see about saving Pike.

After setting the bone and dressing Pike's wounds, the army physician returned to Fort Maginnis. For ten days there was no apparent improvement; so Dr. DePalm was summoned from Reed's fort . . . Dr. DePalm decided that the jaw had been set wrong and that it would be necessary to rebreak it and set it again.

"Go ahead and break it," said Pike. "If I die, I die."

The second operation was a success . . . but his face was disfigured for life.

Upon his recovery in the spring of 1881, Landusky and Hamilton went to the new boom camp of Maiden where they opened a saloon.

---

[2] *Ibid.*

Maiden, located in the heart of the Judith mountains, was then at the zenith of its prosperity. It was here that Pike married Mrs. Descry, a widow....

With "Dutch" Louis and Frank Aldrich, Pike went to the Little Rockies in July of 1884. They prospected for gold and located some placer leads in the bed of a creek that they named Alder. A mining district was organized, and the stampede which followed took more than 2,000 men to the various gulches of the Little Rockies. Eli Shelton, a negro, found the heaviest gold on a high rim and William Skillen uncovered the biggest nugget, weighing $83....

The mining camp for Landusky, the center of a wild and lawless border country perhaps without equal, during its time, at any place on the continent, far removed from the more civilized sections of the territory, was the rendezvous of a number of real "bad men."[3]

Of these bad men none was to have a more evil reputation than the Curry boys who lived on a wild and isolated ranch not far from Landusky. Pike's last and fatal feud was with the Curry gang. One version of the Curry-Landusky trouble attributes the original difficulty to the thwarted romance between one of Pike's foster daughters and Loney, brother of "The Kid" Curry. Loney had fallen in love with the girl, but Pike had forbidden her associating with one of such unsavory reputation. Shortly after this, the Kid was arrested for changing a brand and was left in charge of Pike who, according to the Kid's accusations, brutally mistreated him while he was handcuffed. On his release the Kid swore he would get even with Pike.

The robust life of the town went on but with a growing tension.

---

[3] *Ibid.*

Along in November somebody suggested the camp ought to have a big community dance and dinner at Christmas time. So much favor this suggestion met that a big town meeting was held, where it was planned that the camp should let the world know it was a going concern and that the event should be the biggest social function the country had ever known. Everybody subscribed liberally so there would be nothing lacking. Then Warren Berry got up at the meeting and said they should have something extraordinary on the menu, that pigs and turkeys and chickens and baked hams were not novelties—there ought to be something folks would go home and talk about all winter. When asked what he would suggest, Warren said, oysters. Fresh oysters, not the old stereotyped, canned cove kind but the massive old juicy Baltimore selects. So oysters it was and when the committee left it to Warren as to how many should be ordered he said four dozen quarts ought to be enough and four dozen quarts it was. Orders were given to "Lousy" the stage driver, to wire for them when he went to the railroad. Lousy had never bought any but cove oysters before so he wired to Minneapolis for them, thinking the oyster beds were at the foot of the falls of Minnehaha. The express on them was more than the original cost of the oysters.

From that time until the big day the camp was all feverish activity. The big time was all the topic of conversation and fully a barrel of bourbon was licked up in considering details and devising new features. Word had gone over all that sparsely settled country that Landusky was entertaining; they all heard it and they all came. And such people they were! They drifted in from the badlands 60 miles away, from grassy valleys in the foothills, from the alkali flats farther out, from remote places in the river breaks and from the gulches of far reaches of the mountains. They came in all the vehicles that were known to the time and they brought food enough to feed the multitude in the wilderness, those who didn't get a break on the loaves and fishes.

There were more than 100, the biggest crowd of white folks that country had ever assembled. Everything was the best in the land, but the great achievement of it all was the four dozen quarts of oysters. It wouldn't do to let a novice monkey with these bivalves, they had to be prepared and served by a chef who knew how. So "Tie Up George" the most famous of all roundup cooks, was drafted into service and warned not to get cocked up until the feed was over. The writer's handsome new long bungalow, just completed, was donated for the preparation and serving of the evening and midnight meals; Johnnie Curry, second of the Curry brothers trio, loaned his big new barn for the dance, while Loney Curry, a fiddler of no mean ability, volunteered to lead the home talent orchestra. No such thing as a piano was known in the country, but some folks on a ranch out 10 miles had one of those little organs. A dead ax wagon was sent out to borrow the organ, and everything looked jake.

It was a real old time frontier jamboree. For two days and nights they danced and ate, kept the drinking right up with the procession, and the harsh bark of the six-gun was heard many times, but it was all in good humor, and noise was a part of the show. "Tie Up" made a masterpiece of culinary art of his oyster stew. They liked it so well that, after they had eaten one generous wash boiler of it, he made a second—and George wanted to make a third—but one gets enough even of oysters, to say nothing of four dozen quarts of them. Ranchers and stockmen stayed in town to enjoy the show. It was an outing for all hands, and folks then were not in such a hurry as they are now. . . .

Yet there was a tenseness through all of this apparent gaiety that seemed to forebode a tragic ending. When the gun fighters first came to town they all discarded their guns for the time being. If they wanted to wake the echoes for a moment they'd borrow a gun from the barkeep and have at it. The day following Christmas, in the evening, they all rearmed and everybody clung close to his arsenal. Every man there was watching, he didn't know just what for! The second morning after Christmas, Dec. 27, it came—as all had known it would come eventually.

A light fall of snow brought a chill to the air and the dreariness of the day encouraged the drinking men to hang close to the saloons. Jew Jake's place[4] had the smallest crowd of all. About 10:30 in the morning Pike and a friend dropped into Jake's to have a drink. There were seven or eight other men in the house including Jake and his gunman, Hogan. Just before Pike entered, Loney Curry and Jim Thornhill came in but had passed on to the little trade counter at the rear of the room, where they engaged Hogan in conversation.

---

[4] Jew Jake was one of the most sinister characters in Landusky. He had lost a leg during his long criminal career and customarily used his Winchester as a crutch.

Pike was in the saloon less than three minutes and was in the act of filling his whiskey glass when Kid Curry came in. The Kid walked up directly beside Pike, gave him a good stiff slap on the shoulder and, as Pike looked to see who it was, Curry landed a terrific blow on his jaw, knocking him down. . . .

As soon as Pike fell, Curry was down on top of him with his knees on Pike's arms, holding them to the floor while he began to beat him without mercy. . . .

When the Kid finally finished Pike was a pitiful sight. The entire left side of his face and most of the rest of the face, and his head as well, had been beaten until they looked almost like a black eye. It seems, though . . . that a new spirit of fight came back into the old battler, for when he was finally allowed to get up—he came with a gun—. . . . So quickly did he draw and hold his gun on the Kid, that, for a moment, Curry stood and hesitated.

The drawing of that gun, however, was another bit of hard luck for Pike. . . . It was one of the new fangled automatics that had just come out at that time, and either Pike didn't know how to use it or it went wrong. . . . Anyway, it didn't work. The Kid found himself in a moment, drew his .45 and it was all over. He shot Pike twice in the body—and missed the third time—and Pike battled no more. . . .

Pike is buried on his old ranch holdings a mile down the valley from Landusky town. Just the place where he should lie and contemplate the changes as they come to a land with the passing of the years.[5]

Zortman, founded by Pike's friend, Pete Zortman, drew its wealth from the great Ruby Gulch Mine. The power plant for the mine and the town, when running at full capacity, burned seventy tons of coal every twenty-four hours. This energy was supplemented by wood and water, the latter coming from hot springs at the base of Morrison Butte. Large wooden pipes, bound with wire, carried the water to the power plant a mile away. There it flowed over a huge water wheel

---

[5] John B. Ritch in the *Great Falls Tribune*, January 20, 1935.

to help the wood burners produce the electricity needed by the Ruby Gulch Mine operations.

The town was a lively one; the stagecoach made almost daily trips to Malta during the time that the Ruby Gulch Mine poured out an estimated five million in gold. When the gold was exhausted, the state's first cyanide mill operated for several years two miles below Zortman. It was destroyed by fire and the charred ruins can still be seen.

43

YOGO

IN 1879 TWO BUCHANAN BROTHERS WERE PROSPECTING ON YOGO creek and panned out gold in paying quantities at this point. News of their discovery soon reached the outside and as early in the spring of 1880 as the melting snows would allow, prospectors began coming into Yogo, most of them from Fort Benton and Billings. The trail to Yogo was marked by a board sign near the top of the hill and some wit wrote with chalk under the word Yogo—"Nogo." This really proved true, as Yogo was a No-go.

Near the foot of Yogo hill the rocks came so close together that the passage was not large enough to permit a horse and wagon to get through. A man by the name of Hawkins blasted enough rock away to make a larger passage and then charged toll, from which the name Toll Gate hill was derived. It is known that way today.

The first postoffice in this section of the country was established at Old Yogo in 1879-80, the mail being carried at that time on horseback between the towns of Fort Benton and Billings.

The summer of 1880 saw Yogo creek alive with prospectors, all hunting for the vein or lead of gold from which the small nuggets and dust must come that was daily being panned out.

Several log buildings were built to house a store, postoffice, saloon and boarding house. But the town of Yogo was doomed to live but a short time as, when no lead was found, most of the prospectors drifted to other fields. . . .

In the rush from Fort Benton were several negroes, one of them being Joe Selby, who did the barbering for the camp.

Another negro character familiar to all the pioneers of this section was an old woman, Aunt Milly Ringo, who came to Fort Benton from Parksville, Mo. with Dr. Ringo and family. She was one of the first to arrive in Old Yogo and the last to leave. She kept a boarding house for the miners and even after the town was deserted would keep a long table set with white linen and shining silver that she might be ready when they came. For Aunt Milly had faith that gold would be found and that some day a big boom would come to Old Yogo. She also did prospecting and was always locating claims which she named for our presidents or other noted men. She added log rooms one after another to her long house. But old age and rheumatism crippled Aunt Millie until she became a county charge and she was finally taken to Great Falls for medical care, but she pined for her home in the mountains and they let her go home where she died in the summer of 1916. Her funeral services were conducted in Utica and were attended by a large number of her friends. Rev. Hammer, known as the cowboy preacher, conducted the services. . . .

As far as prospecting is concerned, the Yogo field has never been quite deserted. . . . Besides gold, silver and copper have also been found but never in large quantities. But many old timers and prospectors feel that some day a rich vein or lead will be discovered and that the town of Old Yogo will be born again.[1]

With the Buchanan brothers when they discovered gold in Yogo Creek was Jake Hoover, "Lucky Boy" of the Montana gold fields. At sixteen he had arrived in Montana from Iowa and, in spite of his "tenderfoot" standing, began having phenomenal luck finding gold. In the Gold Creek area he discovered the Tenderfoot Bar; in the vicinity of Pikes Peak Gulch he panned gold from the dirt and gravel of the cabin floor.

At this last site his friend Rich, having heard of Jake's luck, had asked him to help locate gold on a claim. Arriving at the friend's cabin in the winter Hoover

. . . went out and cut poles for his bunk, and proceeded to put it together. In the dirt floor he excavated holes for the outer posts for the bunk, and as he dug out the gravel he scrutinized it carefully and finally put it all in a couple of gold pans. Then he went out

---

[1] *Rocky Mountain Husbandman*, August 8, 1929.

and got three or four good sized boulders from the channel of the creek and put them in the fire which was blazing in the fireplace.

"What's that for?" inquired Rich.

"Wait and see," replied Hoover. "I've seen worse looking gravel than this, and I'm going to wash it."

"There isn't any water, and you will have to wait until morning to chop a hole in the ice," said Rich, "and, anyway, who ever heard of prospecting in a cabin? The colors I found last fall were half a mile below here."

But Hoover went right ahead with his preparations, saying nothing. He found a wooden tub and filled it full of snow. Then he raked out the hot boulders and put them in the tub. After adding snow several times he soon had a tub full of water. Then he took one of the pans of gravel that came from where his bed posts stood and began washing them out in the tub. When the pan had been washed down by Hoover's skillful hands, it yielded dust that weighed out $1.70 in gold.

Rich, who had never seen so rich a strike, was wild with excitement and joy.

"What are our workings worth, Jake?" he inquired.

"Well," said Jake, who had made too many big strikes to get stirred up over this one, "I should say these upper claims would sell tomorrow for [$]100,000."[2]

But Jake was as unlucky in business and love as he was lucky in finding gold. He sold his bonanza on Gold Creek for a paltry sum; his friend Rich beat him out of the Pikes Peak Gulch strike, and Jake moved on to the Judith Basin.

One day in early summer he saddled up his best horse and packed another one for a long trip, for he intended to journey over to the Helena country to look for a lead he had once run across in early days when quartz mining was often too expensive a process to be profitable and the prospector preferred a placer strike. In the afternoon he crossed Yogo creek, which is the north fork of the Judith, and the weather had turned so cold that he decided to camp for

---

[2] *Hardin Tribune*, March 11, 1921.

the night in an old log cabin. The next morning it was fine and warm again, and Jake felt that he should get an early start and push on while the weather was good. But somehow he had a "hunch" to do some prospecting along the creek, his instinct telling him that, because there were a great many gulches running out into the creek in that vicinity, he was likely to find gold that came from some of them. So he took his pan and started to wash gravel along the rims.

The first few pans yielded nothing but a stray color or two, and he was just about to quit and make another start on his journey, when his eye was attracted by some small blue pebbles, smooth and transparent, in the tailings of his pan. He picked them out and tried another pan, getting some more and finding one bigger than the others. A dozen pans of earth yielded a considerable number of blue pebbles. He changed his plans right there for his prospecting trip and rode twenty miles to Utica to the ranch of S. S. Hobson, with whom he was to be associated by agreement in any strikes that he made, Hobson furnishing the money for development.

"What have you there?" inquired Hobson, when Jake handed him the blue pebbles.

"I believe they're sapphires," replied Jake.

Hobson said he was just leaving for Helena, and that he would take them to a lapidarian and find out what they were. Two days later in Helena, a Swiss gem cutter told Hobson that they were fine sapphires, of a quality equal to the best oriental stones. Thereupon Hobson returned and the celebrated sapphire lead was soon located and staked.[3]

Jake's luck pursued him. Within a year he had become involved in financial difficulties and, worse than that, in serious matrimonial troubles. His wife had a violent temper and frequently threatened to kill him. Twice she shot at him and nothing but luck saved his life. He decided that it was time to leave his wife and likewise the country. He sold all his interests, including his interest in the sapphire mines, for $5000 and left for Alaska. His wife followed his trail, even into the wilds of Alaska, but Jake managed to keep a few jumps ahead, and finally she returned to the United States.

---

[3] *Ibid.* Another version of the discovery of Yogo sapphires maintains that Frank Hobson had a schoolteacher friend in Maine who asked him to send her some samples of gold-bearing sand so that she could show it to her pupils. With the sand he sent her some of the pretty blue pebbles that were numerous in the area. When she wrote to thank him, her praise was mostly for the sapphires which he, until then, had not realized to be precious stones.

Later she married a Montana rancher, who eventually shot her dead while she was trying to kill him with a gun.[4]

Today Jake and the gold of Yogo are almost forgotten; a few prospect holes dot the hills, and a few old-timers still believe that the real wealth is in gold. Meanwhile, the area where Jake found blue pebbles has come to be considered the most important gem locality in the United States. Perfect cornflower blue stones weighing up to 110 carats have been found, and the British company that at first controlled the mines has taken out between $20,000,000 and $30,000,000. Yogo, no longer No-go, is the only place in the world where sapphires are found in vein formation, and of this vein only a fraction has been worked up to the present time.

---

[4] *Ibid.*

44

GOLD BUTTE

THE RICH VEINS, THE REAL BONANZAS, OCCURRED MUCH less frequently in northern Montana than in the south. However, in 1885, one important strike was made near the Canadian border in the Sweet Grass Hills. As late as 1942, Jack Monroe, a pioneer of the stampede to the Sweet Grass Hills, still lived in the region.

Born in what is now the state of Wyoming, then a part of Utah territory, Monroe says that his exact age is not known. His parents were Chicagoans, his father a driver for the famed pony express.

When he was sixteen, Jack Monroe was taking a man's place in the world. Because he was small and took a great interest in horses, he naturally took to the race tracks and became a jockey.

With weight a costly premium, the race horse owners did everything possible to keep down Monroe's weight. They encouraged him to chew tobacco in the belief that this would help stunt his growth, and in the event of a close race ahead, where every pound was a handicap, the horsemen sweated off the weight by burying the jockey up to his neck in a compost pile.

It was in 1885 that Monroe went to the Blackfeet reservation. It was the preceding year that Rodney Barnes made the strike in the Sweet Grass hills that drew the attention of gold seekers.

According to Monroe, Barnes dug out $125,000 worth of the precious yellow metal and fully that much more, in the opinion of the old timer, passed through the banks. All this was placer gold and to date all efforts to locate the mother lode have been futile, but Monroe still prospects in the hills with the everlasting hope that he will some day uncover the long-sought vein.

Gold Butte today is a lingering ghost town wrapped in the memories of a half century back, slumbering amid the pitted hills that once meant a prosperous village. It was in 1886 when Monroe first saw the booming gold camp whose chief distinctions were the number of lusty, brawling miners and the numerous saloons.

. . . Battering fights were everyday occurrences and gunplay settled many an issue. Monroe says he lays claim to some distinction or the other in that he helped start the graveyard—Boot Hill—at Gold Butte in assisting with the burial rites of a man who had been murdered.[1]

Besides gold there were important copper deposits in the country; the Brown-eyed Queen produced rich ore for several years, and, after she shut down, an enterprising resident recovered $500 to $700 worth of copper from the tailings at the mine.

Monroe always believed that there were rich uranium deposits also. In numerous places throughout the hills were spots where the snow never lay for very long. Cattle would gather here, grazing and enjoying the warmth from the earth. According to Monroe, whose opinion was backed by scientists who investigated the area, such conditions indicated uranium wealth.

Today the gold and copper mining is no longer profitable; the uranium deposits have not been found or exploited, but the earth has yielded up another source of vast wealth. Petroleum, discovered in the Cut Bank fields in 1929, has since then yielded over $150,000,000, hundreds of times more than the gold of Gold Butte.

---

[1] *Mineral Independent* (Superior), August 6, 1942.

45

LOST MINES AND BURIED TREASURE

NO GOLD-RICH REGION IN THE WORLD HAS BEEN WITH-
out its tales of lost mines and buried treasure. Generally, these stories belong to no particular camp unless,
like the Beartown Chinaman's baking powder can of
gold or Beastly Butler's hoard in Red Mountain City,
the treasure is supposedly buried in some particular
town. They are, rather, repeated around campfires and
in saloons of the entire area, rumors spread by the
nomadic prospectors as they follow first one stampede
and then another.

In the area around Gold Creek, Pioneer, and New
Chicago the most talked of lost mine was the Springer,
or Deadman, Lode. Old man Springer was a lone operator; he had no partners and no confidants. His
life was spent roaming the hills in his search, and,
when he died, he left a legacy of mystery that has
kept many others wandering those hills that finally
rewarded his quest. When he came to town with a
little dust he spent all of it in a wild drinking spree
and often had to be grubstaked for his next try. One
day he came to Deer Lodge with about a pound of
reddish quartz tied in his old bandana. He and an
acquaintance pounded the rotten rock in an old iron
mortar, then began panning. The little bit of quartz
yielded about a tablespoon of clean, coarse gold which

Springer promptly spent on a rip-snorting drunk. When he sobered up, his friend, Sam Scott, tried to persuade him to reveal the source of his rich find. At first suspicious, he refused but finally admitted that, while digging a prospect hole on Bagg's Creek, which is the north branch of Cottonwood Creek, he had found the gold-bearing quartz. Throwing his tools into the hole he had hurried to town to pan out his find.

The next Sunday the two started for Bagg's Creek; while Sam fished, Springer picked up two old tomato cans and went off to bring back more of the quartz. His two cans yielded three ounces of gold, and when Sam asked him if he had staked his claim, he replied, "Not yit. But it's safe enough; nobody'll ever find it." (Nobody ever has.)

From that day Springer was a marked man. He was shadowed constantly by those seeking to follow him to his treasure; knowing his weakness, many generously bought him drinks hoping to loosen his tongue. Neither scheme worked. The old man always succeeded in eluding his spies and never got drunk enough to reveal his secret. On his last trip to Deer Lodge he had a handful of beautiful nuggets and implied that he had struck the mother lode.

Again, after his usual spree, he slipped away, and a few days later another prospector came across his body lying in the trail near his cabin. Apparently he had died of natural causes, but a peculiar old vest that he invariably wore was missing. This gave rise to the suspicion that he may have been killed and the vest, heavy with gold, stolen. However that may be, he took with him to the grave the secret of the Springer, or Deadmans, Lode.[1]

Since then countless people have sought the mine; several times swindlers, claiming to have discovered it, have fleeced the unwary. In 1934 a trio armed with a "doodle-bug" which could locate gold as unerringly as a divining rod can locate water, was sure they could find the vein. Although the location is fairly specific, Springer's gold has never been discovered.

The glamor of romance still hangs around the cabin reputed to have been built over a rich vein of gold ore in the Big Horn mountains in the summer of 1863. It is one of the unsolved mystery classics of the mining world of the northwest. Of the four men who made the remarkable discovery, three were killed in an attack by Indians and one escaped to tell his story. He gave his name as Thompson and forgot to reveal the name of his associates.

Thompson's subsequent arrival at Alder gulch set that camp afire with the tale of the wonderful discovery he and his companions had made. He described the find as being that of a ledge of quartz several feet in width with streaks of pure gold running through it averaging from one to seven inches wide. It was a marvelous tale. If the public mind in Alder gulch had not been in a feverish state on account of the vast quantities of gold then being taken from the placer mines there, Thompson's recital might have been questioned. As it was no one doubted it, for he exhibited several ragged chunks of gold that had the appearance of being broken from a mass of glittering metal.

Describing his experience, Thompson said that he and his three companions, wandering in the foothills of the Big Horns and eager to make their way to the higher altitudes, took little notice of occasional bands of Indians stalking buffalo on the plains and in the grass-covered valleys. They were not aware that the Sioux had laid claim to the country by treaty arrangements with the government,

---

[1] According to the *Helena Daily Herald* at the time of Springer's death, the man's name was Thos. O. Spring (not Springer) and he was not being shadowed by those who coveted his wealth. He simply died of a heart attack while on his way to his claim with two friends.

having been driven westward ahead of the advancing columns of settlers that were pouring across the Mississippi and Missouri rivers. They did not know of the jealousies excited in the minds of the savages at the presence of white men in a forbidden country.

Reaching a point somewhere near the Montana-Wyoming line the travelers were attracted to an outcropping of quartz. On closer examination they were agreeably surprised to discover the streak of yellow metal that ran through it. They had reached the end of their journey and proceeded to build a cabin. It was set immediately over the ledge of quartz. A sense of security followed together with that of a collective appreciation that they were living over something of untold value to them. All thoughts of a lurking enemy in their vicinity was [were] abandoned. The men gave themselves over to the enjoyment of their great find.

Without warning one afternoon several hours before sundown, while the men were at work digging the precious metal from the ledge, a fusilade of arrows and a spattering of bullets struck with fatal effect upon the group of busy men. Within a short time three of them lay dead. Thompson said that owing to the position he occupied, somewhat below the ledge and protected, he was able to drop down the slope and make his way along the mountainside to safety. The Indians lingered over the tragic scene. Whether they took the scalps of the three dead men he did not know. In his haste he moved as far away as possible during the remaining hours of daylight, got into the foothills, followed a stream down into the plains country and with no heart to return, found his way to Alder gulch.

The camp went wild upon hearing Thompson's story. One hundred men stood ready and anxious to follow Thompson to the spot if only he would lead them. But Thompson was not ready to return. The hours of fear and the moments of peril through which he had just passed served as a deterrent; he wanted to go to California. He promised that upon his return he would act as guide to such as would go with him. He exacted an understanding, to which assent was given, that he was to have a certain number of feet on the ledge at each side of the cabin that stood right on top of the exposure.

A few of the excited placer miners in Alder gulch did not want to wait for Thompson's return. They urged him to describe the locality and promised to protect him in his right, the same as if he went along. Thompson would give no information beyond a vague statement that the cabin and the ledge of gold were in the Big Horn mountains.

A few days later Thompson set out for California. That was the last seen of him in Alder gulch. Nothing more was heard of him and it was supposed he was killed by road agents. A report to that effect came back to Virginia City a few weeks after his departure. In the meantime the gold ledge somewhere in the Big Horns had not been forgotten. In fact, it became the general topic of conversation wherever a group of miners gathered. When the news of Thompson's death came to Virginia City a few of the most enthusiastic miners determined to make the trip to the Big Horn country and conduct a search for the treasure deposit. They found nothing. Other parties outfitted and came back empty-handed.

The story of the cabin and the ledge was one that could not be dismissed from the minds of the miners. The searchers kept in mind the fact that the cabin stood right over the treasure, and to find the cabin was equivalent to finding the gold. With the constant effort made to locate the property it came to be referred to as the search for the "lost cabin."

When the Alder gulch placers began to yield less of the precious metal and were pretty well "worked out," a member of the first group that went in search of the cabin from Alder gulch went up to Last Chance, and finally drifted out to California. He was in that state for several years when in company of a friend he went to visit the state lunatic asylum. That was in the winter of 1881-1882. In going through one of the wards his attention was called to a peculiar case in charge of the attendant, who was also his guide through the institution. The inmate was occupying all his time drawing maps, or diagrams, on the walls and floor of his cell. They depicted a mountainous country with a river running through from the south.

A small stream emptied into the larger river in about the center of the map. From a point at the junction of the two streams a line was drawn due south to a peak marked "three miles." The line then continued in a zigzag direction to the south. At the extreme end of the line appeared a circle in the center of which was drawn a cross.

The warden stated that he often had questioned the patient as to the meaning of the map with the idea in mind of getting to the cause of his mental affliction. The patient's only answer was a smile.

Then he would go on with his map making. The visiting miner from Montana took another look at the patient. He seemed to recall, after three years, that he remembered him as having been in Alder gulch. He recognized him as Thompson.

In a lucid interval Thompson had told his story. On going from Montana to California he had lost all of his money and was taken ill with a fever. When he became well enough to leave his room he found that his mind had become unsettled. While not absolutely crazy, he fretted over his condition and was unable to work for many months. At times he would rave about gold mining and a rich mine that he had discovered. He tried to borrow money to go back to the Big Horns. He said, according to the story told by the warden, there was gold enough in the ledge to enrich the world. He made other statements that to a stranger only served as evidence of Thompson's insanity. Finally in 1878 Thompson was examined, adjudged insane and sent to the asylum.

Stepping back to his cell, the warden asked Thompson about his maps again. He seemed to be willing to talk about other matters, but remained reticent about his map making. Questions were put to him in an effort to get a clue to an interpretation of the diagram. Finally the visitor put his finger on the circle on the map and suddenly interrogated:

"Is that gold?"

Thompson sprang at him in a rage, and it was with some difficulty that he was quieted. One of the physicians was interviewed. He knew much of the patient's case. He was impressed with Thompson's condition and held little doubt of the existence of the gold deposit and felt that Thompson, if properly handled, could lead a party to it. The doctor said that Thompson had lucid intervals when his mind functioned in a perfectly normal manner. It was agreed that when he was rational another visit would be made to him.

In a rational mood Thompson appealed for release from the asylum. The doctor offered to secure his freedom immediately if he would show him the way to "that point," indicating it with his finger on the cross in the center of the circle on the map.

Thompson hesitated for a moment. Presently he consented. Freedom was what he wanted. Certification was made as to his cure and his discharge soon followed. An immediate start was made for Montana with the intention of proceeding at once to the Big Horns for the purpose of searching for the treasure deposit.

The party reached Dillon on June 3, 1882. They took a stage to Virginia City where they outfitted, ostensibly for a trip into the Yellowstone national park. After a few days spent there the party was well on its way to the Big Horns where Thompson said the gold mine with the cabin built over it was located. Three more days were spent in reaching the mountains. They traveled up the range toward the south. Up to the 15th of June Thompson had acted in a rational manner. There were four in the party. The doctor, an asylum attendant and the former Alder gulch placer miner, besides Thompson. The guide said that they would be able to reach the gold deposit on the 16th, the day following. Wild with excitement and nervous with anticipations of coming in sight of a new Golconda the party went into night camp in a wild place a few miles from a river. All slept soundly except Thompson. When the morning of the 16th broke, it was discovered that Thompson was gone. It was feared that the excitement of the day before had brought on insanity and that he had wandered into the mountains. The party hunted for him for three days. His body was found at the foot of a cliff over which he had fallen.

The subsequent search was hopeless. The party turned back, the doctor and his attendant went on to Miles City, while the former Alder gulch placer miner went to Helena, where he told the story of his effort to find the Lost Cabin Mine. It was felt, he said, that further search for the cabin without Thompson would result in nothing, for there are more than a hundred localities in the Big Horn mountains that would fill the description given by Thompson.[2]

Montana's other Lost Cabin mine is somewhere on Willow Creek, a tributary to the South Fork of the Flathead River. At about the time gold was discovered in California, a group of Hudson's Bay trappers, guided by a Flathead Indian, made a rich strike on Willow Creek. They dug prospect holes and whipsawed lumber for sluice boxes. The cleanup exceeded anything they had ever seen, and they collected the gold until

<hr>

[2] "Mon Tana Lou" Grill in the *Roundup Tribune*, November 22, 1928. This version differs widely from one recently published by J. Frank Dobie.

water froze and ended their washing. Building a trim cabin they spent the winter at the site; in the spring, after gathering more of their precious dust, they began making preparations to return to civilization. Now the days were warm and the nights cold; water poured down the mountain from the melting snows. One day, when the preparations were almost complete, the whole mountainside, loosened by the action of frost and water, slipped down in a thunder of rock and debris. The cabin and all its occupants, except the Flathead Indian, who had been out foraging, were buried in the slide. The Indian guide made his way to the head of transportation of the Missouri and told his tale of the Lost Cabin mine of the Flathead.

Years later an elk hunter stumbled onto decaying sluice boxes that were almost covered by debris and earth deposited by the spring freshets. The lumber bore the marks of ax and saw. These may have been the trappers' diggings, but their lode was never found.

The lost mines of the Little Rockies are numerous, and all involve the imperturbable Indian. Outstanding among them is the legend of the Lost Keyes Mine, talk of Montana gold camps in the sixties. Keyes' background before he came to Montana is as much a mystery as his lost mine, but in 1864 he and John Lepley were the first to discover gold on Silver Creek and were the founders of Silver City. Keyes became dissatisfied with the claims at Silver City and, packing his horse, started out for richer ground.

Not long afterward he appeared in Fort Benton and outfitted for a trip down the Missouri River. The following spring, in 1865, he returned to Fort Benton, and either wrote a letter to Lepley at Silver City or went there to see him, begging him to drop his mining on Silver Creek and go with Keyes to a gold placer diggings he had found that was extraordinarily rich. . . .

Keyes returned to Fort Benton, or remained there to receive a reply to his letter, and finally becoming impatient, set out down the river with another man, whose name is believed to have been Sam Hooper. Each of the men had an Indian woman of the Gros Ventre tribe. Neither ever returned to Fort Benton and it was learned later that both men were killed by Indians in the vicinity of Rocky Point. One of the squaws was also killed and the other lived, it is said, till a few years ago, on the Fort Belknap reservation. It was through this Indian woman that the fate of Keyes and Hooper later became known.

When Keyes returned to Fort Benton in the spring of 1865, he was very secretive about his affairs, but had plenty of gold dust to make all necessary purchases, and to one or two persons whom he tried to interest in his gold mine, he showed a sack of considerable size filled with the dust. He did not give anyone the slightest information concerning the mine or its whereabouts, and when he left Fort Benton the last time with Hooper and the two squaws, the whole matter was surrounded by mystery.

With news of the killing of Keyes and Hooper, interest immediately was aroused in the whereabouts of his rich gold mine and many trappers on the Missouri began to search for it, but in vain. Keyes former partner, Lepley, always held to the belief that Keyes had struck a bonanza, but he was as much mystified concerning its whereabouts as anyone.[3]

Granville Stuart did not agree that Keyes had found a rich lode. A party of miners from Idaho, carrying with them $25,000 in dust and nuggets, stopped at the Stuarts' en route to the States. On their way down the Missouri they were ambushed by Sioux, all were killed and their gold, of no value to the Indians, was dumped out on a sand bar. This, believed Stuart, was

---

[3] *Bynum Herald*, April 11, 1921.

the gold Keyes found. There is, however, an irrecon-
cilible discrepancy in the date of this expedition, 1871,
and the disappearance of Keyes.

Those who, through deductive reasoning, concluded
that the mine must be near the mouth of the Musselshell abandoned hope of finding it when the Fort Peck
dam backed up the water to cover the probable site.

Someone of those who reject both the Stuart theory
and the Musselshell theory may still solve the mystery
of the legendary wealth of the Lost Keyes Mine.

One of the most ludicrous stampedes in Montana's
history occurred in 1895 as a result of the supposed
finding of the Lost Keyes Mine.

Each spring for twelve years preceding the stampede
a tall, buckskin-clad prospector named Alexander would
arrive in one of the small settlements in northeastern
Montana. He would outfit for a prospecting trip, then
disappear into the Bad Lands where he was convinced
the Keyes mine was to be found. In the fall he would
show up again, taciturnly sit out the winter and try
again the next spring.

The spring of 1895 found him camped on Big Dry
Creek to which he had been directed by a dream. In
the dream a beautiful Indian maiden had appeared to
him, whispered, "Two more sleeps,"[4] and vanished.

The second day on the Big Dry he found an old rubber boot and a piece of plank with a cleat nailed to it.
He paid little attention to his find and continued his
panning which was yielding a little color. A cowboy

---

[4] The instruction, "Two more sleeps," was woven into some versions of the
Lost Keyes Mine story.

wandering by was impressed with the showing and rushed to Glasgow to record a claim.

Alexander, realizing that he had not recorded a claim, rushed after him. This was enough to start the rumor that the Keyes mine had at last been found.

From all directions, men on foot, carrying their blankets on their backs, or leading a pack horse with their outfit, others on horseback driving a pack train, four-horse teams hauling lumber and merchandise, men in buggies, buckboards and descending the river in boats, or on log rafts. And one Red River cart drawn by a mule and a cow. All impelled by the magic power of imagination and moving into the Bad Lands in the general direction of Big Dry creek, but converging on a point where an old rubber boot, a rotten piece of plank and three microscopic particles of gold had been found. . . .

The barren country along the bed of Big Dry creek was, for a time, the scene of great activity, which was named Alexander City. Alexander City was destined to become the metropolis of a vast mining region, and its broad streets and avenues extended for miles into the Bad Lands and the imagination of the real estate man.

One tent in Alexander City was used as a shrine, and the sacred relics were kept there on exhibition. When new arrivals reached the city, they were led to the shrine and allowed to gaze in awed silence upon the old rubber boot . . . and the rotten piece of plank.

A number of prospect holes were sunk to bed-rock along the creek, but nothing like pay gravel was found. . . .

Some men are from Missouri, others are born with a questioning or scientific mind. . . . One of these cold-blooded skeptics stood looking at the sacred relics. He picked up the piece of plank and with a pocket knife scraped away the incrustation of rust from the head of one of the nails which held the cleat . . . The cleat was nailed to the plank with wire nails and wire nails were not in existence in 1871.

News of the appalling discovery spread up and down the creek like wild fire, and the boom collapsed like a pricked toy balloon. Within an hour after the skeptic exposed the fraud, men were rolling their blankets and packing their horses. The next day a cavalcade of disgusted men was stampeding back to civilization and rational thought. In two more sleeps Alexander City had passed into history; nothing remained of the megalomania dream but a row of pegs which marked the course of Main street.

The whole matter was treated as a huge joke by the participants. On the discovery post of one claim the owner left this couplet:

> "The Big Dry gold was our only hope
> Our only hope is gone, we're broke"

One man who evidently realized he had made a monkey of himself by joining the stampede, tacked this notice on the trunk of a big cottonwood tree: "To all whom it may concern: I hereby locate the right of way up and down this tree."

It is told of a German who walked in on the railroad nearly 100 miles, carrying his blankets and provisions on his back, that he arrived in the "new El Dorado" just as the bubble burst. As he was trudging back to the railroad, he was overtaken by a man in a buggy; the man invited him to ride. The German shook his head. "Don't want to ride" . . . . Then rolling his eyes up at the man in the buggy he said by way of explanation, "I'll learn this damn Dutchman something."[5]

The other two lost mines of the Little Rockies were known also only to Indians.

It was on Thanksgiving day, 1868, the white man was first told there was gold in the Little Rockies. Just where it came from there is no one now living, nor has there been for many a day, who knows. The secret belonged to the Indians and they, through fears instilled by the early missionaries, would murder rather than to permit it to leak out. In fact it is believed by old timers that at least one white man lost his life in quest of the gold deposit there.

Fifty-two years ago, so it is said by those who long ago learned the facts, there was a Thanksgiving dinner at old Fort Browning on the Milk river about 50 miles below the present site of Fort Belknap. It was given by the officers to the little command and included several white men.

While the dinner was in progress it is related that an Indian

---

[5] *Terry Tribune*, May 4, 1928.

known as Nepee came into the fort with a little bag containing gold dust and nuggets which he showed to Major John Simmons, Captain D. W. Buck, James Stuart, who afterwards died at Fort Peck, and Major Culbertson. Nepee was a fast friend of the whites and gave the sack to Major Simmons. He was taken into the dining room where the banquet was in progress, and every effort was made to get him to tell where the gold had been found. However, they proved without avail.

There is no doubt, it is said, that the Indian would willingly have complied, but he knew well that if he did it would mean his life. He stated as much at the time that he was afraid his tribe would put him to death as they all had explicit instructions not to divulge the hiding place of the precious metal.

There was made to him at that time all sorts of offers. He was promised protection from the members of his tribe for all time to come, but while he was ready and willing to perform any other favorable act to the whites he would not give up this secret.

However, it is believed that he did reveal it to at least one white man, and that was Joe Hontus, commonly known as "Buckskin Joe," who was afterwards killed on the Milk river. Joe and the Indian were on the best of terms. They had slept together and had been on the prairies for weeks and months at a time and it was well known there was no one whom the Indian thought so much of as he did of Joe.

Hontus, a few years after the Thanksgiving day the Indian came to the fort, while drinking, stated he knew where the mines were located and that he was going out to find them. Shortly afterwards he left and the next seen of him was when his body was found riddled with bullets. It is the general belief of old timers, and always has been, that Joe started out to find the mine and was discovered by members of the tribe and put to death.

Nepee died in 1876 and with him passed the only man, friendly enough with the whites to tell them the place. So far as it has ever been learned, he took his secret with him to the grave.

The story goes that for a long time prior to the Thanksgiving day when Nepee came to Fort Browning the Indians knew of the existence of gold in the Little Rockies and that they had taken some of it out, after their own fashion. About 1865 they were visited by two French priests and the story has it that they showed these priests some of the gold. Thinking that they would be better able to learn the secret of its location, they are said to have informed the Indians that they must never tell the white man that there was gold there, or it would only be a short time before he would manage to take away their land. This schooling was the means of sealing the secret and even the priests were unable to learn its location.

In 1867 one of these priests was put to death by the Indians and the reason for the murder, it is stated, was that he was believed to be possessed with knowledge regarding the location of the gold deposit.

There were in the early days many of the old miners of northern Montana who sought to find out the secret. Weeks of search lengthened into months, and although there have been those who claimed to have found it, no one has been able to bring forth the same class of gold as was exhibited on that Thanksgiving day by Nepee.

There is a legend connected with this lost mine, but whether or not true no one can be found who will say. It is that after the priests told the Indians what would be the result should they divulge the mine they put a guard to the mountain pass leading to it. For years afterward this guard was maintained and even as late as 1875 an Indian sentry is said to have been seen in the Little Rockies.

There has been gold found there since that day, but nowhere in such quantities as was told of by Nepee, and there are men living who believe to this day that the secret of the tribe is their own.[6]

It was many years ago—how long the Indian could not say—but he is now a very old man and this was back in the days when he was a young brave. The Indian married and in taking to himself a wife he found that he had also taken her relatives, who came to make their home with him. In that day there was a trading post where the city of Wolf Point now stands. It had been noticed that once in a great while gold would be brought by Indians to this trading post. After this marriage the Indian discovered that his mother-in-law and her cousin were the two who had been bringing the gold. Being a thrifty soul, even for an Indian, the proposition struck him as having some very good points. It seemed considerably easier to go out and bring back a fistful of gold when one needed blankets, canned tomatoes, tea, and such necessities, in place

---

[6] *Silver State Post* (Deer Lodge), January 20, 1938.

of having to go through the arduous performance of trading ponies or doing actual work. He found, however, that it was not so easy to learn the secret. His mother-in-law told him only this much, that the mine had been discovered by her father and that the secret had been shared by him with no one, but herself and cousin. She also said that it had been her father's dying wish that she tell no one about it. And thus the matter hung while several years passed by.

With the passing of the years one more death in the tribe left the Indian's mother-in-law the sole surviving possessor of the secret and still, with persistent loyalty to the dead man's wishes, she kept the secret from them. In the days gone by she used to go on long trips up the Poplar river and it was upon her return that she would bring the nuggets to take to the trading post. The Indian often begged for permission to accompany her on these trips but soon found that it was of no use. At last one day—and this not so very many years ago—the Indian and his wife spent much time pleading with the old woman to tell them the secret. She was now becoming very old and she knew that it would not be very much longer that she could enjoy the benefits of this knowledge.

Unwilling to break her word to her father she at last laid this proposition before them. "We will go on a long camping trip. You will choose the way and will camp wherever you choose, but if ever we come to a spot where I tell you to camp, look there for gold."

The ponies were harnessed, the teepee and poles packed in the wagon and with all the dogs following, the party set off in a north-easterly direction. For many days they wandered back and forth always working northward and up the Poplar river. For all these days the old woman sat silent in the wagon, for she could not bring herself to break her pledge by saying anything that might direct him. Many times he had looked hopefully for a sign from her but always she said nothing when the time came to pitch camp.

At last one summer evening they drove through a little grove and out on a little strip where the Poplar river rippled around the point of a hill. The water ran musically over the rocks in a sort of rapids and after they passed the point the old woman roused herself at last. "We will camp here tonight, my son," she said.

And right there the story ends. The Indian worked long over those rocks and in that water, and he found no gold and no trace of gold. The old woman remained silent. She would have helped him, but she did not dare. She was an old woman and she knew she had not much time left; in fact that time was soon passed.

The Indian and his wife, still living, have given up hopes of the lost gold mine and now only tell the story impersonally, as a sort of legend.[7]

No particular romance is attached to the Lost Gold Mine of the Yellowstone; yet it may well be more authentic than the others. In 1866 several of the miners of Emigrant Gulch knew about this lode which they supposed to be the mother lode of the gold deposits in Emigrant Gulch. Very late in the fall of 1866 David Weaver, discoverer of Emigrant Gulch, and some other prospectors happened upon this rich deposit in the wild jumble of mountains and gulches near Yellowstone City. The danger from the hostile Indians was great, and, with the threat of the approaching winter, the little group left the location after making mental notes of its whereabouts.

Because of the Indian threat it was two years before anyone of the party could return; then it was spring; trees were in leaf and bushes had grown over many of the landmarks that had previously been noted. All their searching failed to lead them again to the lost lode. That it actually existed—and exists—was vouched for by Weaver, a man of unquestionable integrity. After leaving Montana, he returned to Pennsylvania where, in 1921, he was the only surviving member of the group that found the rich lode. He had in his possession samples of ore from the mine that assayed more than five thousand dollars per ton.[8]

---

[7] *Valley Tribune* (Bainville), September 9, 1920.
[8] *Bynum Herald,* April 11, 1921.

Most of the lodes that fed the rich sand of Montana's gulches have never been found or, if found, have been lost. George Brandt searched for fifty years hoping to find the huge vein that supplied the placer diggings of Confederate Gulch.

At the head of Basin Gulch near Highland City was found a quartz rock weighing nearly six hundred pounds, which, for its richness in gold exceeded anything else ever found in Montana, but the vein from which it came was never located.

Crazy Sal knew where the mother lode of the Last Chance Gulch diggings was, but the information was still locked in her befogged brain when she was laid in her grave.

Apparently Skookum Joe Anderson knew where a fabulously rich vein was located, but he, too, told no tales. The last entries in his diary are a moving record of the final days of a typical prospector. Joe had tramped the long miles from Bozeman to Nye, from Nye to Red Lodge, from Red Lodge to Cooke City. It was he who had discovered gold in Maiden Gulch and other rich spots; yet, like so many others, he moved over the next ridge always seeking "five to the pan and shallow diggin's."

"Aug. 26, 1894. Some gold today. Got very tired today. Feel lonesome. Think the highlode is center of gold leads. Heat is hell. Nearly sick. Got something. Can't tell yet what it is. Weak. Fever. Take coal oil and whiskey. Feel better."

A few days later: "Got a blacktail buck before I got my pants on this morning. Very sick. Used bottle of most bitter truck I ever tasted. Got the mail. Note from 'Bud' McDonnell."

And thus the weary fight goes on. During the summer of 1895 there is [are] repeated references to a new-born hope. "Pan out some rich prospects. Been on a trip after a big thing. Gold in all good places." Beneath that triumph we sense an undercurrent of fear for a man, Davidson, was dogging Skookum Joe day after day, step by step, shrewd, ruthless, ready to jump the claim. Joe, equally shrewd, was outwitting him effectively, covering his finds, leaving no clues. Out in the solitude of Montana's hills a silent, nerve-wracking duel was being waged. Joe writes: "July 3, 1895. Start to dig. Men came along so I panned and quit. Don't want to show them gold. July 5. Prospectors stay around to see what I'm about. Aug. 31. Seen man with horse. Gone up creek about two miles." And Joe, little suspecting his end near, so effectively covered his trail toward wealth, that no one has ever found it. The last entries in his diary are: "July 17, 1895. Note from O'Donnell. July 18. Get to Billings."

Joe arrived, Mr. O'Donnell says, a very sick man. That last night Joe said: "We've got it at last, Bud, richest thing in Montana. I'll draw a map so you can locate it easy. But not tonight. I'm too tired. They kept trailing me, Bud, but nobody'll ever find it without me. Tomorrow I'll draw a map."

Next morning when the landlady went to Skookum Joe's room she found the fire lit, coffee pot bubbling on the stove and Joe dead in his chair....[9]

Besides the gold that nature still hides in Montana, there are numerous buried treasures. Chief legend connected with these is that of the buried gold of the Plummer gang.

Occasionally history bears out to some extent the wild tales of golden caches, with facts that link with what might otherwise be flights of imagination. Such is the case in the story of the road agent gold on Gravelly range in Madison county—gold that is literally blood stained, and guarded by the bones of one of the men who stole it.

The story long ago became a legend; in fact perhaps the old-

---

[9] Glenolin Wagner in the *Midland Empire Farmer*, August 8, 1935.

timers themselves have largely forgotten it. But there was a time when it seemed thrillingly real and plausible and promising to those who heard it. An Indian in whose arms the last of three desperadoes died, gasping the story of the buried treasure with his dying breath, was the only direct source of the information considering the hidden cache, but his tale was substantiated by facts. A stage coach was robbed at a designated time, three members of Plummer's gang actually did disappear shortly afterward, land marks near Romey lake were as described—these were the facts. The remainder of the story which follows must necessarily be consigned to a "believe it or not" category.

During the hectic weeks when the Vigilantes were bringing the Plummer reign of terror to a grim close, three men, believed to be members of the gang, held up a stage coach not so far from Virginia City and confiscated a quantity of gold. Its value has not been recorded by history, but it grew to $30,000 several years later when the treasure hunt was on.

Maybe it was fear of Vigilante vengeance that prevented the trio from bringing the gold to Virginia City. More likely they deliberately decided not to split the spoils with the rest of their greedy crew. They went out through the canyons of the upper Ruby and camped in the vicinity of what was later called Romey lake.

Fearful of pursuit, they buried the gold in the center of a huge tract of sagebrush, after placing it in tin cans. They covered it with several feet of gravel and cleared away four small patches of the shrubbery, each equidistant from the cache, which thus became the center of a square.

This accomplished, they parted, each going in a separate direction. One went to Summit, one to Virginia City and a third crossed the range and came down into the valley presumably where Dillon now stands, proceeding to Bannack.

But thieves in those days trusted each other to about the same extent they do now. The minds of the three road agents held but one single thought—there was going to be double-crossing. Each of them decided at just about the same time that if he was going to get anything out of the stage coach deal he had to hurry.

Thus it was that two of them ran into each other a couple of days later in too close proximity to the cache to leave any doubt as to respective intentions. They apparently laid their cards on the table, however, and joined forces. That night they camped near the lake. The Bannack man, with a longer distance to ride, arrived on the site during the early morning. All his fears seemed confirmed as he saw from a distance the two horses of his erstwhile comrades in crime. Apprehension that he was to lose his share of the spoils must have made him a little careless, for he promptly fell to digging up the gold in spite of the fact that he was in full view of the other road agents.

They awoke, and the sight that met their eyes left them, according to their desperate code of ethics, only one course to take. Both fired at once.

The Bannack man had just uncovered the gold. Across it his dead body fell, and the story runs that it was never moved. The killers filled in the hole, making it serve the double purpose of a grave and a treasure cache. During the process, it is entirely probable that they manufactured numerous crude jokes about the guard they were leaving behind to protect their gold.

They were still fearful about departing from the country with the loot and cautiously decided to leave it in the hiding place until conditions seemed more propitious for its removal. They were apparently the best of friends again.

The friendship was short-lived. Camping that night on the upper Ruby they quarreled, and the following morning one of them shot the other and killed him.

Greed now got the better of caution. The gold belonged to the survivor for the digging, and no time was lost as the remaining road agent hurried back to the cache, trailing the two horses of his dead companions.

When he arrived on the scene, however, he was startled and dismayed to find that a band of Bannack Indians had established camp on the shores of the lake. Moreover, they were apparently there to stay for some time. None too friendly toward white men, the Bannacks eyed him with suspicion and left him to himself for hardly an instant.

Grimly determined to out-stay them, the white man defied their antagonism. Evidently they decided to tolerate him, for within a short time he was engaged in a game of chance of some kind with one of the bucks. The Indian was lucky and the desperado lost all three of his horses.

The record is a little hazy concerning what happened next, or as to the cause of it, rather. But whatever the motive might have been, the fact remains, the road agent was shot by one of the Bannacks and mortally wounded.

Among the Indians was an old buck known to white men as Madison John, who spoke some English. When it was ascertained that the desperado was dying, John was sent for, and into his startled old ears was poured the tale of robbery and bloodshed which has just been related. Realizing that he was gone, the road agent told everything, even to the location of the cache—evidently in a frenzied effort to rid himself of his sins before he died. Life ebbed away shortly after his tale was spun.

The Indians, not understanding that Vigilantes would probably reward them for their act, were frantic with fear of vengeance for the killing of a white man. Burying him hastily, they pulled camp and retreated back across the range.

Several years later we find Madison John again back in the Ruby, making his home with an old friend, English George Thorpe. The secret of the cache had remained locked in his breast but his trust in Thorpe led him to finally reveal the story told him by the dying desperado. Thorpe, intensely interested immediately, took Jim Ptomey into his confidence. The two men, old-timers in the county, remembered the incidents related by Madison John—the stage coach robbery and the disappearance of the three road agents—and comparing notes, they discovered that the story linked with the facts, even to the description of the sage brush covered country on Gravelly range. A treasure hunt was soon under way, with Madison John expressing confidence that he could lead the men to the cache.

But when they arrived in the vicinity of Romey lake, something went wrong. Madison John was forced to the confession that his memory had failed him. He recognized none of the landmarks and was unable to locate the site of the Indian camp.

They searched hard, covering a wide territory, but nothing could be found resembling the site of the cache. Sagebrush patches there were in plenty, but none that contained traces of four clearings, equidistant from each other.

After days of fruitless exploration, they returned to the Ruby and told the story to others. The tale did not bring on a concerted "gold rush," but for many years not a prospector or range rider visited Gravelly range without conducting a search of his own for "four cleared patches, equidistant from each other."

But all were unsuccessful. The bones of the murdered road agent guarded too well the treasure that had cost him his life. Gradually those who knew the story came to treat it as fiction, and, finally, a man who would confess to searching for the "cache" found himself at once on the receiving end of stinging ridicule.

And thus passed the blood stained gold of Romey lake into the realm of the mythical.[10]

When Henry Plummer was faced with the gallows, he begged for his life in exchange for his weight in gold. "Uncle Bill" Owsley, who was there at the time tells the incident and the location of the gold.

There is a possibility that more than $300,000 in nuggets and gold dust is buried near Robbers Roost, a two-story house used as a rendezvous by Henry Plummer and his gang of road agents in the palmy days of hectic Alder gulch, the richest gulch in the history of the world.

That the fortune in gold was buried within 100 yards of one of the corners of the corral at Robbers Roost and as far as known had never been found was the statement made by "Uncle" Bill Owsley, Montana pioneer, member of the famous vigilantes and one of Butte's first mayors. . . .

The gold was buried by Henry Plummer, who while officiating as sheriff, was the leader of the greatest band of road agents in history. The cache was Plummer's private spoils taken with unlisted thousands from the stages and out-going miners of "The Days of Alder Gulch."

Robbers Roost is still standing on the main road to Virginia City and is one of the historic landmarks of Madison county. A family is living in the place, which is still in a fair condition for a house built in the early '60's. The corral, which was an important point in "Uncle" Bill's story, disappeared many years ago.

"When he had to stand the acid test, Plummer was yellow," said Owsley. "I never told the story before, but Col. W. F. Sanders, X. Beidler, myself and others hanged the head of the road agents at Bannack, Jan. 10, 1864.

"Plummer lived near the home of Colonel W. F. Sanders and

---

[10] *Hardin Tribune Herald,* April 10, 1931.

when we entered his house to get him, he was in bed. He put up a great game of bluff when we first got him, as he was the sheriff of the territory.

"When Plummer fully realized that he was to hang on a scaffold that he had erected to hang a man he had arrested, he broke down and groveled like a cur. Of course, none of us was masked, and he knew me pretty well. A few minutes before the rope was settled around his neck he threw his arms around me and said, 'Owsley, I will take you to a place where I have $300,000 in dust cached.'

"I pushed him away and he again grabbed me.

" 'Hanging me will not give back the dust,' the doomed man said. 'I'll take you over to Robbers Roost and if the gold is not where I say, you can cut me to pieces. Just give me a horse after I show you the cache and I'll leave the territory forever.'

"As I started to push him away again," continued Owsley, "Plummer said, 'Oh, God, I tell you it is within 100 yards of one corner of the corral.'

"The rope was placed around his neck and then he asked us to see that he didn't strangle to death, and all the time he kept begging me to see if the vigilantes would grant him a day to live.

"After the rope was attached to the gallows, we boosted him high from our shoulders and let him drop. That ended Plummer."

"Did you ever look for the gold?" Uncle Bill was asked.

The hearty, contagious laugh known to so many, broke out, and wiping his eyes, the trailblazer said: "I felt convinced that Plummer spoke the truth, and I spent several weeks each year digging for more than five years.

"Say, . . . You chaps have no idea what it means to try to dig somewhere around 100 yards from four corners of a big corral. I should have had a steam shovel.

"I have kept more or less of a tab on the place ever since and to the best of my knowledge and belief the gold has never been found."[11]

Another Plummer hoard was concealed—and found —in a cabin on the Sun River. Forest Young of Park City told that his mother, then living in Minnesota,

[11] *Roundup Tribune*, August 18, 1929.

was related in some way to Plummer or to some member of his gang. One day she received word that the outlaws, whose unlawful activities were unknown to her, had concealed four bags of dust and nuggets in a cabin. Careful directions were given for finding the cabin, and Mrs. Young and her son set out to recover the treasure. After an arduous journey, they found the site as described, dug in the dirt floor and found the precious buckskin bags. Concealing them in some blankets, they loaded them on a pack horse and started back to Deer Lodge. The river was high due to heavy rains so, when they reached a ford, they hastened to cross before the water was any higher. Mrs. Young went first, the pack animals came next, and Forest Young brought up the rear. When they reached the middle of the stream, they heard the whine of a bullet and the pack horse carrying the gold began thrashing about wildly in the water. Looking up Forest saw their assailant running through the timber, but he was unable to think of pursuit since he had his hands full getting himself and the horses across the swollen stream. Even then, the wounded horse had to be abandoned. Once on the other side, Young and his mother made camp for the night, cold and wet, without the blankets that had been on the lost horse.

The next morning they followed down the stream until they found the body of the pack horse wedged against a boulder. The gold was gone, whether stolen by the gunman or washed into the mud at the bottom of the river will probably never be known.

Cooke City, at the northeast corner of Yellowstone park, boasts a legend of buried treasure which in recent years has led numerous prospectors and casual fortune hunters to dig over a considerable area near the new Cooke City-Red Lodge highway just east of the town.

An old stump, some six feet high, bearing carved hieroglyphs, lends credence to the legend and inspires various interpretations which send men digging in new spots nearby.

The story is this:

In 1880 two miners had made a stake at Virginia City or in the mining gulches near the town. They decided to return to their eastern homes to enjoy the luxury their new found wealth entitled them to. But, being of a suspicious nature, they trusted no one, and chose a back country route with their burden of gold rather than transmit it by the banking or express route. And, despite an established commonwealth in 1880, there were always tough characters ready to waylay those with money if it could be done with but little danger of capture and punishment.

These miners chose a route which apparently took them up the Madison and across Yellowstone park, thence down Clarks fork. Anyway, they were in the Cooke region when they camped one night about 300 yards from the trail. Unknown to them, they had been followed, and during the night they were attacked. One of the men was killed. They had hidden their pack mule and his cargo a bit away from camp. The surviving partner made his escape into the darkness and, finding nothing of value about the camp, the attackers left.

The survivor took the gold from the pack mule, secured one of his dead partner's boots, placed the gold inside it, and buried the treasure near the camp. He carved a legend on a tree, which is now the tall stump on the supposed treasure site. The pack mule, apparently struck by a bullet which reached his hiding place, was abandoned, and his badly weathered bones may still be seen not far from the stump.

Having made his treasure as safe as possible, after making a map of the immediate locality, the surviving partner went on his way down the old Clarks Fork Indian trail, used only a few years previously by Chief Joseph and his Nez Perce band.

The story is that many years later three men, armed with a map and supposed to be nephews of the survivor, appeared one day at the old Eagle's Nest road ranch near Cody, Wyo., and after showing their map to Sam Launchberry engaged him as a guide. They failed to find the treasure and left the country. Nothing more was ever heard of them or their map.

But the stump with its carved hieroglyphs remains. The legend on the stump shows: At the top a circle eight inches in diameter. Inside this a cross with arms about three inches. Below the circle the date, 1880. Below this a triangle or the outline of an Indian tepee, and under this the large figures 6 and 5.

The figures 65 have been interpreted to mean 65 feet, or 65 yards or rods, from the tree, and at these distances much digging has been done.

The land where legend locates the treasure was patented in 1895 by the Seeright Brothers; it was acquired in 1930 by George Ogden of Cooke City, whose present plans are for the development of a cabin camp and summer resort.[12]

---

[12] *Midland Empire Farmer*, November 7, 1935.

PART II

TRADE & TRANSPORTATION CENTERS

1

TRADE & TRANSPORTATION CENTERS

THERE ARE SEVERAL WAYS OF GETTING INTO MONTANA. HAVING made up my mind to visit it, I took the longest and the pleasantest, which is the shortest after all.[1]

I might, to be sure, have taken the stage at Atchison; and, jumbling across the prairies of the Platte, have had my legs swollen, as though afflicted with elephantiasis, long before we reached Denver. From Denver, then, I might have jumbled along in the same way to the beautiful and wonderful city of the Mormons; and, having revived myself with the sulphur baths and delicious fruits that abound there, have braced myself for another spell of cramps and starvation, on the great Overland Route.

But I heard enough of this style of traveling; enough of the salt fare one has heavily to pay for every time he has a chance to snatch a meal; enough of the drear and achesome wastes one has to sulk over while making the middle part of the trip, and the waters of bitterness he has to quaff; enough of the chances one has to be roasted like St. Lawrence, or punctured to death with arrows like St. Sebastian, for most of the road: I heard enough of all this, from many pleasant authorities on the subject, not to come to the conclusion it was well to avoid.

Were I ambitious of figuring, one of these days, in the Travelers' Club of New York, as an out-and-out Pilgrim of the Rocky Mountains, I might have paid handsomely to walk with a train, and have spent three or four months at the work. But I heard enough of this way, too, of getting to Montana, and shrunk from it with a convulsion of the heart. The world pretty generally knows, by this time, what it is to travel with a caravan of oxen and huge green wagons, in a column of dense red dust, to the cracking of oaths and cow-hides, through a region the greater portion

---

[1] This was by way of the Panama Canal!

of which justifies the description that "it is the worst part of the infernal domain burned out."

A third line was open to me, of which it is fair to say I heard nothing extremely repugnant. This is the line of the Upper Missouri. Early in April, and from that to the end or middle of May, great steamboats swing off from St. Louis for the mountains; and, having panted and shrieked and blowed with all their might against the yellow volume of that huge river, finally take rest at Fort Benton, after a violent struggle of fifty, sixty, seventy, or eighty days.

. . . I came to the determination *not* to face the Upper Missouri, as I have a strong aversion to traveling on anything like a canal —the more especially should it be from two to three thousand miles long, with the risk constantly recurring of being impaled on a snag, running dry on a sand-bar, blown sky-high into atoms, or scalded to death. Then I well knew that fresh provisions were sure to give out on such a trip as that long before it was over, and that a surfeit of ham, codfish balls, sardines, and lamp-oil, and such-like rare and delicate commodities would be our visitation, night, noon, and morning, for days, and it might be for weeks. Buffalo meat would, of course, occasionally come into play; but even that anticipation, novel and refreshing as it was, failed to persuade me. . . .[2]

The Mullan Road may be added as a fourth way of getting into Montana, and each of the ways developed its own legends and its own towns where supplies could be unloaded and weary travelers could rest.

The earliest of these was Hell Gate on the Mullan Road, a settlement that dates back before the great gold strikes.

---

[2] Thomas F. Meagher, *Harper's New Monthly Magazine,* October, 1867.

HELL GATE

INTO HELL GATE RONDE[1] ONE DAY IN THE SUMMER OF
1860 came Frank L. Worden and C. P. Higgins. They
had set out from Walla Walla with a considerable
stock of merchandise, intending to trade at the Indian
agency. With keen business sense they realized that
the Ronde lay on the crossroads of a growing commerce. Unloading their merchandise they set up shop
about three miles from the present town of Missoula.
A string of "cayuse" pack horses brought their supplies the 425 miles over the Mullan Trail from Walla
Walla, and for the duration of Montana's early history the trading post of Higgins and Worden at Hell
Gate played an important role. Worden later built the
first flour mill at Missoula, Higgins gave and sold the
land on which the town is built, and many of the
streets—Hilda, Arthur, Gerald, Ronald—are named for
members of his family.

In spite of its importance Hell Gate never "boomed"
as did the mining camps. It was a trading post only,
drawing supplies from Walla Walla and produce from
the rich farming areas of the Bitterroot and Hell Gate

---

[1] The disagreeable terms "Hell Gate" and "Missoula" reflect the fear the western Montana Indians and the voyageurs had of the spot. Here, as the trappers
and peaceful tribes, in search of furs or buffalo, sought to pass westward through
the canyon, they were so consistently ambushed by the warlike Blackfeet who
dominated the western plains that the Frenchmen called it "Port d'Enfer," or
"Gate of Hell" and the Indians "Missoula," a "place of chilling fear."

Valleys. As the rush to the gold fields continued, the trade became more lucrative. Currency was usually gold dust at about $18 an ounce. Flour sold at $30 a hundred, potatoes at $6 a bushel, yeast powders at $1.50 a box. A small fortune was realized in the liquor which was sold to the Indians. Throughout the territory the standard recipe was:

> 1 part whiskey or alcohol
> 10 parts water
> tobacco) ⎫
> ⎬ for taste, color and potency
> cayenne) ⎭

The going price was one horse for four gallons.

Probably Montana's first marriage between whites was performed at Hell Gate when George White married Mrs. Mineinger in March, 1862.

Everyone was interested in the event, but they had very little with which to prepare a wedding supper. The year before, old Captain Grant had moved back from Ham's Fork and built a house on Grant creek. He had brought a few chickens from Salt Lake and had raised a number of young ones. During the winter the Grant family had gone to Walla Walla, leaving a man in charge of their premises, with particular instructions to look well after the poultry and not to kill, sell or give any away for any consideration whatsoever. A council was held and plots made to get some of these chickens for the wedding feast. The result was that Frank H. Woody and A. S. Blake . . . volunteered to go three miles through deep snow and forage the ranch. They came back the next day with a bag full of chickens. How they got them was never fully known, but it leaked out that Woody talked the man so nearly to death that the matter became easy.

The supper was cooked. Captain Higgins had Justice Brooks out in the corral for a whole afternoon rehearsing the marriage ceremony, and in short the wedding took place. Everybody got drunk

and just before supper Blake stole the wedding cake. After a short
dance the happy couple retired, the men all wishing there were
brides enough to go around.[2]

The first lawsuit tried in Montana was tried here in the same month and is reported by Granville Stuart.

Hell Gate is putting on "States Airs," and has a justice of the
peace, and has held court and tried one of the distinguished citizens
of that section for killing a neighbor's horse.

The trial was held in Bolt's saloon, a long building near Worden
and Higgins' store. Suit was brought by "Tin Cup Joe" against
Baron O'Keefe for killing a horse. Henry Brooks was judge; Bob
Pelkey, constable; Frank Woody, prosecuting attorney; Sterne Blake
was one of the twelve jurors and Bud McAdow was an onlooker.
Baron O'Keefe conducted his own defense. . . .

"Tin Cup Joe" accused the Baron of injuring one of his horses
so seriously as to cause its death. The Baron denied the charge of
malicious mischief and said that the horses had been in the habit
of breaking down fences around hay stacks that he put up for his
own stock and that he had warned "Tin Cup Joe" to keep them
away, a thing he failed to do.

Frank Woody began for the prosecution and he had not proceeded far before some of his remarks about "Good Citizenship"
were taken to be personal by O'Keefe. The Baron straightened up
with eyes flashing and snorting like a war horse yelled, "Who are
you, what kind of a court is this anyhow?" Then addressing himself to the Bench began, "Say Old Brooks, who in hell made you
judge? You are an old fraud. You are no judge; you are a squaw
man, you have two squaws now. Your business is to populate the
country with half breeds. You ———— ———— ————" The Baron
made a lunge at the person nearest him and in an instant the fight
became general. Everybody took a hand, and as both sides had about
an equal number of sympathizers, when the dust of battle cleared
away it was considered a draw. But judge, jurors, constable, and
prosecuting attorney, had disappeared and the fiery Baron held the
center of the room declaring that "no Frenchman's horses can nibble
hay from one of my stacks without suffering the consequences."

---

[2] Louis Maillet in Historical Society of Montana, *Contributions*, IV, 224-25.

Quiet was finally restored, the judge and jury returned and the
trial proceeded without further interruption. The jury brought in
a verdict for "Tin Cup Joe" and awarded him forty dollars damages,
but I do not know that anyone ever tried to collect the money from
Baron O'Keefe.[3]

In addition to being distinguished for these "firsts,"
Hell Gate held another record. It might be inferred
from the early establishment of law and business that
Hell Gate's history was rather monotonous compared
to the rip-roaring events of Bannack and Last Chance.
Not so. Hell Gate's record of violent death in the five
years of its existence could challenge that of any "tough"
town in the state. At no time was its population more
than fourteen, yet nine men died with their boots on
in or near the trading post.

In 1863 a sinister character, Cyrus Skinner, opened
a saloon near the post. Soon other men of like calibre
were seen loitering about his place. If others in Hell
Gate had suspicions concerning the gang, they were
prudent enough to keep their thoughts to themselves.
Down in Virginia City, though, the Vigilantes knew
who the men were, knew they were marked by the
3-7-77 symbol. After an epic ride through the winter night, they closed in on the Skinner establishment.
Within a matter of minutes after their appearance,
Skinner, Alex Carter, and Johnnie Cooper dangled from
a pole fastened to a log corral in the lower part of
town. Bob Zachary, seized on the Baron O'Keefe ranch,
joined his friends the next day.

A couple of months later an Indian attacked a French-

[1] Reprinted by permission of the publishers, The Arthur H. Clark Company,
from *Forty Years on the Frontier*, by Granville Stuart (2 vols.; Cleveland, 1925),
I, 198-99.

man and, being accused, was threatening and insolent, declaring that he would spark a general Indian uprising against the little colony. Alarmed, the whites sent a messenger to recruit aid from Virginia City. Hearing of this move, the Indians delivered up the culprit, son of a Pend d'Oreille chief, and he was forthwith hung on the same gallows that claimed the lives of the outlaws.

In 1864 Matt Craft shot Crow for, according to Matt, insulting Mrs. Craft. Since there were no officers handy and no one liked Crow much anyway nothing was done about the killing.

One afternoon two Irishmen were playing poker in the local saloon. A bitter quarrel developed over the $2.50 settlement of the game. They left the saloon still arguing heatedly. One of the men present at the time concluded their bloody story:

There were no electric lights in Hell Gate. The illumination of the rough interior came from a big fireplace in one side of the room and from candles stuck about. On the night of the day that the Irishmen, McLaughlin and Doran, had quarreled over their cards, there were some of the Hell Gate men seated at a table in front of the fireplace, playing a friendly game, when the two returned— they were quarreling. That night added two more names to the list of Hell Gate's dead. One of the men who sat at the little table has told me this story of the spectacular events of that evening:

We were playing at a little table near the fireplace, from which we got most of our light. We had also a candle on the table. Doran had walked over to our side of the room and stood with his back to the fire. McLaughlin, who had been an employee at the Jocko agency, was sitting on a whiskey barrel, leaning against a brandy keg. He had evidently apprehended trouble, for he had borrowed a big navy pistol from Captain Higgins. He wore an old blue army overcoat and, though we didn't know it, had the gun in his lap under the cape of the coat.

The men came into Cook's quarreling and they continued their argument. They were not talking very loud, but seemed very much in earnest. Standing in front of the fire, Doran reached for his hip under his coat, evidently to draw his pistol. McLaughlin leaped to his feet, exclaiming, "I've a pistol as well as yez." He threw back the cape of his coat. There were two flashes at the same instant. All the candles were extinguished and the close of the tragedy was enacted in the fitful light from the fireplace.

At the table, we jumped up. The men were firing across the way to the front door and we couldn't get out that way. But we wanted mighty bad to get out. There was a thin board partition across the back of the room separating Cook's living quarters from the saloon. Through this we dashed. I was in the lead. We upset a sheetiron stove which was in the living room; we scared Cook's half-breed wife and her baby and they screamed; the discharge of pistols sounded like artillery—it was the greatest confusion I ever knew.

Reaching the back door, the others pressed so hard against me that I could not swing the door. While I was struggling with it, Cook came out and said, "I can open it. Go tell Captain Higgins I am shot." I hurried to the store. Higgins returned with me and we met two men supporting Cook, who was hardly able to move. The shooting was all over. McLaughlin had fired but one shot. Doran had continued his bombardment until he was out of ammunition. He had fled and there was darkness and silence when we returned with our burden.

Cook was laid upon the counter and an examination showed that a bullet had passed through his body, entering above the left hip and lodging right under the skin on the side. Captain Higgins used a razor to extract the bullet, but that was about all we could do. There was no doctor and no means of cleaning the wound. We placed poor Cook in his bed and he died Thursday. . . . Father Grassi came up from Frenchtown to see him, but said the shot had pierced the bowels and it was a hopeless case. Cook was buried near the little church which Father Grassi had built just below Hell Gate.

McLaughlin had died almost immediately; when found he had crawled to the back of the room in Cook's and was breathing his last. Doran fled across the river on the ice and made his way to Stevensville. There was a supposed justice of the peace there, Roop by name, and there was the mere form of a hearing before him. Despite the testimony of John Chafield, who was one of the party playing cards in Cook's when the shooting occurred, Doran was released.[4]

The ninth death? Merely a suicide that served as an anticlimax to the bloody drama.

For a few years after the removal of Hell Gate to Missoula, mounds could be seen to mark the graves of those who died violently in the years 1863-65 at the little trading post. Those hung by the Vigilantes were buried slightly apart from the others. Today no one knows where their bones lie. Various groups interested in the preservation of historic sites in Montana have sought funds for the restoration of Hell Gate, or at least for the preservation of the remains of the two original buildings that are still found at the location.

With the increase in travel over the Mullan Trail and the influx of miners to the camps of Cedar Creek and the Coeur d'Alene mines of Idaho, numerous stage stops were established west of Hell Gate.

. . . one of them being Widow McCabe's stage station, a famous frontier stopping place not far west of Frenchtown. Another famous stop was Peter Rabbit's saloon and stage station which was known as "The Kitchen." Peter Rabbit's place was situated in Mullan's gulch, at the confluence of St. Regis and Clark's Fork rivers. Other roadhouses in Mineral county of the early years were Rothschilds' hotel a mile below the present site of Superior, and St. Regis House at the mouth of Packer creek.

St. Regis house was built by a Colonel Meyers, who had a reputation for great accuracy in shooting, for he was a veteran of several wars. A village called Silver City, sprang up around Colonel Meyers' place, thus named because there was much placer mining

[4] A. L. Stone in the *Missoulian*, March 9, 1912.

being carried on in Idaho just across the Continental divide.[5] A picturesque traffic of explorers, prospectors, stage coaches and overland freight wagons passed along the Mullan road past St. Regis house enroute to the Idaho mining camps and the new settlements of the Pacific coast. A rollicking company of missionaries, soldiers and adventurers passed over Mullan road. . . .[6]

---

[5] The Continental Divide is about 250 miles east of this point.

[6] William West in the *Glacier County Chief*, August 3, 1936.

3

NEW CHICAGO

ALSO ON THE MULLAN ROAD BUT OF A LITTLE LATER origin was New Chicago, approximately three miles south of Drummond. When it was founded in 1872 by John A. Featherstone, it was hoped that someday it would rival the great city after which it was named. Being on the stage road between Deer Lodge and Missoula, it had a promising location, and in the first years of its life numerous businesses were established: two stores, two saloons, a flour mill, a livery stable, and two blacksmith shops. A school was established in 1874 for pupils who ranged "from 6 years to 6 feet."

In 1886 a Methodist Episcopal church was built. The items put in the cornerstone, after the old tradition, were enclosed in the container handiest at the time, an Epsom salts box. Into the box went

. . . a copy of the "Doctrine and Disciplines of the Methodist Episcopal Church," dated 1884; a "Songbook of Gospel Hymns," four newspapers dated August 12 and 13, 1886; a 5-cent piece dated 1883 and, left by a workman, a twist of Cotton Ball tobacco.

Of all the memorable characters who lived in or near New Chicago, none could match in either humor or tradegy the Dennis Mittens who lived on a ranch just out of town. Both Mr. and Mrs. Mitten were huge, uninhibited frontier types whose lack of restraint, particularly in regard to whisky, was perhaps the cause of all their troubles. When word was received that the Nez Perce were on the warpath, Mrs. Mitten, having taken her produce up to Bear Gulch, bought herself a needle gun and a bottle and, thus fortified, began marching up and down Bear Gulch's one street

. . . gun over her shoulder, wheeling, saluting, going through every known military maneuver. At regular intervals she would shout: "Attention! Take aim! Fire!" And then, obeying her own command, she would drop on one knee, aim carefully and fire at the flags adorning the stockade fort.

Finally, urged by hunger, instinct, or possibly by a vaguely troubled housewifely conscience, she went home. At the ranch she found a pardonably irate spouse who had been left with all the chores to do and supper to get. The customary family quarrel ensued. He demanded to know why she had a gun. "To kill Indians with, of course," she explained, heatedly. "You couldn't kill an Indian," he scoffed. "Now, if I was an Indian, what would you do this minute?" "I'd do this," she said, and aimed and fired.[1]

Under his wife's tender care Dennis recovered and, when the Northern Pacific was pushing through Hell Gate Canyon, he set up a profitable saloon to cater to the workmen. One day he and one of the laborers became involved in an argument and the laborer knocked Dennis down. Leaping up as fast as his bulk would permit, Dennis ran for his wife's needle gun, shouting

"I'll shoot you and shoot you until I can knock you down!"

He aimed and fired at the man who apparently deemed prudence the better part of valor, for he was running, as fast as he could, through thick underbrush toward the river, with Mr. Mitten close at his heels, firing every step of the way and with loyal Mrs. Mitten shouting excited advice:

---

[1] *Kalispell Times,* August 6, 1936.

"You're over-shooting, Dennis. You're over-shooting him!"

The thick underbrush proved a benefactor to the fleeing human target and the man succeeded in reaching the river and started swimming across. Dennis fired one last parting shot into the water at random and then returned to his saloon, evidently defeated. But about a month later the laborer's body was found on a sandbar near Missoula with one bullet in the heart. Missoula officers investigated and came up to Hell Gate and arrested Dennis Mitten on murder charges. He was tried, convicted and sentenced to 17 years in the Deer Lodge penitentiary. Gloom settled over Hell Gate for everyone liked the quarrelsome, friendly, kindhearted Mittens.[2]

Dennis served a few years of this sentence but, with the aid of his neighbors and his wife's nephew, who was the warden at the prison, he was soon paroled.

Mr. Mitten's triumphant return home was due cause for rejoicing. He and his wife rode up to New Chicago where all their friends joined in the gay celebration. Everybody congratulated them and voiced their hearty welcome by setting up drinks. Consequently, by evening the whole town was in a drunken uproar, with the Mittens, to each of whom the passing years had added many pounds, the natural center of the festivities. Everyone was happy, although few, at this final stage, could doubtless have explained the primal reason for their happiness. At last the reunited couple, having sung and shouted and laughed themselves hoarse, decided to go home. Kind hands helped them onto their horses where they perched unsteadily. As a parting token a generous bartender gave them each a bottle of whiskey. The whole town stood watching them ride out of sight up the canyon, swaying perilously in their saddles.

For the sombre finale to that gay day of reunion we have only Dennis Mitten's heart-broken confession. It was very cold, he said, and there was about four inches of snow on the ground. When they had traveled within a mile of their ranch, Mrs. Mitten, who had been seeking warmth and comfort from her bottle all the way, toppled off her horse and lay in the snow in a drunken stupor.

---

[2] *Ibid.*

Dennis was in a serious predicament. It was impossible for any one man to lift the huge, limp woman back into her saddle. To leave her in the snow while he went for help meant she would freeze to death. And so, after his liquor-befogged brain had puzzled over the difficulty for some time, the worried husband hit upon a plan which seemed to him a logical answer to his problem. He tied a rope around his wife, secured it to the horn of her saddle, and then, mounting his own horse, led hers home, with Mrs. Mitten dragging through the snow behind. When he arrived at the ranch he hastened to release his wife and discovered, to his horror and deep grief, that she was dead.

And simple Dennis Mitten, who had bungled all his life, was again charged with murder. He was tried, convicted and sentenced to return to Deer Lodge where he died.[3]

Today the old church is gone, having been torn down almost twenty years ago. A bright new sign on Highway 10A points off toward New Chicago, but little is left except the name to indicate its ambitious origin. A name, too, Mitten Peak, keeps alive the memory of the lovable, irresponsible frontier couple of New Chicago.

---

[3] *Ibid.*

4

LAURIN

AS THE RUSH CAME FROM SALT LAKE TO VIRGINIA CITY, a Frenchman, Jean Baptiste Laurin, was quick to see the advantages of a trading post along the route.

The quiet little town of Laurin (pronounced Loray), eight miles south of Sheridan, is one of those "wide places in the road" usually ignored by travelers speeding through Montana. It was not always so. In the bustling days of Virginia City, Bannack, and Last Chance, Laurin, sometimes called Cicero and sometimes Lorrain, was an important supply center of southeastern Montana.

Here in July, 1863, Laurin opened a store in a canvas house. During the same summer he built a log cabin, the second one in the Ruby Valley.

Personally, Laurin was an impressive figure. About five feet seven inches tall he weighed from 250 to 350 pounds; yet, in spite of his fat, he was physically active and mentally alert. From the little store he expanded his business until he had a financial empire that spread over the entire area.

. . . Although unable to make an entry in his books, he is estimated to be worth $500,000. He digs no gold, and would not give a "kiyuse" for the best gold-lead in the Territory to work it. His forte is to traffic with everybody; and the result is that he owns all the stores, bridges, and most of the ranches, cattle, horses, and

mules for fifty or one hundred miles along the valley. The Big
Hole bridge alone yields him eight thousand dollars a year in gold.
He owns the finest winter pastures, and each fall he exchanges
sound and fat oxen, horses, and mules with those unlucky enough
to have broken-down animals, and by spring they are restored, and
ready to be jockeyed off again for two or three times their number
of cripples. His herds are scattered over the Beaver-Head, Stinking
Water, Big Hole and Deer Lodge valleys; and his stores are found
in every settlement, with their supplies of canned fruits and vegetables, groceries, a few dry goods, a profusion of prepared cocktails,
bitters, etc., and every variety of robes and skins.[1]

At the ranch he raised poultry in large numbers; frequently he had a thousand chickens in his yards. He
kept the first hotel at Cicero and also a well-stocked
store as will be seen by an advertisement, put out in
1872, which indicates somewhat the needs of the people
he sought to serve:

Farmers and Miners, Attention
J. B. LAURIN
Cicero   Montana
    Keeps constantly on hand a large
and choice assortment of
GROCERIES, DRY GOODS HARDWARE
    Queen's ware, boots, shoes, drugs,
agricultural implements, miner's tools,
etc. etc.
    Which are always offered at lowest
prices. He also trades and deals in
Grain, Produce, Wagons and Stock of
all kinds.

———————

Toutes mes merchandise sont fraiches
et satisfaction garantie. Venez et
voyez vous memes. J. B. Laurin.

———————

[1] A. K. McClure, *Three Thousand Miles through the Rocky Mountains* (Philadelphia: J. B. Lippincott & Company, 1869), pp. 311-12.

Mr. Laurin loaned money to his neighbors, taking their promissory notes, usually without security. His interest rates were one to two or three per cent per month, depending on whether he had security or not and how he regarded the borrower. Unable to read or write, it was said he could always tell the borrower how much he owed, even if there were many partial payments separated by long periods of time. When he died in 1896, his estate was worth over $150,000.

5

REED'S FORT

AS THEY TRAVELED THEIR LONG MILES BETWEEN TOWNS, the bullwhackers and wagon bosses cheered themselves and their teams with loud and rollicking melodies. "Sweet Betsy from Pike" was a favorite among them, and the little trading posts as well as vast spaces between were enlivened with this vigorous ballad of the trails.

Did you ever hear tell of sweet Betsy from Pike,
Who crossed the wide prairies with her lover Ike,
With two yoke of cattle and one spotted hog,
A tall Shanghai rooster, an old yaller dog?

Chorus
Sing-too-rall-i-oo-ral-i-oo-i-ay,
Sing-too-rall-i-oo-ral-i-oo-i-ay!

One evening quite early they camped on the Platte.
'Twas near by the road on a green shady flat;
Where Betsy, quite tired, lay down in repose,
While with wonder Ike gazed on his Pike County rose.

They swam the wide rivers and crossed the tall peaks,
And camped on the prairie for weeks upon weeks,
Starvation and cholera and hard work and slaughter,
They reached Montana[1] in spite of hell and high water.

---

[1] This song originated during the gold rush to California and the original version has "California" instead of "Montana"; however, it was readily adapted, as are all folksongs, to the circumstances under which it was sung.

Out on the prairie one bright starry night,
They broke the whisky and Betsy got tight,
She sang and she shouted and danced o'er the plain,
And showed her bare ankles to the whole wagon train.

The Injuns came down in a wild yelling horde,
And Betsy was skeered they would scalp her adored;
Behind the front wagon wheel Betsy did crawl,
And there she fought the Injuns with musket and ball.

The alkali desert was burning and bare,
And Isaac's soul shrank from the death that lurked there;
"Dear old Pike County, I'll go back to you."
Says Betsy, "You'll go by yourself if you do!"

They soon reached the desert, where Betsy gave out,
And down in the sand she lay rolling about;
While Ike in great terror looked on in surprise,
Saying, "Betsy, get up, you'll get sand in your eyes."

Sweet Betsy got up in a great deal of pain,
And declared she'd go back to Pike County again;
Then Ike heaved a sigh and they fondly embraced,
And she traveled along with his arm around her waist.

The wagon tipped over with a terrible crash,
And out on the prairie rolled all sorts of trash;
A few little baby clothes done up with care,
Looked rather suspicious, but it was all on the square.

One morning they climbed a very high hill,
And with wonder looked down on old Placerville;
Ike shouted and said, as he cast his eyes down,
"Sweet Betsy, my darling, we've got to Hangtown."

Long Ike and sweet Betsy attended a dance,
Where Ike wore a pair of his Pike County pants;
Sweet Betsy was covered with ribbons and rings,
Said Ike, "You're an angel, but where are your wings?"

A miner said, "Betsy, will you dance with me?"
"I will that, old hoss, if you don't make too free;

But don't dance me hard. Do you want to know why?
Dogone ye, I'm chock-full of strong alkali."

Long Ike and sweet Betsy got married, of course,
But Ike, getting jealous, obtained a divorce;
And Betsy, well satisfied, said with a shout,
"Goodby, you big lummox, I'm glad you backed out!"

It took a hardy breed of men to endure the hardships
and perils of the freighters' life. Alexander Toponce,
one of the few who has written of his experiences, tells
the following concerning a trip to Helena in February,
1866. He and his train had started from Fort Union
with a herd of cattle and a load of flour, sugar, and
coffee.

On the 3rd of January we got to the Quaking Asp River, where
it empties into the Missouri. . . . There a snowstorm struck us, and
we couldn't go any further. . . .

We had to corral our wagons and take our cattle down to an
old Indian camp on the river and the storm was so severe, and so
cold that there was fifteen days we dared not all go to bed at once.
We had big Sibley army tents. We kept a fire in them and some
of the men had to keep fire outside between the tents. . . .

We were unable to save the cattle. We had to shoot them, and
we shot them all in the course of ten days, as their horns would
freeze and burst off from the pith; their necks would freeze and
their legs, so that they couldn't move at all, while others froze
standing up.

The buffalo began to drift in from the north during this storm
and when they struck the timber they wouldn't cross the river,
but crowded in there and all that was left outside the timber froze
to death. In the spring you could walk for miles on buffalo skeletons, your feet never touching the ground. . . .

After we had killed all the cattle and horses, we had but two
mules left, Molly and one other, which we had kept inside a tent
and fed on buffalo meat and cottonwood bark. . . .

About the first of February, 1866, Mann and I started out with my two mules for Helena, a distance of about five hundred miles, with two feet and a half of snow on the ground.

We were unable to carry anything except a pair of saddle blankets, and all we had to feed the mules was cottonwood bark and buffalo meat. We made slow progress for the first two hundred miles. Every night we would have to kill a buffalo, take his hide off and lay the flesh side down on the snow for a bed. We lived on buffalo meat for about thirty days.

We would take a quarter of buffalo meat and hang it up in a tree by means of a long pole and build a good fire under it and roast it as well as we could, and when it was done we would lay it on the ground before the mules. They would set one foot on the meat to hold it steady, and start in and tear off big chunks of hot meat and fat with their teeth and chew it just like hay. The two mules would gnaw the meat clean to the bone on a quarter of buffalo.[2]

To protect freight and passengers from Indian raids along the various routes, the government set up military posts. In 1874 such a post was established at Camp Lewis near the present site of Lewistown. The two companies of soldiers stationed there for the summer served to protect the wagon trains during the season of heaviest traffic. When November arrived, and only stragglers were found on the trail, the camp was discontinued.

Opportunely on hand were Alonzo S. (Major) Reed and J. J. Bowles. Realizing the need for a trading post at this point, they purchased the commissary stock, moved it down river about two miles to where the Carroll Trail crossed Big Spring Creek and built a trading post.

The post, from the best description, consisted of two log cabins

---

[2] Alexander Toponce, *Reminiscences of Alexander Toponce, Pioneer, 1839-1923* (Ogden, Utah: Mrs. Katie Toponce, 1923), pp. 121-25.

built with the ax and auger and with no nails but pegs to hold it
together, and a dirt roof. They were inclosed in a stockade built
by standing poles on end in a trench joined close together so as to
form a high fence around a quadrangle about 100 by 150 feet. On
the south end towards the river was a big gate through which they
could drive inside the quadrangle or stockade. On the north was a
corral to protect horses from Indian raids. During this period their
main business consisted of trading with the Indians, mainly in wet
goods. . . . The traffic in liquor with the Indians was condemned
and outlawed by the federal government, so, in fact, it amounted
to a bootleg joint in the Indian country. In addition they would
keep travelers, who stopped on their trips along the Carrol trail.
During this period this was the only station from Martinsdale on
the forks of the upper Musselshell, more than 75 miles southwest,
and Carroll on the Missouri river, 75 or 80 miles northeast. . . .

   During this period, except for three or four months in summers
of 1874 and 1875, when the government kept soldiers at Camp
Lewis, there were no authorities for maintenance of order for 100
miles or more from this trading post. Reed and Bowles were in
themselves kings, maintaining their position and prestige by guns.
They had a reputation as killers all over the territory and many a
tale has been told of the mysterious disappearance of customers and
of their private ground where they buried victims. As their traders
usually remained around the post for days and even weeks at a time
consuming Indian whiskey, many an argument between trappers,
wolfers and Indians were settled by guns. . . .

   Reed and Bowles, now having established for themselves a permanent home, felt they should take unto themselves a woman. The
only ones available were Indians. . . .

   How Bowles got his wife is a well known story, having been
published a number of times.

   Bowles stood outside of Reed's fort, or station, one morning talking in sign language to a considerable party of Crow Indians, when
a fine looking young Indian girl, the daughter of Long Horse, head
chief of the Crows, walked up to him and startled him by spitting
at him. As soon as she did this she ran away, laughing.

   Bowles was offended and did not hesitate to express his feelings
to men of the tribe around him whom he knew were his friends.
They laughed and explained that the girl was in love with him and
had taken the method used in the tribe in a case like that to let him

know of her affections. They informed him further, that he was expected, in the event that he liked her, to pursue the girl. If he caught her she became his wife.

Bowles had been an admirer of the girl so he immediately started running. In three minutes he found himself with a wife. He considered the whole transaction as a most satisfactory method of courting and saving lots of time. To celebrate his wedding he gave a sumptuous feast to relatives of the girl.[3]

Reed did not have as good luck with his Indian woman. For two years he lived with Emma Shane, a half-breed French-Crow maiden. She bore him one child and might have been a faithful wife had she not become enamored of a big Negro cook that Reed had hired to work in the kitchen.

. . . Reed, without their knowledge, found out about it and without letting them know and while drunk, ordered the negro to dig a grave. The negro complied without suspicion, that not being an uncommon occurrence, and reported to Reed that the grave was completed and was good enough for anyone. Reed whipped out his gun, shot the negro and threw him into the grave. At the point of the gun he forced Emma Shane to fill the grave. Emma took advantage of the darkness and the drunken condition of Reed and, with her child, escaped on horseback to Fort Benton.[4]

The relationship between Bowles and Reed, often strained, erupted one day into a near-fatal fight. It is supposed that both men had been drinking and the major had become extremely surly. After a heated argument, Reed stabbed Bowles in the stomach with a bowie knife; whereupon, wounded as he was, Bowles beat Reed mercilessly, breaking his jaw, dislocating his shoulder and inflicting other terrible injuries from which

---

[3] Oscar Mueller in the *Lewistown Daily News,* December 18, 1949.
[4] *Ibid.*

Reed nearly died. However, he finally recovered and left the country.

Meanwhile, friends loaded the wounded Bowles into a wagon and started the 150 miles to Fort Benton for medical aid. After days of jolting over the prairie in the wagon, Bowles was in serious condition on reaching the fort. The skill of a doctor, combined with his rugged constitution and the care in a hospital started him well on the way to recovery—so well that, chafing under the inactivity, he left his bed and sauntered down to the saloon. There he found many friends and a few enemies—wolfers, trappers, miners. After a few drinks, he again became involved in fisticuffs. He knocked down his opponent, but he himself collapsed from weakness, and his partially healed wound was broken open.

The hospital attendants picked him up; the surgeon sewed him together again, and before long he was as good as ever. He remained in Montana for many years but, finally, as the state became more civilized, he moved to Alaska about the turn of the century.

Montana is still a frontier state, always too busy with the future to be much concerned about the past. Visitors from older regions are surprised that so little has been done to preserve the landmarks and relics of the state's fascinating history. One of the few of these that has been preserved is the old post office of Reed's Fort. The building, appropriately marked with a commemorative tablet, was presented to the city of Lewistown by the Daughters of the American Revolution and can be seen today in very much the same condition as when Alonzo Reed handed out the mail that was brought in by weekly stage from Fort Benton.

OPHIR

THE ROUTE OF THE GREAT RIVER, "WILD MIZZOURYE," "Old Muddy," captured the imagination of those who sought a fortune in trade. Since 1846, Fort Benton, thirty miles above the mouth of the Marias, had been the head of navigation on the Missouri. By 1864, it was in the heyday of its prosperity. The Missouri, from St. Louis north, was alive with stern-wheel steamers carrying supplies and adventurers to the thriving gold fields of Virginia City, Bannack, and Last Chance. Detachments of troops, with all their supplies and equipment, disembarked here for assignment to more remote places that needed protection from the Indians. Miners coming from rich diggings swelled the crowds and the wealth as they waited for a steamer back to "the States" or just drifted in to stay the winter.

The money these men spent during their short stops in Benton represented, in the aggregate, a colossal sum. Plummer and members of his bandit gang, with the loot of many robberies in their possession, made their expenditures for pleasure there, because they were afraid to spend too much money in Virginia City. Hurdy-gurdies, gambling houses, and saloons never closed. Gold dust abounded. Merchants and hotel men and all who catered to the river trade were very prosperous. It was the metropolis of the young territory of Montana.

Natually the idea would occur to enterprising frontiersmen, "Why Fort Benton?" From the Musselshell to the Marias the Missouri was extremely dangerous to navigation. There were sand bars and rapids, treacherous currents and more treacherous Indians. Wouldn't a town farther down the river avoid some of these hazards and, being closer to "the States," capture most of this lucrative traffic?

In July, 1864, Captain James Moore, of the stern-wheel steamer *Cutter*, arrived at the mouth of the Marias River, thirty miles below Benton. He had with him a number of immigrants from Minnesota. Something went wrong with the machinery of the boat, and the passengers continued the journey on foot. The boat was tied up for the winter.

While lying at the mouth of the Marias, Captain Moore conceived the idea of founding a town there which would rival Fort Benton. His dream was to build a river metropolis. He squatted on ground for the townsite, which he decided to call Ophir, platted the townsite in a rude way, and set off for Virginia City, then in the first flush of its placer prosperity, with the idea of interesting capital in his enterprise.

Alder Gulch had given up her riches lavishly that season, and Moore found eager listeners. He told of the desirability of the townsite, of the deep harbor, and dwelt on the fact that his town was thirty miles down the river and would be the first town of any consequence that the voyagers would reach after the long trip from St. Louis. He sold lots right and left at inside property prices and experienced no difficulty in interesting a considerable amount of capital in his

scheme. Laden with gold dust which was the treasury
of his townsite company, and accompanied by twenty
men who had put money into his undertaking, Moore
started in the middle of winter back to the new river
town of Ophir. The season was too far advanced to
permit much activity, but a large double long cabin,
the offices and headquarters of the company, was constructed. When it was completed, the promoters spent
the rest of the winter dreaming of the rich harvest of
next year.

The residents of Fort Benton were naturally much
incensed at Moore's designs on their prosperity. They
became so antagonistic that he was warned to keep
away from their town. Several of his associates who
ventured to make necessary purchases were compelled
to make a hurried and unceremonious exit.

About this time a Blood Indian, on a spree with a
half-breed, was murdered near Fort Benton, and his
body was thrown into the river. His tribe decided to
make reprisals on the white men. Fort Benton was too
large and strong for them so they selected Ophir as the
place of vengeance.

A few days after the Benton murder, ten white men
and a Negro from Ophir went up the river to cut
timber for the new settlement. Calf-Shirt, a Blood
chieftain, with a strong party of 180 warriors, ambushed the group. The Indians "employed the usual
tactics of circling around them as they endeavored to
reach the river and friends. They fought valiantly,
using the bodies of oxen killed by the attacking In-

dians as breastworks, but it was a losing fight and the party was exterminated."[1]

This tragedy was the death blow of Ophir. The settlers lost heart and one by one moved on. The repairs to the steamer having been completed, the boat dropped down the river, and its departure marked the end of Moore's project.

Today a monument stands beside U.S. 87, moved there in 1959 from its original location at the site of the massacre on the right bank of the Marias.[2]

---

[1] Tom Stout, ed., *Montana, its Story and Biography* (Chicago: American Historical Society, 1921), I, 338.

[2] This account is essentially that of Dan Conway in the *Kalispell Times*, February 17, 1927.

7

KERCHIVAL

THE NEXT ATTEMPT TO CAPTURE FORT BENTON'S TRADE
came in 1866. Many miles farther down the Missouri
at the mouth of the Musselshell, the land fell back
from the river in a pleasant valley. From here, roads
led to the gold fields. During low water or other conditions adverse to navigation on the upper Missouri
goods were frequently unloaded here and freighted to
Benton, Virginia City, and Last Chance; in fact, one
of the notorious Slade's first freighting assignments in
Montana was over this road from the mouth of the
Musselshell to Virginia City in 1863. Furthermore, the
economy was diversified. Not only would the wealth
of the mines flow through a town here, but it was also
the logical center for the Indian trade, the wolfing
business and the wood-hawking industry that kept the
necessary supplies of fuel for the steamers plying the
river. With all these factors in mind, a group of men
organized the Rocky Mountain Wagon Road Company
and in 1866 opened a regular freight route between
the spot and western Montana. A townsite was laid
out and the town named Kerchival City in honor of
an old steamboat captain who was a partner in the
enterprise. A trading post was built and plans for a
city were drawn up.

Although Kerchival's hope of monopolizing the Missouri River freighting did not materialize because of the powerful opposition of Fort Benton, the post did thrive briefly on the Indian trade.

The trading method was very simple, for everything was purchased with a robe, such as a robe's worth of sugar, or a robe's worth of coffee. The Indians did not understand at that time that they could divide the value of the robe, and buy part in coffee and part in sugar. This made trading especially easy and many robes could be purchased in a short time.

The prices on goods were high then. A gun sold for six or eight robes, while groceries were measured out in a tin cup. Three cups of coffee cost one robe, while ten cups of flour or six cups of sugar had the same price. . . .

When the Indian came to the fort to trade, he always brought his wife along, for she had to carry the family purse. And hard it was to manage the carrying of that purse, for it was simply a huge load of robes which she had piled on her back. . . . She marched to the counter where the man unloaded her one robe at a time.

He threw each robe over the counter and called for what he wanted, until only a couple of robes were left. Then it was the squaw's turn to buy what she wanted. These were spent for beads and she was very careful in choosing her colors. . . .

As the Crows were the best customers of the Kerchival fort, great care and experience was necessary to bring the right colors of beads and proper merchandise to be traded in order to get more robes and to satisfy the customers. Their styles in beadwork changed just as our dress styles change today, so the trader had to keep in touch with their changing styles and demands.[1]

The legislature named Kerchival City as the county seat of the newly formed Musselshell County, but even this distinction failed to bring sufficient life to the little post. Business and interest declined steadily; then one spring day high water washed even the site of Kerchival City into "Old Muddy."

[1] Eva Town Murphy in *Midland Empire Farmer*, December 20, 1934. For twenty years she lived within three miles of Kerchival City townsite.

8

MUSCLESHELL CITY

IN 1868 A MORE DETERMINED ATTEMPT WAS LAUNCHED
to establish a trading post at the mouth of the Musselshell. This time the Montana Hide and Fur Company, an organization of Helena businessmen, sent James
Brewer to the spot with instructions to establish a town.
He arrived in March, 1868, did as he was commanded
and called the town Muscleshell City.

During the summer months many people from down river points
and from the mountain settlements flocked to the new town; and,
before winter set in, eight buildings were ranged in line fronting
the river bank. The town then had a population of fifty people,
while there were usually many transient trappers, woodhawks and
river men. About this time, a company of troops under Captain
Nugent of the Thirteenth Infantry arrived at Musselshell from Fort
Cooke. They built a stockade with bastions at a location just a
short distance below the town. . . .[1]

Wolfers, perhaps, as a class, the toughest of the men
who roamed early Montana, made Muscleshell City their
headquarters. Peter Koch, who lived at Muscleshell during the winter of 1869 and 1870 describes the wolfer:

. . . As soon as cold weather began, he would start into his chosen
field. Generally two went together for company and greater safety.
Their outfit consisted of their blankets, coffee, sugar, flour and a
liberal supply of ammunition and strychnine. It was necessary to

---

[1] Dan Conway in the *Kalispell Times,* May 19, 1927.

go to the buffalo country, because the wolves followed the buffalo
herd, and yet, if possible, the place selected must be one where the
Indians do not hunt much, or too many carcasses would be left
lying around on the prairies. The first thing to do was to put out
baits in convenient places where buffalo were killed. These were
partly skinned and three or four bottles of strychnine, containing
one-eighth ounce each, were sprinkled over the carcass after gash-
ing it well with the knife, and the strychnine was rubbed into the
flesh and the blood with the hands and then left. Another buffalo
was killed a mile or two from the first and prepared in the same
way and so on, until frequently thirty or forty baits were put out,
generally forming a circle. During mild weather it was necessary
to visit the baits every few days to skin the poisoned wolves, or
the hide would become loose and the skins spoil. Where the country was not too dangerous the wolfer managed to take advantage
of the mild spells throughout the winter and keep his wolves well
skinned up; but if he couldn't do that, the dead wolves, when frozen
stiff, were piled up to protect them as far as possible from the mag-
pies, which birds spoiled many skins in spite of all precautions. Towards spring a final visit was paid to the baits, all the wolves were
skinned and the furs carried to the nearest trading post, where each
skin was worth about three dollars. . . . It was an exceedingly rough
and dangerous life, but for that reason all the more attractive to
the class of men engaged in it, and a successful wolfer made considerable money. . . .

Frequently the wolfer was "set a-foot" (i.e. had his horse stolen)
on the prairie and had to make his way to the nearest post, as best
he could. His work was mostly in the open plains country, where
he suffered greatly from the winter blizzards. I have heard many
tales of frightful sufferings and know of several instances, where
the hapless wolfer was reduced to feeding on the carcasses of the
poisoned wolves. Strangely enough I have known several old wolfers
who always fried their batter-cakes in wolf fat, when obtainable,
alleging that it gave a much finer flavor to the cakes than if fried
in any other kind of grease.[2]

Not only did the Sioux harass the wolfers, but they
also threatened the whole town of Muscleshell just as

[2] Historical Society of Montana, *Contributions*, II (1896), 301-2.

they had threatened Kerchival City. A series of letters from Muscleshell City published in the *Weekly Herald* of Helena, in 1869, graphically, if a bit ungrammatically, tells of the Indian trouble.

DOWN THE RIVER

Muscelshell, Apr. 27, 1869—All the sufferers from the late Indian raid, so far as bodily injury is concerned, have nearly recovered, excepting the woman who was scalped. She is doomed to wear a wig the rest of her days while Mr. Lo[3] (the noble red man who the government arms and feeds) dances and shouts his war songs around that portion of her physical economy that once adorned her upper works. But such is life and such will be the condition of things just as long as the Northwest Fur company are allowed to conduct Indian affairs and control Indian agents along the river. When it comes to protection against the ruthless savages we have only our own nerves and trusty rifles.

May 1st, 1869—To the Editor: I wrote you a communication on the 23rd of April and which I sent out by our private mail, but the friendly Assinaboines, that recently scalped Jordan, Long and Foster, and wounded "Big Dan" at Joe Bushaway's wood yard, took possession of the letters and papers destined for Helena and I fear they must have neglected to forward them in the right direction.

On the 29th of March a party of men from Thompson Gulch and Diamond City arrived here from the Black Butte where they had been wolfing and had been surprised and attacked by Major Collin's contented, reconstructed, friendly Crows. They were compelled to fight incessantly for three days and finally creep away in a dark night after losing many valuable horses and several hundred dollars worth of valuable furs. They arrived at this place on foot, worn out and destitute as vagrants.

Smith and Andrews were getting out timber from the Muscle-

---

[3] Lo, the poor Indian! whose untutor'd mind
   Sees God in clouds or hears him in the wind;
     Pope, *Essay on Man*, Epis. i. l. 99.

Pope's expression, twisted in both meaning and grammatical use, appeared widely throughout the West, sometimes as Mr. Lo, Poor Lo, etc., as a derisive term used to ridicule what frontiersmen considered the too-lenient and unrealistic treatment of the Indians by the government in Washington.

shell, employing four hands in the woods and three teams in hauling. Major Brewer and Captain Andrews were driving two of the teams. A white woman and some squaws had gone to carry dinner to the men. Brewer had unloaded in town and was about 500 yards on his return. Andrews was about a half mile from town coming, and the women on the road between the two when sudden as unexpected, the dreaded warwhoop was heard, and 60 naked, yelling painted warriors came charging down the hill and in a moment were close upon their victims.

Brewer jumped from the wagon firing as he went, and after running a fearful gauntlet through the storm of leaden hail, safely reached the stockade. The poor woman ran with the speed of a frightened deer but was soon overtaken. One of the squaws was shot through the thigh and the white woman stopped to pick her up but had only got the squaw to her feet when she herself was shot through the neck and fell and the Indians rushed upon her and tore the scalp from her head.

Captain Andrews in the meantime, being much further out than any of the others, and having all the Indians in front of him, came slowly down the road firing at long range at the Indians in pursuit of the women. After a few shots he missed his cap box, and turning to look for it saw another large band of Indians in his rear. Then came tall running, comic dodging and fine strategy in the game of life and death.

Andrews left the road and made for the trees along the Muscleshell, but being cut off from these he took a course more toward the village, shots and arrows at all times falling thick around him. His clothes were literally cut into ribbons and his hat shot from his head, yet he kept on his course, frequently turning and leveling his now useless gun, making the savages fall in the brush to avoid his supposed fatal shot and thereby losing time in the pursuit.

The Indian shots were finally exhausted and Andrews' oft repeated ruse had become old, when a few Indians rushed upon him with their war clubs and soon found that an old soldier (even with an empty rifle in his hand) would not die like a dog.

While the fight was going on, hand to hand, club to clubbed rifle, a small party headed by Colonel Clendenning and C. M. Veits, rushed to the rescue just in time to prevent old Cap from passing in his checks. Clendenning's party pressed to the rescue of the men in the timber and found them in safety. Andrews went to camp calling for volunteers to assist in finding the woman. They soon found her scalped and shot in two places and bruised with war clubs, revealing a sight well calculated to curdle the blood in one's veins and render his dreams horrible for days to come. They found her in a semi-conscious condition, faintly calling for help and water. She was taken to her cabin.

May 8th, 1869—We have but a few quiet days here. We have even to fight for the wood with which to cook our grub. This morning about eight o'clock, a white man and two squaws went out about 400 yards from camp to pick up wood. While thus engaged a band of Indians suddenly arose from the sage brush within a few yards of them and commenced yelling and firing. The wood party fled, as only people can who are pursued by Indians, and their clothes completely riddled with bullets, reached the city unharmed.

The Indians now appeared in full force, swarming through the sage brush—Santee Sioux numbering between one and two hundred. But the men of the Muscleshell were not daunted nor did they falter. Immediately upon the alarm being given, the men grasped their everready breech loaders and with a yell that would shake even an Indian's nerves, went flying across the field to attack the savage foes.

A running fight now ensued for a distance of half a mile, when some eighty of the Indians took shelter in a deep and crooked coulee emptying into the Muscleshell. The men charged their position and were unable to dislodge them. In the charge Jacob Leader was shot in the brain, dying instantly. The men now divided themselves into several parties and took possession of every side of the coulee save that next to the river in a vain endeavor to find a position from which to bear their rifles on the Indians. Although a heavy rain was falling and the position of the Indians seemed impregnable, the shower of shot and arrows coming like hail from the coulee, none seemed willing to turn their backs, leave the fight or draw the game.

The fight went on for six hours with no results save the killing of one or two Indians and Mr. Greenwood, who was seriously wounded. Some of the boys now became desperate. Frank Smith, Jim Wells and Frenchy went below, waded the thick willows and continuously made their way upstream until they reached a point immediately opposite and in easy range of the coulee that concealed the Indians.

Here was presented such a hornets' nest as seldom falls to the lot of a white man. Being in point blank range, they turned loose their Henry's with such fatal effect as to make a good Indian[4] at every fire. The red devils realized their position in an instant and saw nothing but certain death on every side. With a yell of rage and a howl of despair, they fled like frightened elk.

The whites now completely surrounding them, arose from their cover, closed in and death and destruction on every side. Law! You should have been there to see Mr. Lo the poor red man pass in his checks! Thirteen fell on the spot while many more went floating down the stream, or crept wounded or in a dying condition into the thick willows along its bank. Their loss in killed and wounded could not have been less than fifty.

The woman recently scalped at the place is alive and on her pegs. She perched herself upon a high bastion while the fight was going on and when the boys came in with 13 bleeding scalps at their belts, she felt somewhat consoled for the loss of her top knot. . . .

Captain Andrews—or Dr. Andrews—has dressed Greenwood's wound and is now busy cleaning scalps.

It may seem to you in cities and safe places that it is barbarous to scalp and maim dead Indians, but our everyday experience teaches us that we must, however revolting it may be to our feelings, resort to their own savage mode of warfare, in order to make our arms feared and our strength respected. . . .[5]

The scalping of the Indians was not the most barbarous act of the battle. The following day Andrews went out and cut the heads from ten of the dead Sioux. After severing and preserving the ears as souvenirs, he boiled the heads until the skull could be cleaned. He then impaled each skull on a stick fastened to the stockade; from this vantage point they grinned down at the horrified passengers arriving on the steamboats from the East.

---

[4] Livereatin' Johnson's motto, widely adopted on the frontier, "There is no good Indian except a dead Indian."

[5] *Kalispell Times*, May 19, 1927.

... a little to one side, as if guarding them, stood a trapper, well known throughout eastern Montana, by the sobriquet of "Liver-eating Johnson."[6] He was leaning on a crutch, with one leg bandaged, and the day being hot his entire dress consisted in a scant, much shrunken, red undershirt, reaching just below his hips. His matted hair and bushy beard fluttered in the breeze and his giant frame and limbs, so freely exposed to view, formed an exceedingly impressive and characteristic picture.[7]

From this time on the enraged Sioux harassed the whites up and down the Missouri. Wolfers and wood-hawks were murdered and mutilated. This constant danger, combined with the failure to win the freight business from Fort Benton, discouraged those who had started out with such high hopes. Within three years after the town's founding, it was being abandoned. Finally, in 1874, the military garrison was dismantled and moved to Carroll. About two hundred cords of wood valued at $4.50 per cord were left behind to be burned by the ever-vengeful Sioux.

Today the blood and ashes of Kerchival City and Muscleshell[8] City are buried deep beneath the waters of the Missouri where it was backed up by the building of Fort Peck dam.

---

[6] A detailed treatment of "Liver-eatin'" Johnson has no place here as he belonged to the earlier era of trappers and scouts, an era during which the wilderness was unmarred by "cities." The origin of his nickname is hotly disputed. After the Crow Indians had killed his wife and unborn child, he dedicated himself to the extermination of the Crow nation. However, according to one of his friends, he never actually ate the liver from those who fell before his wrath. One day, however, admits his friend, he did cut open a Crow corpse, remove the liver and, holding it aloft, dripping, ask if any of his comrades wanted a bite. The other extreme is Raymond Thorp, who, in his recent biography of Liver-eatin', would have us believe that the vast prowess of this mountain man was attributable chiefly to his diet of Crow liver.

[7] Historical Society of Montana, *Contributions*, II, 293.

[8] The troublesome spelling of Musselshell caused the early inhabitants much confusion beginning with at least three variations in the Lewis & Clark journals. "Muscleshell" was the most common in early days.

9

GAUGLERSVILLE

ANOTHER LANDMARK ON THE MUSSELSHELL THAT HAS disappeared is Gauglersville. What was once Frank Gaugler's store building at Gauglersville has been torn down. In the interest of sightliness, the old building on the Settle ranch has been razed and removed, and one more "first" structure has vanished. . . . This dilapidated building was all that remained of the town that was once a rival of Clendenin, later to become "old" Martinsdale. Gauglersville saw plenty of excitement. Its old logs were full of bullet holes and the punctures of Indian arrows. An old picture of the interior of the store shows rows of lanterns hanging from the ceiling, bolts of flannel and calico on the shelves, and heavy-booted men lounging around the big stove.

The original building of the settlement was L-shaped, with dirt roof and floors, with the trading post in one end. It was about 12 by 16 feet, with a bar across one end. In early days trinkets for the Indian trade were the most prominent display, and the shelves were packed with "sourdough" clothing. "Two-bits" was the minimum price on any item, no matter how trivial.

And what of Carroll, that seemed to profit always by the deaths of these other towns? After its founding in 1874 it prospered greatly for several years. The Diamond R, greatest freighting concern between the

Mississippi and the Pacific, was linked closely with Carroll, and it became an important landing place on the Missouri. However, with the coming of the Utah and Pacific and the Northern Pacific railways, river traffic fell off, the famous Diamond R disbanded, and the town of Carroll declined until today it is only a memory.

10

GALLATIN CITY

AT THE THREE FORKS OF THE MISSOURI RIVER, BELOW the junction of the Jefferson and the Madison rivers and near the mouth of the Gallatin River, was a settlement located before Montana became a territory and given the rather imposing name of Gallatin City.

It was said that Gallatin City was laid out by certain enterprising Missourians who expected it to prove the head of navigation of the Missouri River, forgetting that there was a slight obstruction below in the shape of tremendous falls, and that after receiving a few lessons in geography most of them abandoned the location.

However, Gallatin City did become quite a promising town for a brief period; it had a townsite company, was temporarily the county seat of Gallatin County, and sessions of the district court were held there.

After the incorporation of the county of Gallatin the first meeting of the county board was held March 11, 1865, at the residence of A. F. Nichols, near Gallatin City, and at the meeting of June 28, the same year, it was agreed that the county should rent from J. B. Campbell his residence at Gallatin City for the use of the county clerk at two hundred dollars a year. The board also appropriated $10,000 for the erection at Gallatin City of county buildings, which, however, were never built.

At the election of Sept. 4, 1865, thirty-four electors appeared and voted at the polls in Gallatin City.

The first district court in Gallatin County was held in Major Campbell's house in Gallatin City in July, 1867. Owing to the clouds of mosquitoes present, court was held in the midst of dense smoke created by burning pine boughs, which dispersed the mosquitoes and well nigh dispersed the court.

Gallatin City, after its initial boom either did not look very good to the sole newspaper in the territory, the *Montana Post* of Virginia City, or else community jealousy prompted it to belittle the new community:

Sept. 3, 1864 GALLATIN CITY
We have got the headline, and being leaded looks well on paper. Not wishing to say by any means this is a paper town, "Oh, No!" The old mountaineers frequently resort thither when game becomes scarce in the settled portions of the territory to hunt and antelope are readily brought down in the city limits. We don't know the town company but presume when they laid off the city was like the fellow that set the hen on 100 eggs, he wanted to see her spread herself.

We learn at latest advices from a gentleman who had just passed through the city that it contained one family, but they were daily looking for another. There was a certain Mr. Campbell who was some two months in the country last year, and who sometimes writes for the Chicago Tribune. This gentleman went home with "sore feet," published a pamphlet giving all the particulars of our territory, in which Gallatin fills a prominent part.

The picture in the pamphlet shows a church with a somewhat tall spire, a military post, with paper soldiers, of course, a steamboat at the wharf busily discharging cargoes, etc. We don't know how much he received for all his trouble, but if he got nothing he must have been taking "a drop of the critter," until steamboats, soldiers, churches and large townsites danced in his imagination, for surely none before or since have been able to discover any of these things. Having thus briefly described the city and having ourselves been sold, thinking at one time to locate there, we of course feel a little tender on the subject.

Whether Gallatin will be able to hold her "oats" remains to be seen but she is certainly at the present in bad condition, let it be recorded. . . .

In 1876 Lieutenant Bradly, en route with General Gibbon and troops from Fort Shaw to the aid of Terry, Custer, and Crook in the Big Horn country, camped near Gallatin City and under date of March 26, 1876, wrote:

Soon after crossing the ferry. . . . We passed the few straggling houses known as Gallatin City and camped on the plain half a mile below. . . . Two of the locators of Gallatin City, W. J. Beal and D. E. Rouse, abandoned the place within two years of their arrival in the valley. . . . It was in the fore part of July, 1864, while Beal and Rouse were returning from Virginia City, where they had marketed their crops of potatoes and other vegetables at 40 cents per pound, that they met John M. Bozeman, whom they had known in 1863 and he had returned east that fall.

Bozeman told them he was piloting an immigrant train from the east over what is now known as the Bozeman cut-off. He advised them to move up the valley and to take up land and start a town on the present location of the city of Bozeman. He also asked them to locate a claim for him.

During the same month Beal and Rouse located adjoining claims or farms on the site of the present city of Bozeman and built the first two houses there. . . . As Bozeman went up Gallatin City went down.[1]

---

[1] Wilchey in the *Kalispell Times*, October 23, 1941.

11

JUNCTION CITY

THE SITE OF JUNCTION IS A SMALL FLAT OF BOTTOM LAND SUR-
rounded by some low bluffs. Much of the original site has of recent
years washed into the river. It is located a short distance to the
right after crossing the river bridge from Custer, almost directly
below a neglected graveyard which is intersected by the road. The
main street of Junction faced the river, a wide thoroughfare, in its
thriving days filled with bull teams and wagons. A row of cottonwood trees was between the street and the river. The old road grade
may still be seen, coming down at right angles to the main street
from the north. . . .

The first stage station at Junction City was kept by "Muggins"
Taylor, who had been at Fort Pease and afterwards was a scout with
Gibbons, taking the message of Custer's disaster to Bozeman and
Helena. Taylor later came to Coulson where he was killed while
acting as deputy sheriff and is buried in Boothill cemetery. A stream
through Pease bottom is known as Muggins creek. . . .

Junction City long had a reputation as a wide open town. In
1883 there was 14 saloons and three dance halls in the village.
During the building of the Northern Pacific railway, however, it
escaped some of the flood of undesirable citizens that made construction towns along the line places of bloodshed. About ten miles east
Kurtzville had the reputation during its brief existence of being
the worst town in the territory. When the railway built on beyond
the Big Horn river, Kurtzville was, however, soon abandoned.

. . . A number of episodes . . . give some of the western flavor
that belonged to the little cowtown which kept its frontier char-
acteristics long after the towns situated on the railway had almost
forgotten what a cowboy looked like.

Billy McCormick . . . was arrested for striking Frank Campbell
with an ax. Billy . . . was the mail carrier, and on his arrest claimed
immunity, but Burr, the justice, held him for trial. He placed the

bonds at $50 and when Judge J. R. Goss, who was county attorney, protested at the smallness of the bail, Burr replied that an ax was not a deadly weapon but an instrument to cut wood with. The bond was raised to $250, however, but McCormick left the country after placing the bond.

There was at Junction a German violinist, known as Professor Glab, who was employed in a saloon as an orchestra leader. A bully, who was the terror of the town, appeared in the street with a Winchester and revolver and ordered everyone to come in the saloon and drink with him. The professor said that he did not care for anything. But when the town terror shot a hole in his hat he took the enforced drink. The professor then quietly borrowed a shotgun and concealed himself until the bully passed, when he let him have both barrels at once. With howls and yells the bully fell on the ground and begged for mercy. A physician later picked about 200 fine bird shot from his back.

During the time when horse stealing was rampant in central Montana, Junction City was on the trail of a large band of thieves operating between Wyoming and the Canadian line and Junction City merchants got a good share of business from the passing bandits, particularly the saloons and dance halls. There was an unwritten agreement by which the property of the townsmen was unmolested while the Junction City folks did not interfere with the rustlers' movements. But Granville Stuart and his "regulators" shortly afterward cut off this source of revenue.

On April 5, 1883, Junction was visited by a destructive fire that, starting in the Brown & Davis saloon and lodging house, destroyed several adjoining buildings at a loss of $10,000. . . . The townspeople formed a bucket line to the river. As most of the places threatened were saloons, jugs of whiskey were sent down the line, each third bucket of water being followed by a jug. By the time the fire was out there was only five sober men left in the town. . . .

Before the railroad was built steam boats came up the river regularly. In 1878, nine steamers made 15 trips up the Yellowstone. Most of them came as far as Junction City but some went to Camp Bertie near Pompeys Pillar, while, under favorable conditions, they got as far as Huntley or Coulson. The arrival of the boats made business for the freighters who hauled the goods on as far as Bozeman, and for the stage lines. . . .

About 1884 there was some Indian trouble and there were reports of the Sioux and Cheyennes coming to fight the Crows. . . .

The accidental death of an Indian boy of 14 or 15 brought on one of the most exciting episodes in the history of Junction City. A housewife noticing an Indian dog skulking about her henhouse fired a shot at it with a small caliber rifle. It struck the boy, whom she did not see, in the temple but it was not until the Indians missing the boy discovered his body that the tragedy was made clear. The boy was the son of Big Ox, who had been a great friend of the whites. He was with a band of about 100 families of Crows who were camped across from Custer. The death, coupled with the fact that several Crows had just been placed in jail at Billings for horse stealing, aroused the bitterest feelings among the Crows.

Day and night, the Indian camp resounded with blood-curdling howls and shrieks of lamentation, while the relatives cut their fingers and went through their customary manifestations of grief. The hostile flare first showed itself when a young Indian threatened the woman, who had unintentionally shot the boy, with a knife. Her friends took measures for her protection while at the same time every effort was made to quiet the Indians.

Paul McCormick loaded up a great wagon with flour, meat and other provisions and took it to the Indian camp, with several other citizens as escorts and they endeavored to explain the accidental nature of the death. Those who remained in town were warned to be on their guard night and day. The boy was offered a white man's burial and his family was given all manner of gifts for an atonement. It is said that but for the labors of Father Prando of the Catholic mission that even then the efforts to placate the Indians would have been in vain. The father, in spite of the death of the boy, remained a friend of the whites. The Indian boy is among those buried in the cemetery above Junction. . . .[1]

About nearly everyone buried in the Junction cemetery there could be told a fascinating tale.

There were a number of suicides who are buried there, a young gambler named Gillman, a woman called "Tex" and a Chinese who took strychnine because his squaw left him and went back to the tribe. In 1878 a young soldier, J. C. McCullough, shot himself

---

[1] W. H. Banfill in the *Billings Gazette,* February 1, 1931.

on an island below Junction. He had several thousand dollars and was to be discharged soon. Sergeant Wessenger came down the night before with $30,000 to pay the men stationed at the cantonment. McCullough, who had planned to go home, lost all his money in a poker game that night. He was buried beside two large sandstone rocks on the Ben Green ranch in Pease bottom.

A Negro called Andy, whose feet were frozen off and who was interpreter for Paul McCormick with the Crows, was killed by a man named Sam James Reed, who was killed by James Carpenter at Wolf Springs in a quarrel over Reed's Indian wife, was buried at Junction where his brother, Joseph Reed lived. David Conklin, who died under suspicious circumstances of poison, was buried the same evening that he died on the Junction bluffs.[2]

All of these, however, are forgotten, but one citizen of Junction City, "Muggins" Taylor, won lasting fame when he carried the news of the Custer massacre to the outside world.

[2] Ibid.

12

COULSON

AS THE RAILROAD MOVED WEST, IT, TOO, SPAWNED towns across the state that were to live and die with the coming and going of men working on the rails.

"Bud" McAdow stood on the banks of the Yellowstone (in the early fall of 1877) and, gazing for miles across the Clarke's Fork bottom, saw, like Jacob of old, that it was good. And like Jacob, he had a vision; the railroad, then at Bismarck, Dakota, would bring to the spot a city; hundreds of farmers would be drawn thither, now that the Sioux no longer menaced the settler; it would become a cattle center; the hub of a vast area potentially rich. Perry W. McAdow was not an illusionist nor a dreamer; he was a practical Missourian who had good horse sense. He at once acquired a large tract of land at the lower end of the bottom and built a store, stocking it with goods hauled by team from Bozeman or the nearest landing place of the river steamers; for boats, before the advent of the railroad, came up as far as Junction City, at the mouth of the Rosebud, one, the Josephine, reaching a point nearly opposite to where Billings now stands.

The trading point was named Coulson, presumably in honor of one of the steamboat captains, and by 1881, had become a place of some importance, being provided with a postoffice, an eating station for the overland stage, a saloon, a gambling hall, a livery stable, a blacksmith shop and was the center of railroad grading operations. Coulson was about to occupy a place on the map.

The winter of 1881 brought the adventurous pioneer by all manner of means, stage coach, wagon train, on horseback and on foot. It became apparent that at this point must arise one of the great centers, a "Denver of the North." The winter was cold, bitterly cold, for those who had to abide in the hastily built shacks, floored and covered with dirt. Those there were who were privileged to sleep in McAdow's store. Not infrequently a Crow Indian, high in his council, became an occupant of these quarters, announcing the duration of his stay by the height in which he hung his headgear on the wall. . . .

In this pleasant company, partaking of "Bud's" open hospitality, provided he furnish his own blankets, was "Muggins" Taylor, a soldier of fortune, who, but a short time previously had been in the employ of the government as a "Trailer" or scout. It was he who took the message of Custer's Massacre to the wires and gave the New York Herald readers an account of this memorable tragedy. . . .

"Liver Eating" Johnson was another member of Coulson society. For a time he held the office of deputy sheriff, and while he had no jail in which to incarcerate his prisoners, this was not necessary. For when "Liver Eating" finally came to the conclusion that it was time to act, he acted so thoroughly and so effectively that the wrong-doer was more in need of a hospital than a lockup. . . .[1]

Next to McAdow, John Alderson was considered Coulson's leading citizen. With his wife and child he had arrived in Coulson and staked out his acres on a beautiful bend of the Yellowstone. Unfortunately another pioneer, Dave Currier, chose the same land and a bitter feud developed.

Currier, seeking to get the law on his side, boarded the stage for Bozeman, the nearest recording office; Alderson, getting wind of this, saddled his fastest horse and made a record-breaking trip to Bozeman beating his opponent's time by several hours.

Currier, still unwilling to cede the land, took justice into his own hands, and a few days later, while Alderson was perched atop the ridge pole of his ice

---

[1] A. K. Yerkes in the *Hardin Tribune*, April 16, 1920. Yerkes published a newspaper at Coulson.

house, Currier, gun in hand, sought to slip up on him.
However, Mrs. Alderson saw the little drama, hurriedly
passed a rifle up to her husband who, from his superior
position settled the dispute once and for all.

After establishing himself, Alderson made far-sighted
plans for the growth of his city. He erected a dance hall
and imported seductive ladies from the East. He pro-
moted saloons and other business to attract the miners,
freighters, and cowboys. Soon wolfers and buffalo hunters were making Coulson their headquarters. In 1880
one fur dealer shipped 32,000 buffalo hides and 12,000
robes worth $164,000 down the Yellowstone.

Coulson was on the path of the growing cattle industry, and cowboys, horse thieves, and speculators
crowded her busy streets.

Coulson . . . had a main street of creditable length, and log houses
for the families were on every hand. It had a newspaper, lawyers,
doctors, real estate agents, and all that go to make up a city. The
leading citizens, voicing the sentiments of the principal land owners,
McAdow and Alderson, were unalterably of the opinion that no
power on earth could cheat Coulson of its ultimate greatness.[2]

The *Coulson Post* shared the optimism:

With every prospect of the early building by the Northern Pacific
of a principal feeder to Fort Benton from this point, the commence-
ment of the track laying season and the opening of the boating
season, the presence of a vast amount of lumber, Coulson can truthfully be said to have the most glorious future of any Yellowstone
City.

But almost within sight of this hustle and bustle, men set to
work to lay out another city and what they did to Coulson was
a-plenty. When June came and the railroad had left Miles City

_____
[2] *Ibid.*

on its way to the coast, Herman Clark, a townsite boomer, appeared and at once and forever stilled the pulsating hope and life of Coulson. He had builded better than the backers of Coulson knew. For he had gone to headquarters, secured the sanction and land of the railroad and by modern means of advertising and boosting stirred the whole western country with its promises and predictions. Lots were sold in Chicago, Duluth, St. Paul and Minneapolis, from the map, and then began the trek to the land of promise. People came from every direction and by all manner of conveyance, some even walking from the end of the track miles away. When the townsite was opened to sale at the town of Billings, then but the headquarters of the railroad engineers, people stood in line to get their first payment accepted.[3]

The *Post* editor, seeing the rising star of Billings, tried to reassure the citizens of Coulson.

Tis the same story. Towns that are now large cities have passed through the same experience. Only the daring and faithful will win.[4]

And the editor exhorts the people:

Let no man sit down and await developments. Life is too short to waste in waiting for new towns and enterprises to start up. Take hold and help and build up the country.[5]

On April 8, 1882, the *Post* reported the community was laboring "under anxiety, excitement, rumors, dispatches, schemes, reports and etc." and cautioned its readers not to be misled by hearsay accounts "of what the Northern Pacific is going to do for this section of the country." However, reality finally had to be faced: "Coulson is to be left out in the cold."

[3] *Ibid.*
[4] *Billings Gazette,* November 4, 1934.
[5] *Ibid.*

It was not the nature of the frontier spirit to languish long. A week later, along with its foreboding story of Coulson's doom, the paper splashed a vivid account of plans for the new town of Billings under the headline:

A SECOND DENVER

A bitter dose for Coulson, the town that had begun its career as the "Denver of the North."

After the establishment of Billings, activity was sporadic in Coulson. Its days were extended somewhat by the establishment there of a brewery by William Boots and George Ash of Billings. As part of Billings' promotional scheme a streetcar service had been established between the new town and Coulson. This service was conducted by two gaily painted streetcars shipped in from Minneapolis and pulled over their rails by a team of lively cayuses.

There was no definite schedule of arrivals and departures. The cayuses were kept in a pasture belonging to John Shock. . . . The animals were wise after their kind and sometimes Conductor Mann spent half the morning chasing them around the 40 acre lot before he could start his daily schedule. There were also likely to be delays through the car leaving the tracks. The curves were not built according to the most scientific principles and they occasioned much grief. As the months passed, dips and sways developed along the roadbed and rotting ties caused the rails to give as the car passed over until every trip became an adventure.

If the car derailed, the passengers helped in getting it back on the track or if this was too much of a task, teams were brought out to hoist it back while the passengers, if they were in a hurry, continued on foot, as the entire length of the line from Minnesota avenue to McAdow's store at Coulson was scarcely two miles.[6]

---

[6] W. H. Banfill in the *Hardin Tribune*, July 19, 1929.

Since the streetcar ride to Coulson was a popular pastime and since water had to be hauled to Billings but not to Coulson, Boots and Ash decided to locate their brewery (Boots Billings Beer) in Coulson.

A beer garden was conducted in connection with the brewery and the owners and the street-car proprietors struck upon a happy idea for bolstering up the diminishing travel to Coulson. A round trip ticket from Billings to Coulson was provided which bore a stub good for one schooner of beer when presented at the brewery. As the brewers correctly reasoned, one schooner on a hot day would not be enough for the average man and many more purchases would follow.

During the days of the brewery, Coulson also provided drilling grounds for Webbs' guards, an organization of the state militia that flourished for a few years. The brewery was usually visited after the drill period. There was also an early day sportsmen's association which had its target range near Coulson. A keg of beer from the brewery was an important part of the day's program.[7]

It would be gratifying to report that in such and such a museum could be seen one of these first streetcars of Montana. Unfortunately, like the town of Coulson, they are only a memory. One was sold to a farmer who set it up on the riverbank to be used as a milkhouse. One spring, during high water, it was washed down the river.

As a matter of sentiment, "Judge" Mann got possession of the other car and housed it in a barn at Billings. About 15 years ago, the Elks going to a convention at Miles City, after much cajolery and promises of safe return, got the car, put it on a flat car and took it to Miles City. It received such rough usage there that the Elks did not consider it worth while bringing it back. Judge Mann saw it once or twice afterwards, a wreck of its early grandeur, but the last time he was here he could find no trace of it.[8]

[7] *Ibid.*
[8] *Ibid.*

13

McCARTHYVILLE

AMONG "GHOST" TOWNS OF MONTANA IN WHOSE PALMY DAYS
flourished the romance of hard and fast living that gave the state
its early-day western flavor, probably none will live longer in the
memories of pioneers than McCarthyville, still declared by Montanans who sojourned there to have been "the toughest town in
the world."

It was a city for only 18 months, and that was some 50 years ago.
Then its population, always Arabic in disposition, wandered away,
the workers following the rails that Jim Hill was laying towards
Puget Sound and the adventurers in search of new excitement.

The garish false-fronted, frame dance halls, saloons, hotels, and
stores were wrecked for the lumber and the sturdier log buildings
finally succumbed to the weight of many deep snows. Now Mc-
Carthyville is represented only by a quartet of untenable cabins
squatted on the little prairie far below the Great Northern grade,
whose constuction was its sole reason for establishment and being,
and somewhere in the dusty records of Missoula county, by the
recorded plat of the townsite.

The town's founder and first mayor was Eugene McCarthy, who
later was police magistrate and justice of the peace.

"That town in its palmy days was a real, live settlement. It was
a place for rough men and there was nobody else there. From Cut
Bank west there was no other town and we were the metropolis of
miles of country full of working men. All the supplies for the
camps went out from McCarthyville and all the men from the
camps came in for their pay," McCarthy said of the town some
years ago.

Winter and summer the construction on the big grade from the
summit down was pushed and the camps held from three to four
thousand men. That made an enormous payroll for one town.
Teamsters got $40 a month and board and laborers around three

dollars. There was no regular pay day. Any man could get a check any time for what was due him, so there always was big money circulating in town.

McCarthyville also had the company hospital and in the winter of 1890 and 1891 that was the busiest place in town. Laborers were scarce in the west, so the company brought them out from the east, most of them picked up in cities. They'd come by train to Cut Bank and from there on had 80 miles of hiking across the prairies and over the summit.

It was about as tough a jaunt as any man would want and it was a whole lot more than most of these city fellows could stand. They weren't used to the altitude and hardly any of them had enough clothes. They'd start out from Cut Bank, in the dead of winter, and usually they'd get caught by a blizzard out on the flat. Then a couple of days later they'd wobble into McCarthyville and drop into a bunk with pneumonia.

Well, there wasn't many of them lived through. Buryings got too frequent and others began to take notice. Not that they bothered much in the way of attending services, because most residents didn't have time for funerals and anyway, there was no minister in town.

It got so that every morning just at daylight a big Swede that was a kind of nurse in the hospital would come outside with a hand sled. He'd have a body on it, wrapped in a two-dollar blanket, which was the first thing the company sold a new workman. Then he'd start off up the creek and perform the obsequies by digging a hole in the snow and rolling the corpse off the sled.

After this had been going on for some time Will Hardy, one of McCarthy's close friends, remarked one day, "I'm going to kill that Swede; he's getting on my nerves with his everlasting funerals at daylight."

"No," said McCarthy, "we don't want to get the Swede, the doctor's our man."

This doctor had come from Great Falls, where it was understood he had built up a fine reputation as a veterinarian. He had a contract with the construction company to look after the sick and injured men for a dollar per man per month. But these men who had just come in weren't on the payroll yet, so the men figured the doctor wasn't doing much to bring them back to the full vigor of youth.

It was agreed that the doctor probably was to blame for all sudden demises, so a committee of prominent citizens was organized which went to the hospital that night. Among those on the committee were McCarthy, Hardy, Mike Conley, Jack Lamey, Hiram Briggs and Ed Fox. The hospital was right in town and at that time was one of the poorest buildings there. It was a low, log cabin, no floor, and the only window was a hole covered with a canvas flap.

The committee went over in a body and McCarthy knocked on the door. The Swede opened it part way and then when he saw who it was he tried to shut it again but Hardy reached over and tapped him with the butt of a gun. He dropped like a beef. Then the men cast a glance about for the doctor, just in time to see his heels following him through the window. The canvas dropped and that was curtains for him. McCarthyville never saw him again.

Another doctor was secured and the death rate decreased. In the spring, when the snow went off, you could tell that the grim reaper had been amongst the residents. Sometimes the burial parties had gone through the six feet of snow and a short ways into the ground, but lots of them were just let down into the snow. Those that did get under some dirt were scratched out by the coyotes.

As an aid to maintaining population, McCarthyville's citizenry does not come in for glory. On one side of the ledger is a death list, which, while never kept account of, is estimated to have been several hundreds, and on the other side, one birth. A boy was born to a family named Cady.

"Yes, there was a good deal of shooting and one incident that I remember as the most depraved case of murder I know of in 40 years' living in Montana," McCarthy used to say in telling of the famous town.

"On Jan. 16, 1891, two brothers, Joe and Pierre Beaudin, had pitched a tent five miles above McCarthyville. They had quit their blacksmith shop at Two Medicine crossing and were coming over to our town to start a saloon. That day they stayed inside the tent playing freeze-out with three other men, LeBlanc, Winner and Warner.

"Along in the evening, while they were still at the game, the door was opened and two masked men ordered them to get their hands up and face towards the tent wall. Pierre Beaudin turned around once and one of the men said, 'if you look this way again I'll kill you.'

" 'Kill him anyway,' said the other and then they started shooting.

"Joe Beaudin was shot dead in the tent and all the others were hit except Warner, who made a dash when the shooting started and got away. Winner dropped to the floor with three wounds from a forty-five and crawled under a bunk. He managed to cut through the back wall of the tent and into the snow, but one of the men ran around and shot him twice in the head. Both shots were glancing and didn't kill him, though he was stunned. LeBlanc was fatally wounded and Pierre Beaudin was killed.

"Winner came to before long and managed to make his way to a camp and get word to town. I was deputy sheriff as well as mayor and I started for the tent with a posse. We found the dead men there and later heard that Warner had reached a camp to the east. On the way back to McCarthyville my horse shied at something in the road and jumped clear off a little bridge we were crossing. On the road we found Pierre Beaudin with nine holes in him. It looked like the murderers had shot him up after he was dead.

"It was known that the Beaudin boys and the others had about a thousand dollars among them, so we supposed it was a case of robbery, but in Joe Beaudin's pocket was a wallet containing $115. Then it looked like the coldest kind of murder.

"We took up the trail of the men and caught them. One was a half Mexican named Jim Cummins, who was known as a bad man from Oklahoma to the Canadian line. The man with him was Charlie Hart and we learned there was a fellow named Al Johnson, who had held their horses, but we never got him.

"Bill Houston was sheriff of Missoula county then and he took Cummins and Hart to Missoula. But it took the courts a long time to work in those days and it was a year afterwards when they came up for trial. By that time McCarthyville wasn't any more and the witnesses were scattered from Alaska to all points south. As a result they were all turned loose," stated McCarthy years ago.[1]

---

[1] Wilchey in the *Silver State Post* (Deer Lodge), October 23, 1941.

14

DEMERSVILLE

DEMERSVILLE OWES NOT ITS BIRTH BUT ITS DEATH TO the railroad. It was a rollicking, busy little town in the Flathead area about three and a half miles from the present city of Kalispell.

At the head of navigation on the Flathead river, 30 miles from the head of the lake, is found the town of Demersville, a thrifty and progressive settlement, the largest in the valley. Congenial, hospitable and enterprising citizens indeed, are those who today are making Demersville the nucleus about which a promising city is to form, and all honor to them for doing so. . . .

The city was founded by the late T. J. Demers, who bought an 18-acre tract from M. Gregg in 1887. Four short years ago, there was not a house within its limits. Today it possesses a town hall, a two-story structure that would be creditable to any city, the Cliff House, Inter-lake office, Stanton's well-equipped livery stables, money order postoffice, Clifford & Stannard's, Missoula Mercantile company, (late T. J. Demers' store), Adams General Store, Casey's blacksmith shop, Foy's saloon, Dr. Sanders' office, McFaren's saloon, Captain Wilson's buildings. . . .

The unprecedented growth of Demersville from Demers' tent store a few years ago, to the rank of a garrison town and steamboat terminus, justifies the interest with which it is regarded. The causes of Demersville growth and prosperity are many:

1st—Its central geographical location.
2nd—Its accessibility by land and water.
3rd—Its hotel accommodations.
4th—Its superior stores.
5th—Its magnificent climate.

6th—Its unsurpassed saw and grist mill sites.

7th—Its possession of United States troops and the advantages
obtained therefrom.

8th—Its pure water.

9th—Its inexhaustible forests and timber.

10th—Its matchless hunting and fishing.

11th—The public spirit and enterprise of its inhabitants.

12th—The mining and agricultural interests.

Demersville has practical, energetic companies who can insure
success to any locality they take hold of and wish to build up.[1]

The steamers *Tom Carter, U.S. Grant,* the *Crescent,*
and many others carried eager passengers up the river
to this paradise north of Flathead Lake. The stores and
hotels were crowded; the population grew to 2,500,
all optimistic promoters of the growing town. Life
here had the zest and gaiety born of frontier life and
optimism in the future.

Quite a number of people residing in Flathead and Lincoln
counties will readily recall a character who lived and operated in
Demersville, later in Kalispell, and who was locally known as
"Jimmy-the Nibbler." The writer never knew his real name and
we are of the opinion that few who live now are any better posted.

The Nibbler's business had to do with gambling, saloons and dance
halls. At times he operated his own places in the two towns, and in
later years located at Libby. At the time we are writing about, in
the late fall of 1900, when he pulled off his novel woodsawing social
function, he was proprietor of a place on First avenue, west, near
the then restricted district.

Jimmie had accumulated some half-dozen cords of four-foot
wood, much of it taken in payment of bills owing his bar. Along
toward the end of November of the year mentioned it became de-
sirable that this wood be sawed up into stove-length, and he evolved
a novel scheme to accomplish this work at little expense.

There was always a fair-sized sprinkling of loafers waiting for

---

[1]Dan Conway in the *Froid Tribune,* November 26, 1926.

free drinks, attached to all the principal saloons of the town, and to those harboring about his place Jimmie one day announced that any of the boys who would saw up that wood would be given a schooner of beer every time he completed the severance of five cord-wood sticks. To accomplish the expected demand he set a keg of beer, with a spigot in place, on a platform at the rear of his saloon.

Thus started the most laughable program that ever transpired in a space 40 feet square, the dimensions of the open ground which accommodated the Nibbler's woodpile. There was but one sawbuck in the neighborhood. This was seized by one of the loafers and he proceeded to demolish five sticks of cord-wood and collect his drink. Fired by this the congregation of hangers-on scattered to search for bucks and saws. Where they got the tools was never known, but within 10 minutes there were a half-dozen men vigorously at work earning the free beer, and within 30 minutes there were a total of 33 men at work, taking up much of the space—the rest being occupied by hilarious spectators, watching while the bullets of severed wood came sailing through the air as if a steam saw was at work.

Soon the men chose a mock sheriff to keep order and prevent chiseling. His fines went and the men enforced them. The fun grew more furious and the crowd grew larger and larger as minutes passed. Quite soon the pioneers of the novel function were incapacitated from their labors and from the load they were then carrying and left off. But no matter, others took their vacated places at the sawbucks and the beer steins.

Within less than two hours the half-dozen cords of wood were sawed and piled, while at least half the workmen could scarcely navigate. At the end the Nibbler treated each one to a big bowl of Irish stew and a slab of cheese, which was devoured with gusto. That slices of yellow laundry soap were substituted for the cheese to some of the furthest gone was apparently not noticed save by the wag who made the substitution and his friends.[2]

If, now and then, misfortune struck, the townspeople worked together in true Western fashion.

In the month of June, 1891, there was a big fire in Demersville

---

[2] G. M. Houtz, *Missoulian*, January 29, 1939.

that wiped out practically an entire block of the town. This fire
started in the evening from either the exploding or the upsetting
of a kerosene lamp in Ed Gales's general store in the center of the
block. From this point it spread rapidly in both directions. In the
next block to the north was the Racket store on the corner, owned
by Hall & Johnson. The building that was to be used as a printing
shop by the Flathead Journal came next, one or two small offices
and the InterLake shop on the other corner. Efforts of the entire
town fighting the fire were directed to saving the last named buildings. . . .

Hope of saving anything in the doomed block was early abandoned, and work was concentrated on the Racket store building.
The nearest water was two blocks distant, in an "old oaken bucket"
well, water raised by a pail at the end of a rope. A bucket brigade
was formed and water passed rapidly to the Hall & Johnson building.

A half dozen lusty young men climbed to the roof of the Racket
building, hanging blankets over the comb and keeping them well
wet down. Later, after the greatest danger was past, these men
yelled for beer, and a tub full of bottles was sent up to them. Between the water and the spilled beer, the building was saved. But
at the end only two of the men were able to descend by means of
the ladder—the other four were helpless.

The goods of the various threatened and burning structures were
carried across the street—all that could be saved before the fire
spread too far. Men were hired to guard them. Later it was noted
that the two who had been hired to guard the pile of liquors from
the saloons were in a very dopey condition. Any sober man could
have carted off the entire stock of wet goods, the guards with it.

Eugene Desarmo, a 13-year-old boy, was the only kid who worked
right along with the men carrying water, with a pail in one hand
and supporting half a tub with the other. Next day Gene was called
into the Racket store, and the grateful proprietors offered him a
pair of three dollar shoes (he was barefoot) or the same amount
in fireworks. Gene laughed and said: "Give me the fireworks; it's
summer and I don't need shoes."[3]

The Great Northern doomed the energetic town

---

[3] *Ibid.*, February 21, 1937.

when it laid its rails through Kalispell townsite about 3½ miles southwest of Demersville.

As the railroad became a certainty for the (former), Demersville began to lose her citizens and to disintegrate. The town began to be moved bodily to the railroad. Some of the buildings occupied in Kalispell today were dwellings and business houses in old Demersville.[4]

Today no trace remains of "Bad Rock" Tom Stanton's stable, the "Red Light Saloon," or the other establishments founded by the citizens who could "insure success to any locality they took hold of and wish[ed] to build up!"

---

[4] Verne Linderman in the *Roundup Tribune*, December 8, 1927.

15

ROBAR

FORTY-SIX YEARS AGO ROBAR, LOCATED NEAR GLACIER PARK WHERE the Great Falls-Glacier Park highway crosses Birch creek was a flourishing western town. Today there is not one stick of timber or a habitation in sight as far as the eye can see over the wind-swept plains as evidence that there ever was a town.

The businesses at Robar were selling whisky and gambling. Blackfeet Indians from the reservation, Bloods from their Canadian reservation and wandering Crees bought food and blankets and celebrated. As many as 200 Indian tepees at a time used to be pitched in a big circle on the flats east of the town.

The cheapest whisky was used for this trade and saloon keepers added a generous amount of water to each bottle as it was drawn from the barrel.

Indians would form a big ring on the ground within the tepee circle and a quart bottle would be started around, each Indian taking a drink. At a big gathering it would take several quarts to make the round once. When the "fire water" had begun to produce the usual results, the dance and songs would start around the bonfire.

Members of the tribes would tell tales of the great deeds they had done. Stories led to bragging, bragging to fights, and these would gradually involve entire families. Before morning saloon keepers would lock up supplies, barricade buildings and refuse further trade.

To the north, in Canada, where local option was practiced, there was a big demand for whisky, but the Blackfeet Indian reservation had to be crossed to reach Canada. If a smuggler was caught, he lost his load and he went to the penitentiary.

Robar was the center of an immense cattle country. A number of big cattle outfits were on the Blackfeet reservation and others ranged to the east. On occasions when wagon trains camped in the vicinity, there would be hilarious nights, with hundreds of dollars on gambling tables.

There were organized gangs of horse and cattle thieves, with headquarters in Robar. Teton county, which in those days comprised seven of the present counties, Toole, Pondera, Teton, Hill, Liberty, Cascade and Glacier, had a sheriff and a few deputies at Fort Benton, which was then the county seat. There were a few justices of the peace at some of the other widely scattered towns, Dupuyer, Choteau, Havre and the like, but with such great territory to cover, law enforcement was feeble.

In 1884, there came drifting into Robar a party of three men with a string of mules they had stolen in Canada. Description of the mules had preceded them to a few of the regular inhabitants of Robar, bartenders, gamblers and cattle thieves, many of whom have since become industrious and respected citizens. They organized a committee, representing themselves as vigilantes, but one of the mule thieves overheard a part of the conversation and told his comrades, who, being well armed, strongly barricaded the log cabin in which they were spending the night.

When the pseudo vigilantes surrounded the shack they found themselves unable to storm the barricade and get the men so they entered into negotiations instead, promising the three men a trial at Fort Benton. The men gave themselves up at once but instead of keeping their promise, the vigilantes took the three prisoners to a spot half a mile up the creek from the present road crossing and hanged them to a cottonwood tree, not for the sake of law but to procure the mules and sell them to their own profit. This false committee was arrested and taken to Fort Benton for trial, but because of lack of evidence the case was dismissed.

Three unmarked graves in willows at the edge of Birch creek are the only evidence at the spot of this happening and the cottonwood tree has long since been cut down.[1]

---

[1] Told in 1930 by Mike Shannon, veteran Glacier Park guide, in the *Billings Times*, January 9, 1930.

BIBLIOGRAPHY

DIMSDALE, THOMAS J. *Vigilantes of Montana.* Virginia City, M.T.: Montana Post Press, 1866.

LANGFORD, N. P. *Vigilante Days and Ways.* 2 vols.; Boston: J. G. Cupples, 1890.

LEESON, M. A. *History of Montana, 1739-1885.* Chicago: Warner, Beers & Co., 1885.

McCLURE, A. K. *Three Thousand Miles through the Rocky Mountains,* Philadelphia: J. B. Lippincott & Company, 1869.

MILLER, JOAQUIN. *An Illustrated History of the State of Montana.* Chicago: Lewis Publishing Company, 1894.

Montana Historical Society, *Contributions,* Vol. I-, 1876- . Helena: Rocky Mountain Publishing Co., 1876-.

RICHARDSON, A. D. *Beyond the Mississippi.* Hartford, Conn.: American Publishing Company, 1894.

SANDERS, HELEN F. *A History of Montana.* 3 vols.; Chicago: Lewis Publishing Company, 1913.

SASSMAN, OREN. "Metal Mining in Historic Beaverhead." Unpublished Master's thesis, Montana State University, Missoula, 1941.

SMET, PIERRE JEAN DE. *Life, Letters, and Travels.* 4 vols.; New York: Francis P. Harper, 1904.

STONE, A. L. *Following Old Trails.* Missoula, Mont.: Morton John Elrod, 1913.

STOUT, TOM, ed. *Montana, its Story and Biography.* 3 vols.; Chicago: American Historical Society, 1921.

STUART, GRANVILLE. *Forty Years on the Frontier.* 2 vols.; Cleveland: The Arthur H. Clark Company, 1925.

TOPONCE, ALEXANDER. *Reminiscences of Alexander Toponce, Pioneer, 1839-1923.* Ogden, Utah: Mrs. Katie Toponce, 1923.

INDEX

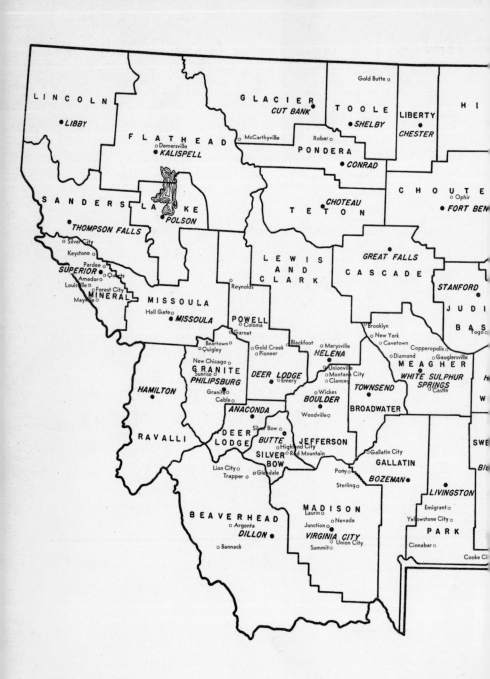